People Count!

 Mark A. Boyer, University of Connecticut, Series Editor

Titles in the Series

People Count!

Networked Individuals in Global Politics

James N. Rosenau

Paradigm Publishers

Boulder • London

Paradigm Publishers is committed to preserving ancient forests and natural resources. We elected to print *People Count!* on 30% post consumer recycled paper, processed chlorine free. As a result, for this printing, we have saved:

5 Trees (40' tall and 6-8" diameter)
2,035 Gallons of Wastewater
819 Kilowatt Hours of Electricity
224 Pounds of Solid Waste
441 Pounds of Greenhouse Gases

Paradigm Publishers made this paper choice because our printer, Thomson-Shore, Inc., is a member of Green Press Initiative, a nonprofit program dedicated to supporting authors, publishers, and suppliers in their efforts to reduce their use of fiber obtained from endangered forests.

For more information, visit www.greenpressinitiative.org

Copyright © 2008 Paradigm Publishers

Published in the United States by Paradigm Publishers, 3360 Mitchell Lane Suite E, Boulder, CO 80301 USA.

Paradigm Publishers is the trade name of Birkenkamp & Company, LLC, Dean Birkenkamp, President and Publisher.

Library of Congress Cataloging-in-Publication Data
Rosenau, James N.
    People count! : networked individuals in global politics / by James N. Rosenau.
      p. cm.
    Includes bibliographical references and index.
    ISBN 978-1-59451-414-2 (hardcover : alk. paper) — ISBN 978-1-59451-415-9 (pbk. : alk. paper)   1. Globalization.   2. International relations.   3. Political sociology.
4. Political geography.   5. Political participation.   6. Civil society.   I. Title.
    JZ1318.R668 2007
    327.1—dc22

                                                                    2007023086

Printed and bound in the United States of America on acid-free paper that meets the standards of the American National Standard for Permanence of Paper for Printed Library Materials.

Designed and Typeset by Straight Creek Bookmakers.

11 10 09 08 07   1 2 3 4 5

Contents

Preface and Acknowledgments

This book is about you and me, and everyone else. It seeks to explore a number of roles that are salient in communities. It does so in order to stress that the course of events is sustained by ordinary individuals as well as officials and governments. Such a perspective runs counter to prevailing ways of thinking about the world. Most people see large macro entities, from corporations to states, from trade unions to universities, whereas here the stress is on micro actors, on the people who maintain or undermine the macro organizations and institutions that are the usual focus of concern.

A micro perspective is difficult to develop and maintain, so fully ensconced are most people in macro thinking. Yet, it does not take much reflection to appreciate that the macro organizations and institutions rest on the conduct of the individuals of which they are composed. The problem is, and always has been, one of tracing the ways in which individuals at the micro level shape and are shaped by the macro organizations to which they belong. It is not an easy problem to solve, so complex are individuals and so complex are macro organizations and the links between the two. No claim is made here that the analytic micro–macro problem is solved in the ensuing chapters, or even that taken together the chapters adequately address the problem, but I hope the emphasis on the micro will give pause to those who proceed from a thoroughgoing macro approach. That the macro rests on the micro wherever organizations are active seems so obvious as not to be worthy of intensive discussion. Such is not the case, however. Once one begins to ponder the nature of micro–macro links it immediately becomes clear that one has taken on degrees of complexity that are not readily resolved. Or at least I have yet to resolve them.

In short, the central idea underlying the analysis of all the chapters is that as time and space continue to shrink with the continuing advent of new technologies for moving ideas and individuals around the world, people become increasingly important. The title of the book succinctly summarizes this theme: whatever role they may occupy, people make a difference, they COUNT!

I hope the analyses that make up the ensuing chapters at least suggest the complexity of the micro–macro problem and provoke readers to explore how to address, if not to solve, the problem. I would welcome outlining the solutions that readers may develop. A couple of caveats are in order. First, the individual roles selected for analysis are far from complete. Societies are composed of many more roles than could be considered in one volume. The logic of selecting those roles subjected to analysis in Chapters 5 through 23 is simply that each chapter focuses on a role salient in modern life, even though I fully realize that many more could have been added. Second, the analyses of the roles in the various chapters are admittedly truncated. One could write a book about each of the roles. I preferred to summarize some general features of each role that may not apply to every situation or person, but that generally are descriptive of each role as I have come to understand them. Third, there is an underlying theme that runs through all the chapters subsequent to the fourth. It is outlined in Chapter 2 and concerns the way in which the roles may be caught up in the clash between those forces at work in the world pressing for integration and those pressing for disintegration. However, this theme is not as pervasive as it might have been in order not to detract from the presentation of micro roles.

Acknowledgments

I am indebted to Miles D. Townes, Ysbrant Marcelis, and Sally Montague for their help in preparing this book for publication. They made a complex task much easier. The encouragement and advice of Jennifer Knerr, surely one of the world's finest editors, is also happily acknowledged, along with the fine Paradigm production team headed by Melanie Stafford. As always, the support of Hong-ying Wang was unstinting and greatly valued. In their own way too, our young children, Fan and Patrick, contributed to the creative environment that facilitated completion of this work.

James N. Rosenau
Manlius, New York

CHAPTER ONE

Teachers and Scholars

Let me recount my experience with the study of world politics. More than fifty years ago, when I was earning my doctorate in political science, the field focused mainly on diplomats and heads of state. That was the prime way in which individuals were considered relevant to international affairs. Since then, I have watched—and helped—my discipline expand beyond the interaction of states and their diplomats: today most scholars focus on nation-states, organizations, and institutions. For a long time, this seemed a reasonable and rational approach to the study of world politics.

In the past decade or so, I began to think that this might no longer be the case. More and more I saw anomalies that could not account for the standard frameworks of the field. I wrote a trilogy of books that attempted to identify and explain the sources of these anomalies: first, a book about change, called *Turbulence in World Politics;*[1] then *Along the Domestic-Foreign Frontier,*[2] about governance; and finally, *Distant Proximities,*[3] my contribution to the globalization literature. These books were written primarily for other academics—college students and professors of international relations—but lately I suspect that they may be relevant to an even larger audience.

One theme of the three books recurs and stands out as central, namely, the increasing skills and capabilities of individuals. I call this the "skill revolution" and first discussed it as a parameter of change in *Turbulence.* My point, put simply, is that people are becoming more skilled and that, as they do, their orientations and relations to each other and their organizations undergo change. They become more engaged, more involved, more able to shape their world.[4]

Many mainstream scholars in political science tend to ignore this trend, but it is becoming increasingly evident in the news and elsewhere. Consider that in the summer of 2005 a California woman, Cindy Sheehan, who had lost a son in Iraq, camped outside the president's vacation ranch in Texas in the hope of getting an interview with him in order to ask why her son had been sent off to die in a remote war. President Bush refused to see her, and her one-person protest soon escalated into a large crowd of supporters who came from far away to share in her protest. Subsequently, antiwar protests mushroomed across the country, giving rise to a noticeable shift in the nation's political climate. In effect, that one person activated a dormant network that proved consequential.

In short, it is misleading to think of world affairs as being driven exclusively by large collectivities such as governments, corporations, universities, churches, and the like. Such macro organizations are surely central to the course of events, but so are people at the micro level. They have become important in a variety of ways, from individuals whose reputations, accomplishments, and positions enhance their public judgments to people who collectively share an organization's policies that are publicized for others to consider.

Thus the central idea in this book is that PEOPLE COUNT! As economic, social, and political changes accelerate at ever-greater rates, as time and space continue to shrink with the relentless innovation of new technologies for moving people and ideas around the world, people—as people—have become increasingly important. To make that claim useful, however, requires that we introduce analytical rigor—in this case, the concept of "roles." The next chapter elaborates on this concept, but it is easy enough to put succinctly: each of us has different roles that we play in our lives. Why this matters for world politics is that, increasingly, we are able to choose the roles through which we engage our world and to define those roles once we have chosen them. This is nothing less than a radical shift in international affairs and a challenge to all of the organizations, institutions, and governments that try to assign or constrain the roles of the people in their jurisdiction.

The Classroom as Home

Before proceeding to more analytic concerns, I want to share more about the role I have occupied for more than five decades in four universities: that of a professor. For me, as for many of those who spend their working lives with students—either standing in front of them, sitting around a table with them, or consulting with them individually—teaching is more than a form of earning a living. It is, rather, a means for me to serve a commitment to sharing ideas, elaborating thoughts, and exchanging perspectives. Indeed, if one wants to maximize income, teaching is not the right profession to enter. Teachers at every level are not well paid and could make more money in a number of other pursuits. Yet most chose to stay on in the classroom. It is a kind of home, a setting where ideas flow, thoughts are contested, information is provided, and minds are expanded as part of the processes of growth—qualities that cannot be measured in terms of income.

Besides their offices in which they engage in one-on-one sharing of ideas, teachers have a variety of classrooms, depending on where they work. In elementary schools their classrooms are filled with low tables and chairs at which students play, draw, and learn to read. In high schools their homes are rooms with chairs in rows for some thirty or more students. In colleges and graduate schools their homes vary from large lecture halls to small classrooms and laboratories. Despite the variation, however, each type of room is a home, a place where teachers practice their craft, impart information, cope with challenging questions, and raise some of their own.

Whatever its size and however it may be arranged, the classroom has one indispensable piece of furniture: the chalkboard (and the chalk with which to write on it). The chalkboard serves several purposes, depending on the students in attendance. For younger students the chalkboard is used to present new words and how they are spelled; at more advanced levels it is used to enumerate concepts, solve equations, and pose questions. It can also be educational in the sense that most teachers do not erase what they put on the board when their class is over, thus presenting the next user of the room with ideas and connections that seem both unintelligible and intriguing. I have long made it a practice to ostentatiously pause and read what is on the board when I arrive to start my class, hoping thereby to demonstrate the uses and virtues of curiosity to the students as well as to find out what goes on in other classes.

Training the Citizen and the Specialist

Depending on the level of students they are instructing, teachers engage in different forms of presenting ideas and eliciting student reactions. Elementary, junior high, and high school teachers are responsible for providing the skills and basic knowledge children need to become mature adults and responsible citizens. College teachers are charged with introducing students to academic disciplines in several fields as well as helping them to begin to acquire expertise by majoring in a particular discipline. Those who give graduate courses are responsible for training students in a discipline as well as introducing them to the frontiers of their field. They are also expected to engage in innovative research that is eventually published and serves to push back the frontiers of their discipline. Their research commitments often lead to their being called "scholars" or "academics." It is in this capacity that I have been teaching for several decades. I think of myself as both a teacher and a scholar, with this book being only the latest in a long line of publications.

Many students and some teachers derisively view the expectation that professors in colleges and graduate schools engage in research and publication because of a requirement that they "publish or perish." It is true that untenured professors who do not engage in research and publish their work are unlikely to retain their jobs. Academics do not devote time to writing up their findings and ideas for publication in order to avoid "perishing," however, else those who have tenure would not publish, a possibility that describes very, very few tenured professors. Most academics seek to publish their work because they feel an obligation to contribute to the expansion of knowledge in their field. This can best be done by sharing the results of their inquiries as widely as possible, that is, by publishing them and thereby reaching unknown others. Thus a more apt phrasing of the expectation is "communicate or perish." Furthermore, teaching and research are not antithetical. The ideas one develops in seminars often become the basis for research inquiries, just as the latter subsequently serve as the focus for ideas discussed in seminars.

To teach at the graduate level is often to serve as a mentor for those students who aspire to writing a dissertation and then going on to a career in the academy. There is considerable satisfaction in mentoring, in seeing one's students move on to establish their own careers as professors and researchers. In effect, one's students eventually become one's colleagues, fellow investigators whose research findings often carry the work of their mentors to new levels. Thus does knowledge in a discipline expand and get refined.

Rivalries

If mentoring and pushing back the frontiers of knowledge are the positive side of life as an academic, the negative side involves needless and unproductive rivalries among scholars in the same field—rivalries for prestige, research funds, and influence. Most scholars are not caught up in such rivalries, but those who are tend to allow their competitive impulses to dominate their teaching and research. Such rivalries can be debilitating for those caught up in them and for the discipline in which they occur. They can become debilitating because otherwise neutral scholars are pressed to take a position on the merits of one or another side of the rivalry. Some of the pressure comes from those who have taken sides in the debates, but it also originates in the press and among people whose professions may be affected by the competition. More often than not, the rivalry peters out as other issues come to the fore.

Twice in my career I have been involved in a rivalry with colleagues. In both situations I had administrative responsibilities that led me to differ with some members of the department's faculty who did not view research as a major aspect of their responsibilities. In one of these situations I was eventually ousted from the administrative role, in good part because I was unable to encourage or otherwise reward unproductive senior colleagues whose annual reports struck me as reflective of mediocrity. We differed on the balance between teaching and research as well as on what kind of research advances the discipline. In effect, the rivalry—which was ideological—was supplemented by personality clashes. It also served to teach me that I was not cut out to be an academic administrator. Except for these brief moments of administrative digression, however, I have thrived in my academic role and deeply believe in the expectations and goals of universities.

Public Service

Economists, sociologists, and political scientists often have opportunities to either serve or advise governments. Depending on the issues involved, occasionally those in the hard sciences, history, and other disciplines are also sought by public officials for advice. Most academics are pleased to respond to requests for their presence and advice, and indeed, some even take government positions for brief periods of time.[5] Aware that knowledge in their fields has implications for the conduct of public affairs, such academics are flattered that their work is sought by their governments and thus feel an obligation to make their knowledge available to public officials who seek their guidance. On the other hand, some in the academy adhere to a contrary position and view public service as an intrusion upon their time or as possibly distorting their inquiries if they are motivated to have an impact in the realm of government. Such academics, of which I am one, feel that if their work can be of value to public officials, it will reach into the halls of government circuitously through either their former students, journalists who learn of their inquiries and use them as the basis for their articles, or perhaps a number of other indirect channels. Conceivably, for example, some of the observations set forth in this book will follow one or another circuitous path into the offices of public officials.

New Boundaries

But to avoid public service is not to be out of touch with the transformations at work in the world. On the contrary, as a student of international affairs I find myself endlessly aware of the changing world scene. More than that, as I fly across oceans to conferences and talks, e-mail colleagues and students around the world, and publish work in languages I do not speak, I am increasingly aware that the boundaries of the classroom have blurred into the boundaries of the world. Here, too, in the world at large I can act out my commitment to the exchange of ideas and perspectives. It is my hope that this book will serve as a sort of chalkboard, a repository for ideas that I hope the reader will find provocative and useful.

Conclusion

In all likelihood many readers will object to my inclination to avoid either advising or serving governments. If they do, they will give voice to the basic premise of this book. In effect, they will be saying that people count, that what individuals do or do not do matters, and that academics should thus be ready to contribute their perspectives directly to public officials.

I have always defined my academic role less as a specialist in international relations and more as a theorist of the subject. I have never tooled up in the dynamics of particular countries or regions—becoming what is generally known as an area specialist—but rather have sought to move ever higher on what I call the ladder of abstraction in order to depict the underlying processes and challenges that unfold in any country or political system. Accordingly, before examining how people count in the various roles examined in Chapters 4 through 23, in the next two chapters I revert to my role as a theorist by way of highlighting the central concepts that recur in the subsequent chapters.

CHAPTER TWO

Roles in a Fragmegrative World

Notwithstanding the prime concern here with individuals at the micro level, note must also be taken of the macro forces that both shape and are shaped by their actions. Some would lump all those forces under the term *globalization,* but that is overly broad and not very helpful. A more incisive perspective posits two overriding, continuously interactive forces at work on a global scale: one involves all the tendencies toward localization, decentralization, and fragmentation, whereas the other is manifest in all the dynamics in the opposite direction that foster globalization (in the useful sense), centralization, and integration. The available analytic vocabulary lacks terminology for capturing the innumerable ways in which these contrary tendencies continuously interact and impact each other. Other authors have coined words that highlight these tensions between coherence and collapse—such as *chaord,* a combination of chaos and order, and *glocalization,* which combines globalization and localization.

I prefer my own term, *fragmegration*—an admittedly ungainly and grating label, but one that captures in a single word the fragmentation and integration that marks the changing dynamics in world politics. An understanding of world affairs at both the micro and macro levels is greatly facilitated if these changes are viewed through fragmegrative lenses. Indeed, in a number of ways fragmegrative dynamics highlight the diverse ways in which people count. As will be seen throughout the ensuing chapters, they are frequently caught up in fragmegrative situations, in conflicts between the fragmenting and integrating expectations built into their roles.

Change

A prime characteristic of fragmegration is the degree to which it is rooted in the dynamics of change. Indeed, neither integration nor fragmentation is a static process. Both impose continuing and extensive change on individuals and collectivities. And the more the two interact, the greater are the transformations they initiate and sustain. Needless to say, this is also the case for the roles individuals occupy. Those roles and the expectations that sustain them are undergoing transformation as the dynamics of fragmegration continue to alter the conceptions that people have of themselves. Active citizens, for example, can no longer draw a clear distinction between local and foreign issues: fragmegration is merging the two types of issues in such a way that perforce the active citizen must pay attention to how each type impacts on the other. More than that, fragmegration imposes on individuals the need to become sensitive to both the integrative and disintegrative potential of any issue. In effect, fragmegrative dynamics tend to elevate the capacities of both active and passive citizens. They may not fully grasp the interaction between the forces promoting integration and fragmentation, but they cannot avoid an awareness that their long-standing routines are being crowded and expanded by new forces from both within and outside their previously established worlds and that, consequently, the new routines are altering the expectations to which they must be responsive.

For social, economic, and political systems, the changes wrought by fragmegrative dynamics necessitate the abandonment of some old procedures and the adoption of new ones, processes of change that can be wrenching for their institutions as well as their citizens. For individuals the changes can be no less disconcerting, inasmuch as they can involve a reorientation of their loyalties, a shift in their priorities, and an assumption of new responsibilities. As they undergo this process, individuals are better able to engage and affect world politics—to "count," in the most meaningful sense of the word.

Stated more generally, as information technologies, jet aircraft, and other innovations make the world more intimate, so too do people and the roles they occupy increasingly serve as foci of concern. Or at least it seems that the orientations, resistances, and activities of individuals and publics have increasingly become salient for observers of all walks of life. Perhaps it was always the case, but today attention to large, aggregated, and abstract structures such as states, societies, and corporations appears to have waned in relation to the attention that is paid to concrete and identifiable people. Although aggregated structures served as the context for inquiries and analysis in the past, this is less so today. Current agendas include heightened focus on demographic trends, social capital, immigrants and reactions to them, the role of networks and smart mobs, emergent identities, corrupt officials and executives, winners and losers in the global economy, the potency of the human immunodeficiency virus/acquired immunodeficiency syndrome (HIV/AIDS) and severe acute respiratory syndrome (SARS) epidemics, suicide bombers, soldiers and planners, and a wide range of other issues in which human beings as well as aggregated structures are the center of attention. Put differently, the world has become increasingly messy and complex as its populations continue to grow and the distances between people continue to shrink.

Aggregated structures may have once been understandable in the sense that they seemed to determine how issues were sustained and resolved, but the collapse of time and distance has shrunk the world into a complex of distant proximities[1] and thus led observers, pundits, politicians, and concerned citizens to refocus their attention on the people who constitute the structures. They have not abandoned or replaced their interest in structures—rather it has been augmented by a growing realization that the structures cannot be comprehended without an understanding of the ways in which they are founded on the roles, attitudes, habits, support, defections, and activities of the individuals that sustain or alter them. It thus seems reasonable to conclude that the world has entered a new epoch, that the age of the nation-state has been supplanted, or at least been supplemented, by the age of the networked individual. In other words, people count, no matter what aspect of public affairs may be of concern. By "count" I mean the substantial contribution that people make to public affairs, to how the course of events is shaped by what individuals do or do not do, either alone or collectively. This is not to suggest a concern with what are commonly called "human interest" stories, such as the men who were trapped for days in a coal mine or the girl found months after having been abducted from her room at night. Such stories are gripping not because they have an enduring impact on public affairs but because they momentarily evoke our admiration or sympathy.

Even though it may seem obvious that people count, understanding how they count—how their influence and roles shape or constrain events—is anything but obvious. Only in the more recent years of my career as an academic have I begun to appreciate the overriding centrality of the micro level, of individuals who, by responding to expectations of their roles, engage in their various pursuits that culminate in macro collectivities. And it is only in recent years have I experienced awe and perplexity over the processes whereby macro collectivities and their micro components shape each other. And I am not alone in this newfound preoccupation. I call it the micro-macro problem, whereas others refer to it as the agency-structure problem. This terminology is also of recent origin.

The task of probing and comprehending the interactivity of micro and macro phenomena poses difficult analytic challenges and perhaps even a few leaps of faith. Put more directly, tracing the impact of people amounts to nothing less than assessing how the orientations and actions of individuals at micro levels do or do not get converted into commitments, policies, and structures at macro levels.[2] The task is not easy, as the processes of conversion are not easily observed.

In order to investigate how people count, it is not necessary to delve into their personalities and other individual traits. Rather their impact is explored through the attitudes, skills, and actions they bring to a variety of roles they may play as, say, activists, elites, officials, voters, travelers, worshippers, soldiers, corporate executives, workers, identity-seekers, and purveyors of information. It is in playing out these roles that people have a collective impact on demographic trends, social capital, the workforce, social movements, networks, immigration patterns, wars, and a host of other aggregates that underlie and sustain political issues and public policies. Such is the purpose of this book: to demonstrate that people count by tracing their behavior in the various roles in which they are counted. Each of the substantive chapters that follow includes an assessment of how fragmegration may be changing the roles and individuals that occupy them.

Needless to say, the ways in which people count can vary considerably across societies, polities, and economies. Their rights and practices in traditional societies are quite different from those in liberal democracies, just as people in developing countries have much less access to modern technologies of communication than those in developed countries, thus inhibiting their capacity for networking that underlies the formation of social capital. What follows, however, is not organized on the basis of societal, political, and economic types of regimes. Rather, in order to maintain the focus on individuals and to avoid slipping into analyzing them in terms of the usual aggregate categories, the various chapters focus on the capacities and limitations that underlie their conduct in the diverse roles they occupy in the family, the community, the workplace, and wherever else they may be active.

Roles

But what are roles and how might they change? The key to comprehending any role is to view it as a complex of expectations. Roles—all roles—are defined by the norms embedded in the expectations that people have of the occupants of those roles and the expectations that the occupants have of themselves. Some expectations are derived from formal requirements evolved by the system in which the role is located—by court decisions, by legislative regulations, by decrees of chief executives, and by organizational bylaws as well as any other codes that the system maintains.

Other and more numerous expectations are informal, those requirements that members of a system consider binding even if they are not recorded in documents. Indeed, informal role expectations usually consist of shared norms that may not be inscribed in documents. Rather, they emerge out of the recurring practices and interactions that comprise the nature of the family, community, workplace, and other situations in which the roles are located. As such, they are just as powerful, if not more powerful, a source of behavior as the formal requirements. Nothing in the Constitution of the United States, for instance, says that cabinet secretaries should testify before congressional committees, but all cabinet secretaries have and all are likely to do so in the future.

In short, some informal roles are embedded in large-scale organizations and institutions, whereas others are fashioned as a consequence of individual actions. Needless to say, there is a tendency toward convergence between the expectations that the macro collectivities have of a role and the expectations held by the individuals who occupy that role. If they lack a modicum of convergence, either the collectivity undergoes transformation or, much more likely, the individual is ousted from the role.

Convergence may be insufficient to define expectations because there is a third realm of any role, what might be called the realm of "individual discretion," that accords its occupant the freedom to employ all the talents, habits, prior experiences, and unique qualities that he or she brings to the role. This dimension of every role accounts for why conduct in the role differs from one occupant to the next. There is an outer limit to the realm of individual discretion, however. To repeat, once the occupant moves outside this limit he or she is either removed from the role or the nature of the role will have been changed to encompass the deviant behavior. The conduct of U.S. students during the Vietnam War offers a good illustration of the limits of how this third realm of any role operates. Students in several universities expressed their opposition to the war by occupying the offices of the university presidents. But many of the universities, instead of ousting the students from their student roles, adopted new procedures that gave students a voice in the policymaking processes of their university. In effect, the system altered its rules with respect to the formal and informal requirements attached to the student role.

Important as the realm of individual discretion is, here we are not interested in the family background, childhood experiences, and other sources of personal traits and history that people bring to their roles. Rather, our focus is on the orientations and conduct of individuals that derive from the expectations of the roles they occupy in the systems that sustain one or another aspect of public affairs. Although it is certainly the case that the behavior of people is to some extent a consequence of their personal characteristics as these interact with the expectations built into their roles, and although each of their social roles provides some room for the expression of the idiosyncratic values, experiences, and talents that distinguish their personalities, the central tendencies that mark their aggregated and collective impact stem from exposure to the common expectations, tasks, and circumstances of which any role consists. And it is these central tendencies that are of concern in the ensuing chapters.

Just as every role is composed of role expectations, so does every role occupant bring a set of skills to his or her conduct in the role. For a host of reasons, people vary considerably in the skills they possess and use. Whatever the variations—and they can be substantial—people everywhere, however, are undergoing what I call in the next chapter a "skill revolution," by which is meant a continuous enlargement of their ability to grasp the analytic, emotional, and imaginative dimensions of the situations that impinge upon their roles. Irrespective of their circumstances, their analytic and emotional skills are enlarging in every community and at every level of society. This is not to say that they are converging around the same values. Every person's skills are expanding in the context of his or her own culture, so that the French sophisticate is more skillful than his or her predecessors, just as the same is the case for the Islamic fundamentalist, the Vermont farmer, and so on across the full spectrum of human experience.

Role Conflicts and Change

It is common experience that people are simultaneously subjected to conflicting expectations in two or more of the roles they occupy. Such conflicts are often not easy to resolve, but they have the virtue of compelling role occupants to prioritize their obligations. Given the numerous clashes between integrative and fragmenting dynamics as well as those between the local and global that characterize the present era, the potential for role conflict is considerable. Involved in a fragmenting organization, does one opt to enhance the momentum in that direction or does one seek to reverse the process and encourage integration? Given tendencies toward organizational integration that one finds distasteful, does one oppose such processes and opt for effort to maintain the fragmented system? The answers to such questions depend on the person and the organization, but nonetheless they are not easily answered. Furthermore, one has to consider whether the resolution of a role conflict is likely to promote renewed conflicts along the same lines in the future.

As the dynamics of fragmegration accelerate and become ever more complex, so do the expectations to which role occupants are subject. Although the expectations that define roles tend to be fixed under normal circumstances, the advent of fragmegrative dynamics has loosened up the rigidities and led either to revisions or replacement of the roles that worked in prior times when fragmegration was much less prominent. Indeed, under current conditions role occupants are likely to use the realm of individual discretion to alter their roles in order to adjust to the new challenges. Professors, for example, are likely to adjust their teaching roles to encourage students to exploit the resources of the Internet, a change that some academics may resist on the grounds that their long-standing practices have worked in the past and there seems no reason to alter them. Similarly, the Internet can tempt students to plagiarize—not that the Internet is the core of the temptation, but rather it is a means to view such temptations as permissible within their role. Students who succumb to this temptation often fail to realize that the Internet also enables their professors to find the documents from which they plagiarized. I recently had an experience along these lines, and I found it so unpleasant that I now seek to enhance the antiplagiarism expectations by adding a statement to my course syllabi that asserts the expectations in no uncertain terms. In effect, the advent of the Internet has led to conflict in my roles, forcing me to be more of a disciplinarian—and I much prefer being a teacher than a disciplinarian—and has led me to be more careful in specifying my expectations of the role occupied by my students.

Conclusion

This may seem like a minor example—although it was not at all minor to me or to the student in question—but all over the world people are facing similar challenges. Fragmegration has had huge effects on role expectations, and these are likely to continue as long as the simultaneity of fragmenting and integrating processes continues and leads them to overlap and reinvigorate each other. To be sure, earlier eras also experienced links between integration and fragmentations. But in those times when information and people took a week or more to cross the seas, the links between fragmentation and integration were not conspicuous and certainly they were not simultaneous. Likewise, roles in the world of public affairs have undergone profound transformations, subjecting individuals to an ever-greater set of expectations and ever-greater tensions as the expectations derived from the ever-greater number of roles they occupy conflict.

This suggests that the roles people occupy hinder their capacity as individuals to be, as it were, their best selves. Such a suggestion rests on the false premise that there are times when people do not occupy one or another role. Individuals do not exist apart from the roles they occupy. They may experience tensions through occupancy of one or more of their roles, and the tensions may be lifelong in duration, but they cannot vacate all their roles without occupying still others. Some may be dismayed by this reality, feeling it indicates people are forever prisoners in their roles. To be dismayed by this reality, however, is to miss the more encompassing reality that much more often than not, people retain the choice as to which of their available roles they will occupy at any particular time and how they will conduct themselves in their chosen roles. In short, both people and their roles count! That is why world affairs has entered the era of the individual, an era that is bound to be different from those in the past and that will doubtless witness intense upheavals as governments have to be more responsive to domestic pressures to accommodate their neighbors and to be more attentive to their responsibilities to the United Nations and the other international organizations to which they belong.

CHAPTER THREE

The Skill Revolution

For years I wrote articles and books with a pencil on yellow pads. When the computer came along, I had trouble breaking with my yellow-pad habit and recall saying to my young daughter, "If I could have one thing, it would be the capacity to go from my head through my hands to the computer keyboard." Some years later I experienced this breakthrough and with it a huge advance in my talent as a writer. Not only could I get more quickly from my mind to the keyboard, but the scope, versatility, and precision of my writing markedly improved. I have always felt that this was a key moment in my own skill revolution.

A Global Revolution

Although the expectations attached to different roles can vary widely, there is one dimension that cuts across all of them—namely, the skills that people bring to their roles. The way in which individuals interpret and perform their roles may stem not only from idiosyncratic sources—such as their values and prior experiences—that can vary widely within the range of expectations that constitute their roles, but also from the skills they bring to the interpretation and performance of their roles. These can also vary systematically in response to their exposure to education, information technologies, foreign travel, and urban life. These variations serve as the main sources of their impact in the public arena and are thus crucial to most issues on political agendas as well as to the effectiveness of nonpolitical organizations. Governments seek to enhance the skills base of their populations through immigration programs, through taxing policies designed to alter birthrates, through educational policies intended to prepare students for careers in an information society, through training their armed forces for modern warfare. Nongovernmental organizations (NGOs) also rely on the skills of the publics they seek to mobilize, and corporations need to train their personnel for particular lines of work. And such needs are felt across every realm of human endeavor.

With more and more people acquiring access to the Internet every year, there is no reason to anticipate a slowing of the momentum underlying the skill revolution.

Time and distance seem destined to continue to shrink, and as they do, so will they facilitate, even necessitate, the further development of new, extended, and diverse skills. This is not to say that people are increasingly more informed (they may not be), but rather that they have an expanding working knowledge of how the world—its governments, its corporations, its advertisers, its communities, and its other institutions—operates and where they themselves fit in the course of events. Stated in more vernacular terms, people are increasingly "street smart," more and more able to cope with the complexities of a shrinking world even if the intelligence, education, and information at their disposal are limited.

This is not to suggest that the future is bright because people everywhere are undergoing transformation of their skills and increasingly sharing sensitivity to the interdependencies that govern their lives. The skill revolution has caught up all people in its undertow, including those who are self-serving, rigid, prejudiced, and resistant to change. Indeed, the skill revolution has intensified and broadened the extent to which many people are self-interested even as it has also had similar consequences for those who tend to be altruistic and civic-minded. Nor is it to imply that people are becoming equally skilled. There is a digital divide, a vast distance between those who have extensive access to information technologies and those who do not. There is an educational divide, a huge discrepancy between those with advanced education and those with little or no education. And there are certainly socioeconomic differences that enable some people to develop their skills more extensively than those whose opportunities are severely limited. Rather, the skill revolution hypothesis simply asserts that whatever resources people may have, they are all becoming increasingly competent. The distinctions among them may remain and they may even become greater—it is likely, for example, that the digital divide may widen with the passage of time—but the persistence of the differences does not negate the idea that the skill revolution enables each person to expand his or her storehouse of competencies, whatever these may be. Stated differently, the changes at work in the world are making it easier for people to expand their skills even as the changes are also requiring that people enlarge their skill base in order to survive.

Nor does the skill revolution underlie a worldwide convergence around the same values. Although there may be a growing commitment to democracy in many parts of the world, this trend stems from a variety of sources and historical dynamics quite unrelated to skill levels. Rather, the hypothesis that skills are undergoing a worldwide transformation merely presumes that people are becoming more skillful in terms of their own cultures, that the Islamic fundamentalist is a more skillful Islamic fundamentalist, that the Russian farmer is a more skillful Russian farmer, and so on across all the varieties of people that comprise humankind.

A Controversial Hypothesis

Although it is easier to identify sources that justify claiming a skill revolution than it is to provide convincing evidence of the claim's validity, both the sources and the evidence are bound to be controversial. The hypothesis is so closely linked to our view of ourselves and the human condition, to our optimistic or pessimistic natures, that people tend to react strongly to any grand claim that, on balance, asserts that ordinary persons, from urban sophisticates to rural peasants, are increasingly competent. "Look at the declining test scores of school children," say the pessimists, "or consider how readily adults join rowdy mobs, or adhere to the dictates of autocrats, or yield to emotional appeals of advertisers, or lose themselves in front of television screens"—to cite but a few of the many anecdotal bases for rejecting the hypothesis. "No," retort the optimists, "think about the worldwide trend toward more and more education, or the ever-greater number of persons who are increasingly able to roam the World Wide Web, or the learning that accompanies the movement of people around the world, or the capacity of most individuals to adapt to increasingly complex urban environments"—to mention some of the anecdotal themes that mark arguments in support of the skill revolution hypothesis. To a large extent, in other words, our view of human capacities and their openness to change, along with any evidence in support of one or another perspective, is shaped by our temperaments, by our fundamental conceptions of who we and others are and who we and others can be.

If both the optimistic and pessimistic lines of reasoning can seem persuasive, it is probably because the skill revolution does not trace a clear-cut and steep upward trend. Rather, the skills involved are acquired incrementally and selectively, thus forming a gentle upward slope that at moments can be jagged as events impel some people to revert to simple and stereotypical characterizations. Any effort to probe the hypothesis, in short, requires nuance and the avoidance of sweeping conclusions. Yet, even if the reasoning and evidence in support of the hypothesis are carefully set forth, the controversy over its validity is unlikely to be resolved. Some observers, those prone to cynicism and doubt, are bound to reject even the most solid evidence that the skills of people are expanding. To repeat, the premises embedded in the hypothesis are too central to the values people hold dear to enable those with pessimistic worldviews to accept the notion that the competence of individuals everywhere is on the rise. And since the evidence offered here is, at best, only partially systematic and clear-cut, it is unlikely to be persuasive for some readers. I can only hope they will at least momentarily suspend their skepticism and ponder whether there may be a germ of truth in the hypothesis.

Despite its controversial foundations, however, one overall statement about the hypothesis does seem justifiable: namely, it is an important proposition. It matters whether or not the world's populations are increasingly competent in terms of their analytic, emotional, and imaginative skills. If the trend line traces a gentle upward slope, then the capacity of governments to be effective and democratic, of economies to be productive and equitable, of cultures to be inclusive and creative is likely to be greater than if the line is flat or a downward slope. Alternatively, if the line remains even or is in decline, then the prospects of leaders and publics confronting their problems and surmounting their challenges are not encouraging.

What Skills and Why a Revolution?

It is important to stress that the skill revolution does not refer to levels of information or intelligence. It is doubtless the case that the more information and intelligence a person has, the more skillful that person is likely to be. Still, there is no one-to-one correlation between the two. One can think of numerous persons who are well informed and highly intelligent but who use these capacities in skewed and absurd ways. Likewise, there is more than a little evidence that people with scant education and limited intelligence handle situations wisely, sensibly, and with aplomb. The Oxford PhD and the Asian peasant may have vastly different degrees of sagacity and information, but they may also be equally capable of grasping the underlying dynamics of situations, anticipating their outcomes, and imagining alternative resolutions. Indeed, it is not inconceivable that in some situations the street smarts of peasants will prove more insightful than those of their well-educated counterparts.

Put differently, skills are needed to convert information into applicable and usable understanding. No matter how plentiful it may be, information is not useful unless it can be organized in ways relevant to its user. It follows that people do not have to have detailed information in order to grasp the nature and potential of situations or the range within which the situations may evolve. As previously noted, what counts is their working knowledge—the combination of information, premises, understandings, experiences, and values that cohesively constitutes an understanding of the rules of the game. This understanding, articulated at many levels of the system, determines how individuals, groups, and nations are likely to confront new situations and manage long-standing ones. Many observers tend toward apoplexy when confronted with findings as to the sizable proportion of people who haven't heard of the World Trade Organization (WTO), but it is an apoplexy that rests on the premise that only with specific information can people reason their way through to a keen grasp of current situations. It may well be sufficient to know that tariff rules imposed by an international organization of which one's country is a member will have consequences for the price at which one can sell one's products without knowing either the name of the organization or the specific rules it is obliged to follow. In short, there is no necessary correspondence between the working knowledge and the level of information one brings to situations, and it is the expansion of working knowledge, analytic as well as emotional, imaginative, and experiential, that lies at the heart of the skill revolution and enables people everywhere to partake in it.

An insightful example of the operation of working knowledge is provided by an experiment conducted in the early 1970s with samples of chess players and non–chess players. Each sample was exposed to a screen on which was flashed for five seconds the same chessboard and then asked to re-create what they saw. The chess players, having working knowledge of the game, had no trouble with the assignment, but the non–chess players, not knowing the rules of the game, were helpless. They could not re-create what they observed. More telling, the chess players were then subdivided into two groups: one was shown a chessboard with pieces arrayed from a game, and the other was confronted with a chessboard with the pieces arrayed at random. The former again had no trouble re-creating what they saw in five seconds or less, whereas the latter were as helpless as the non–chess players. Confronted with an unfamiliar situation, with a situation for which their working knowledge was not appropriate, they could not cope.[1] And so it is with all the situations that arise in the lives of people everywhere in the world. Increasingly the situations are familiar; increasingly the underlying rules through which situations unfold correspond to earlier circumstances; and thus increasingly the working knowledge of people expands, whatever their levels of information and education.

It follows that working knowledge, unlike information and intellectual erudition, is acquired through experience, through observing one's self or others handling or failing to handle the diverse situations that arise every day. Experiential knowledge is more likely to leave residues of understanding than other forms of knowledge. Neither great intelligence nor a backlog of information is required for experiential knowledge to cumulate. That which is experienced or observed firsthand is not easily forgotten or garbled. It lingers, and as it does, it builds upon itself. The commonalties and discrepancies of situations get merged in the senses and understandings of people, with the result that working knowledge evolves an expanding base on which people can draw.

If it is the case, as previously suggested, that the working knowledge people acquire evolves incrementally, on what grounds can it be labeled a "revolution"? It is a misleading label if the notion of revolution suggests that skills have been expanding in a linear fashion. Rather, they expand at a fast pace at some times and at a slow pace at other times. During still other periods they may remain stagnant and even undergo retrogression. Moreover, if the label implies a huge change, even a parametric reversal, then clearly the expansion of skills is not of such a quantitative scope. Even though millions of people are well off today, many still lack sufficient resources to live a good life and extend their skills. In part the answer to the question lies in the large qualitative consequences that can follow from incremental changes that unfold on a worldwide scale with respect to the competence of publics. These may well involve parametric transformations, or at least even a gentle upward slope can significantly affect the way in which people respond to events that impinge on their lives. Partly, too, such a label involves a measure of poetic license: the skill hypothesis is so counterintuitive relative to the way many people think about such matters that referring to enlarged competencies as a skill revolution arrests attention to the potential importance of this development.

Further justification for the label lies in the large degree to which the pace of the skill revolution, incremental as it may be, has accelerated. With the Internet and many other recent technological innovations having collapsed time and distance, the learning curve has of necessity steepened for most people. It may still be only a gentle slope, but its angle of growth seems likely to be much less infinitesimal than was the case in earlier eras.

It is important to stress that the skill revolution is not conceived as one tributary of the larger stream of literature that focuses on the "knowledge revolution" (also designated as the knowledge "explosion").[2] The latter, exemplified by the fact that the processing power of computers doubles roughly every eighteen months, tends to be equated with technology and the ways in which societies apply the knowledge that is generated in industrial and academic laboratories. The trend toward service-based economies, for example, is seen as a major consequence of the knowledge explosion. But here the focus is on individuals and not on economies or technologies, on how individuals have become increasingly competent. Some part of that increase can be traced to the knowledge revolution, to be sure, but as will be seen at greater length in subsequent chapters, an even larger part of the increase derives from a multiplicity of fragmegrative sources that are only indirectly a consequence of economic and technological advances.

A Multiplicity of Skills

Different roles, of course, require different skills if they are to be performed well. But is it possible to generalize about the types of skills that are built into the expectations of all roles? Three are particularly central: what I call analytic, emotional, and imaginative skills, no one of which is more important than the other two and all of which together sum to the abilities that people bring to their roles and responsibilities. Each skill, moreover, not only consists of its own dynamics but also contributes to the expansion of the other two.

Analytic skills help individuals connect cause and effect in situations that are of interest to them. Everyone thinks in terms of scenarios—of what interactions give rise to what outcomes such that each stage of a scenario then moves on to the next stage. The ability to trace the links out of which cause-and-effect chains are fashioned is founded in a respect for nuance and a tolerance of ambiguity. The causal chains are ever-more complex, circuitous, and rapid in the present era of instant communications, thereby necessitating a greater readiness and sensitivity to tracking how situations unfold. Viewed in this way, it is safe to assert that all roles require their occupants to construct scenarios that will enable them to know how and when to perform the tasks built into their roles. Some roles require elaborate scenarios and some involve straightforward ones, with roles located higher in organizations tending to entail the construction of more elaborate scenarios than do those lower down in organizations. In addition to the endogenous skills that attach to role expectations, the analytic skills of all people are shaped by a variety of exogenous sources, such as increases in their education, irrespective of where they may be located in organizational hierarchies and even if they are neither occupants of organizational roles nor active in public affairs organizations.

Emotional skills take the form of the capacity to recognize how one feels about situations, to judge them as good or bad, as welcoming or threatening—capacities that have also been expanded as a consequence of the world's shrinking and imping-ing ever-more closely on the daily lives of people. Emotional skills can be the result of role expectations even though they may also stem from private convictions that people may have apart from their roles. Needless to say, the greater the discrepan-cies between the judgments built into role expectations and the private convictions of their occupants, the more difficult it will be for the occupants to live up to the expectations and perform well in their roles. Obviously, too, emotional skills exert a pull on analytic skills and can readily skew the judgments that people make in the course of carrying out the expectations of their roles.[3]

Imaginative skills involve the ability to appreciate and empathize with the circum-stances of others, to conceive of situations, lifestyles, and cultures that one has never personally observed. Persons who encounter other cultures in one way or another, say, through education or the Internet, are more likely to have higher imaginative skills than those whose distant contacts are minimal. Some roles require extensive contacts with other cultures and subcultures, but many do not, with the result that imaginative skills often develop either prior to or outside the occupancy of roles located in the realm of public affairs.[4] Enlarged imaginative skills derive from a greater ability to conceive of situations, lifestyles, and cultures that one has never personally observed. Given the advent of global television and the vast movement of people around the world—immigrants as well as tourists, students as well as businesspeople, terrorists as well as professionals—who return with tales of what they have seen, more and more people are better able to imagine the benefits and drawbacks of life in distant places and thus draw on skills they did not previously have.

Although knowledge of a role's expectations can tell a lot about how its occupants are likely to act and think, there is no magic in role analysis. Recall that roles accord their occupants some room for the pursuit of their own values and the expression of their own idiosyncrasies as they construct their analytic scenarios. Much the same can be said about their emotional and imaginative skills: there is a range within which people are accorded a free rein to exercise these skills. Still, and to repeat, all roles have a core set of embedded expectations and even though people can vary their conduct within this core, they risk ouster from their roles if they stray too far beyond these core expectations.

Whatever may be the repertoire of skills people develop, and irrespective of whether the skills are fostered by roles' expectations or acquired through any of the sources analyzed below, the result is an expansion of the working knowledge through which people perceive and respond to the worlds around them. Legend-ary are the farmers with little or no education who nonetheless have considerable wisdom—working knowledge—about the way their world works. Alternatively, highly prejudiced persons with a great deal of education may have little wisdom and thus, in effect, a working knowledge composed of unsubstantiated convictions and simplistic, polarized assertions. To repeat, neither the level of education nor the amount of information individuals have is necessarily a measure of the extent of their working knowledge. Information may well enhance skill levels, but the level of a person's skills is not dependent on the information he or she possesses.

An Upward Trend

Both anecdotal and systematic evidence trace an upward slope in the competencies of people around the world that amounts to a skill revolution. Perhaps the most persuasive anecdotal evidence is to be found in the large and worldwide crowds rallying in protest against the war in Iraq. These testify not only to the importance of information technologies, but they also indicate widespread engagement with the course of world affairs. To be sure, sizable protests have occurred in the past, but none have seemed as enduring and expansive as those of recent years. Even more important perhaps, the anecdotal evidence is amply supported by the few systematic studies that have been undertaken. In a study I conducted with Michael Fagen, we focused on the "integrative complexity" through which people assess situations; in our work, we discovered a growth of some 11 percent for seven types of elites across three cultures and three issue areas separated by some sixty or seventy years.[5] Another study found that intelligence quotient (IQ) scores for twenty countries have been rising for more than six decades—a finding not confined to elites and thus even more telling.[6] To be sure, there is little agreement on what IQ scores mean and what IQ tests measure. Some explanations focus on improved nutrition, whereas others simply point out a number of factors that might account for the systematic rise,[7] but the multiplicity of explanations is precisely the central point. The skill revolution is conceived to derive from a variety of sources, no one of which is paramount. Several seem sufficiently powerful to highlight the diversity of sources that underlie the expansion of skills.

The Education Factor

Globally, these patterns of interconnectedness are marked by a long-term trend toward more and more education. In virtually every country the trend line is up for primary, secondary, university, and vocational education. This upward slope is clear for women as well as men in every country for every type of education.[8] To be sure, educators and politicians worry about the quality of education provided at every level, but such worries have not hindered the tendency for people everywhere to seek more schooling and formal training. Likewise, there is no one-to-one correlation between education and analytic, emotional, and imaginative skills, but there are good reasons to believe that the correlation is considerable—that one's skill level is likely to be higher the more education one has had.

In addition to the skill-generating dynamics of formal education, there is more than a little speculation that some informal aspects of youthful experience have also facilitated the acquisition of talent. Most notably, there is cogent speculation—developed too recently to be subjected to systematic testing—that the on-the-spot problem-solving capacity of people is likely to improve across time. Steven Johnson, the most noted proponent of this "cognitively demanding leisure" hypothesis, developed it from observing the recent explosion of new visual media, especially video games and other interactive visual media, and how these media pose "an implicit challenge to our brains: we have to work through the logic of the new interface, follow clues, sense relationships." Johnson sums up the potential consequences of such "brain-boosting media" by stressing that "this is a generation of kids who, in many cases, learned to puzzle through the visual patterns of graphic interfaces before they learned to read. Their fundamental intellectual powers weren't shaped only by coping with words on a page. They acquired an intuitive understanding of shapes and environments, all of them laced with patterns if you think hard enough."[9] Nor are the habits of playing electronic games confined to young people. It has been reported, for example, that some 40 percent of all adults in the United States engage in such pursuits.[10]

Information Technologies as a Source of Skill Enlargement

The advent and rapid spread of diverse technologies for acquiring and exchanging ideas, pictures, and information are surely a major source of the skill revolution. One need only observe how adept young children are at using the computer and accessing the Internet to appreciate how extensive the impact of these technologies has been. The data descriptive of increasing computer access and the reach of global television in most countries of the world are stunning.[11] And for those who own neither a computer nor a television set, the proliferation of Internet cafés and community centers with television hookups continues in rural as well as urban areas. In the United States, 98.9 percent of its libraries offered free access to the Internet in 2005, an offer seized by 1.5 billion visitors.[12] Again a qualification is in order: neither computers nor global television necessarily lead to greater skill levels, but the probabilities are high that more people than not are enlarged by their ability to acquire, circulate, and assess ideas through such communications media.

Nor are computers and global television the only technologies that have accelerated the skill revolution. Cellular phones, a more recent technology, have also served to enlarge the talents of people in all parts of the world by connecting them to distant others and ideas and information that would not otherwise be available. The impact of wireless communications is perhaps most noticeable in Africa: from 1999 through 2004, the number of cell phone subscribers in Africa jumped from 7.5 million to 76.8 million, an average annual increase of some 58 percent. Since there are parts of Africa that still communicate by beating drums, the advent of ever-increasing numbers of cell phones amounts to "a technological revolution akin to television in the 1940s in the United States."[13]

Still another recent trend expressive of the skill revolution is the use of computer technology to record personal thoughts, what have come to be known as blogs. Again the data are stunning. In the United States, some 14.2 million blogs existed in 2005, with nearly 80,000 new ones created every day and with some 900,000 blog postings made on a daily basis. The blogosphere, as the sum of all blogs has come to be known, was doubling in size every five and a half months.[14]

Of course, as is the case with all new innovations, there is a downside to the advent of new and diverse means of electronic communication. Some concern has been expressed, for example, that the proliferation of information technologies has led more than a few persons to become excessively dependent on them, even to the point of compulsively turning to one or another electronic technology for messages, data, and ideas so frequently as to disrupt the normal routines of their lives and families. For such persons the dependence is like a drug addiction, what has been called OCD, or online compulsive disorder.[15]

The Mobility Upheaval

Although occasionally slowed by war and epidemics, people are on the move everywhere. From business executives to artists, from tourists to terrorists, from academics to athletes, from immigrants to expatriates, from workers to refugees—to mention only some of the more salient groups—the mobility of people is growing on a scale that can appropriately be called an upheaval. According to the International Air Transport Association, "There have been two years of conservative increases in worldwide passenger traffic."[16] A host of skills is required to adjust to new circumstances elsewhere in the world. In addition, as the mobility of those who directly move about the world multiplies encounters with other cultures, imaginative skills are also multiplied through the letters, pictures, and messages those on the move send home. The data depicting the mobility upheaval are no less stunning than those descriptive of the exposure to education and information technologies.[17]

Urban Life as a Source of Skill Enlargement

There are no hard data on the ways in which the challenges of surviving in large urban communities enlarge the skills of people. But the number and size of such communities is growing dramatically, and with that growth, skills at coping with crime, strikes, traffic jams, water shortages, polluted garbage, and many other urban problems also seem likely to grow. For people at all rungs on the income ladder, coping with the complexities of urban life is an education in itself.

Conclusion

It is worth stressing again that pessimists will doubtless argue that both the premises and perspectives of the foregoing discussion are far-fetched, that ordinary people have little consequence in world affairs—that they don't count. Not only are skeptics likely to contend that assessing individuals in terms of their roles is more confounding than clarifying, but many critics may argue even more adamantly that the skill revolution is an exaggeration, that huge multitudes of people are as dumb as ever. And even if skill levels are rising, such reasoning would conclude, nothing would change because the leaders of states and other large collectivities pursue their goals without regard for the wishes of individuals, irrespective of whether or not they are mobilized and aggregated.

Even though this line of thought may be widespread, it is rooted in a belief system that takes a dim view of the competence of people and is nourished by contrary evidence that seizes on anecdotes indicating the public is ill-informed and superficial. "Just think," many doubters exclaim, "polls show that huge majorities of people don't know the name of the capital of Pakistan, a sure sign of public ignorance." As suggested, however, such reasoning wrongly equates the level of information with the quality of working knowledge; knowing that Islamabad is the capital of Pakistan is not necessary to grasping what may follow from a coup d'état there. This reasoning rejects the relevance of the identified sources of greater skills, and it is composed of links that do not hold up in the face of the welter of data and anecdotes pointing to a powerfully pervasive and growing wisdom among people everywhere in the world.

To repeat, because the point is so crucial, at some basic level our view of the skills and relevance of people in world affairs springs from our temperaments, from our underlying and fundamental philosophical (and perhaps psychological) presumptions about human nature, its flexibility, its receptivity to evidence, and its capacity for change. Some of us see others as static, whereas others of us perceive people as open to learning and able to enlarge their working knowledge. My nature tells me that people increasingly appreciate the ever-greater complexity and fragmegration of world affairs—they can hardly avoid it—within the context of their own culture and immediate circumstances. In short, people count! They count, moreover, in a wide variety of ways, as the ensuing chapters seek to demonstrate.

CHAPTER FOUR

Demographic Trends

Am I supposed to have a child to save the system?

—Jan Delaror[1]

We have become so selfish, so greedy. Did your parents sit you down with a spreadsheet and figure out whether they could afford to have two or three children? No, of course not. Did this ever happen before anywhere? No, of course not. We live in the richest place and at the best time, and everyone is worrying whether they can afford to take their next vacation or buy a boat. It's kind of sickening.

—Ninni Lundblad[2]

Before turning to the dynamics—the talents, fears, and goals—whereby individuals count, note can usefully be taken of the more mundane, formal way in which they are counted, namely, the census, which is a quantitative depiction of the number of people in a community or society. As the above epigraphs imply, a census traces large patterns of data, but it cannot capture the motivations, tensions, and aspirations that individuals possess or the challenges they face. Nonetheless, it is important to acknowledge the demographic dimensions of people prior to probing the more informal and intimate aspects of their lives. The former do not predict the latter, but censuses do provide a broad context for assessing different roles, the expectations that attach to them, and the variability of the behavior within them.

Although the task is difficult, complex, and often controversial, nearly all societies and communities conduct periodic censuses to count how many people reside within their boundaries. They need to know how many are men and women, how old they are, whether they are partnered, how many children and relatives live in their household, and so on across all the categories that comprise a census. Such demographic data are needed for a variety of reasons: they outline the prospects for population growth or decline, commercial activities, military potential, educational attainment, ethnic rivalry, and a host of other aspects that underlie a society's viability both in the near and long term.

Counting people in a census requires a large organization composed of planners, interviewers, computer specialists, and analysts, all of whom have to devote weeks, months, even years, to framing and conducting the census so that the results are as accurate as possible. The task is difficult because members of the public may be uncooperative or not home when the census taker arrives. It is complex because asking the relevant questions requires a clear notion of what kinds of information are needed. It is controversial because some groups often feel their members have not been adequately counted and that the results of the census are thus unfavorably skewed against them. In the United States, controversy is further heightened because the results of the census conducted every ten years determine the number of seats in the U.S. House of Representatives accorded each state, thus often creating conflicts over whether or not the tallies should be based on sampling techniques to offset the people not at home when the census taker called.

In short, it is not possible to account for every member of the population, with the result that some groups argue that samples and extrapolations have to be used, while others insist that the gathered data are sufficient because sampling techniques are biased. Despite such difficulties, however, periodic census data are necessary to the planning of public policy, corporate programs, political campaigns, and many other features of a society's future.

When controversies over the framing or results of a census do arise, they can readily be seen as expressive of fragmegrative processes. Those groups that want to accept the census results view them as serving to integrate the society, whereas those who argue that the results are skewed in undesirable directions have the consequence of at least momentarily fragmenting its ties.

This is not to imply that all countries ask the same questions in their censuses. Quite to the contrary: every country probes for patterns particular to its own situation even as they all seek to tabulate the number, gender, and age of the people in the country at the time of the census. In some cases, for example, a country's census avoids asking people questions that might yield patterns better left uncovered, such as items about minority status, because the aggregate answers lie outside the bounds of political discourse and might unduly heighten tensions.

The Demographic Cycle: Birth and Death Rates

The size of a population is not constant. Depending on the excess of deaths over births, or vice versa, it will grow or decline in size, and its future growth and decline can be projected on the basis of the proportion of women in the population at a child-bearing age as well as the factors affecting their decision to have children (or not). These decisions can be affected by the state of the economy, by whether more or fewer children will contribute to a family's well-being, by religious precepts, by the taxing and family policies of governments, by world affairs and whether they are conducive to children living a normal life, and by a number of other factors that make it difficult to extrapolate the central trends that determine the direction of population size.

Demographers have a standard theory for projecting a population's trend line. History records that, on average, death rates decline some fifty years before the birthrate because new medical and sanitation facilities enable people to live longer. During this period the population grows at a rapid rate, crowding cities, depleting resources, and otherwise making life more difficult and eventually, some fifty years later, generating a wide range of incentives for families to limit their size and thus to initiate a decline in the birthrate and to slow the absolute growth of the population. This period of slowed growth has been called one of "incipient decline" because each year's growth is less than that of the previous year. The theory projects that after a number of years the aging of the population and the diminution of women in their child-bearing years will increase to the point where an absolute decline in the total size of the population will set in.

The theory explains well why India and China have such large populations. The West brought these countries sanitation and medical practices that reduced death during childbirth and enabled people to live longer. By the time large and complex urban communities arose to reduce the incentives for large families several decades later, the Indian and Chinese populations were already huge. In the case of China, the population was so large that its government adopted a one-child policy that penalized families who had two or more children, albeit with more effect in cities than in rural areas. The theory has also been borne out in most industrial countries, none of which employs coercive penalties. Not only has the rate of growth in their populations been reduced, but also many countries, including every country of Europe, have passed the peak of population growth and started down the slope of incipient decline. Although those countries that seek to increase family size by offering tax deductions, cash payments, and job leaves have slowed the decline,[3] they have not reversed it. In rural South Korea the decline has been so precipitous that it has transformed the "rural landscape, shuttering schools, shrinking class sizes, setting off village celebrations for the rare birth of a baby."[4] Consequently, South Korea reversed its policy of providing government support for vasectomies and tubal ligations. These reversals are now given free,[5] as is care for a couple's third or fourth child. In some Japanese communities, parents are offered $4,600 for the birth of a child and $460 for ten years. Singapore offers $3,000 for the first child, $9,000 in cash and savings for the second, and as much as $18,000 each for the third and fourth.[6] In Russia the problem has been especially acute since the end of the Cold War. Owing in large part to a weak economy, the Russian birth rate fell from an average of 2.62 children per woman in 1958 and 1959 to 1.89 children in 1990 and 1.24 children in 2004. At the same time the Russian death rate declined to the point where the average Russian man lived 58.9 years, or much less than in other industrial countries and some two decades less than the comparable figure for the United States. In 2004 only 10.4 babies were born for every sixteen Russians who died. Little wonder that the Russian president, Vladimir Putin, devoted most of his 2006 annual address to the Parliament to announcing financial incentives and subsidies to encourage women to have children.[7] In effect, he sought to reverse an annual population decline of some 700,000 a year since 1990.[8] In other parts of the world, such as Israel, a more effective means of preventing incipient decline is to reiterate that the population of neighbors is growing at a rate that could prove threatening.

Some of these problems derive from the fact that standard demographic theory is marked by one glaring problem. No analyst has come up with a convincing explanation for a basic determinant of population size, namely, why some families have a third and fourth child and others settle for only one or two. Stated more generally, what determines the number of children that couples have?[9] Clearly, this gap in the theory is important, as it can inhibit accurate projections of how a population's size will evolve in the years ahead. One plausible explanation of the theoretical gap concerns the new roles and opportunities available to women in developed societies. As a thirty-three-year-old Swedish woman put it, "There are times when I think perhaps I will be missing something important if I don't have a child. But today women finally have so many chances to have the life they want. To travel and work and learn. It's exciting and demanding. I find it hard to see where the children would fit in."[10]

Whatever may be the proper explanation for the pervasiveness of incipient decline in the developed world, the data are troubling in a number of ways. At this time the number of young and old people in the world is roughly equal, but the data indicate that by 2050 the number of old people will be double that of young people and Africans will outnumber Europeans by three to one. Among other things, this prospect means that the labor of young people in industrial countries will not be sufficient to pay for the retirement years of old people. In sum, a demographic catastrophe may lie ahead: in the words of a Swedish strategic planner,

> Nobody on earth can tell you what is going on here. Sometimes I think it must be just a blip—we've had them before—and everything will turn out the way we expect it to. But I guess I don't really believe that. I believe we are seeing a fundamental shift in human behavior. We have lived for 200 years on the idea of progress. That the future will be better than the past.... But I think these days have ended now. I have no data to support my views. But young people now seem to have a sense that living for today is about the best they can do.[11]

A Japanese gynecologist had a simple and straightforward answer to the question of why the size of the population in his country was undergoing decline:

> "Japanese people simply aren't having enough sex," Dr. Kunio Kitamura, the director of the Japan Family Planning Association, told the *Japan Times,* adding that more sex is needed to reverse Japan's plummeting birthrate. He spoke after an association survey of 936 people between the ages of 16 and 49 showed that 31 percent had not had sex for more than a month "for no particular reason." Last year, Japan's fertility rate—the average number of children a woman bears in her lifetime—fell to an all-time low of 1.25. Demographers say a rate of 2.1 is needed to keep a population from declining.[12]

The Census as an Indicator of Power and Weaknesses

As mentioned above, in some countries the census is a key tool for governments to assess their capabilities relative to others in the international community, especially for those countries whose population trends may put them at a disadvantage relative to their neighbors. Depending on how it is conducted, a census can tell policymakers at home and abroad a lot about various dimensions of power, about the number of people of military age, about the types and levels of education attained and a society's potential for innovation, about the ethnic and religious makeup of a society and thus its potential for internal rivalries and conflicts, about the economic circumstances of a people and thus their capacity for achieving or maintaining an independent foreign policy, and so on across a variety of indicators examined in subsequent chapters. Perhaps more important, when censuses are taken periodically, comparisons among them offer trend lines as to whether a society is gaining or losing out in its effort to remain competitive in the international community.

Europe offers a striking example of how demographic trends can affect the relations of states. Whereas the median age in the United States will increase only slightly by 2050 to 35.4 years, in Europe it is anticipated to rise from 37.7 to 52.3 during the same time period. Translating these projections in terms of the relative capabilities of the two regions, it seems clear that the growth of U.S. economic and military power will continue to outpace that of Europe. As one observer noted, "the European countries are aging in a world that is becoming younger. And in a global economy, they're not going to share in the energy and vitality that comes with a young population."[13] Stated in terms of policy, "with its population not only aging but shrinking as well, Europe seems to face two broad possibilities: either it will have to make up the population shortfall by substantial increases in immigration, which would almost surely create new political tensions in countries where anti-immigrant parties have gained strength in recent years, or it will have to accept being older and smaller and therefore, as some have been warning, less influential in world affairs."[14] Put differently, it has been estimated that "one million immigrants a year into Europe would be the same as women having on average one more child. But one million immigrants a year would mean 50 million by 2050, and that alone would be a demographic shift that many Europeans find culturally and politically unacceptable."[15]

At an earlier time—most notably prior to the advent of the birth control pill in 1960—it could be argued that demographic circumstances such as these could be reversed through governmental tax policies. The pill and other changes in social norms that have led women to postpone childbearing—or not to have children—make it increasingly unlikely, however, that governmental policies can substantially resolve demographic problems. Nevertheless, governments continue to frame policies designed to solve their declining birthrates. Germany, for example, is seeking to halt the decline through extensive tax breaks and free child care for families with small children.[16]

Of course, there are limits to what a census can reveal. As will be seen in the ensuing chapters, there are innumerable aspects of power that do not lend themselves to quantitative tabulation. The capacity to carry out a reliable census, for example, is a subtle aspect that is not easily assessed. Nonetheless, demographic data are crucial to sound evaluations of the ways in which people count.

Immigration Policies

One major way countries seek to compensate for incipient decline, especially when that decline portends a shortage of persons with the skills necessary to a modern economy, is by admitting into their ranks new people from abroad whose talents are viewed as relevant to the economy's needs. The United States, for example, has addressed its persistent shortage of nurses by giving special immigration privileges to nurses from abroad, especially from the Philippines (thus resulting in a shortage of nurses in the Philippines). Similarly, computer specialists deemed to have special skills that are crucial to the functioning of the economy are classified in such a way as to ensure their admittance, either temporarily or permanently, into the country they seek to enter. Indeed, to cite a specific example, the White House resorted to importing cheap technical skills by hiring a company that imports workers from India to upgrade the president's correspondence-tracking computer system.[17] Perhaps there is no better indication of the skill revolution than the advantage that potential immigrants with advanced technological training have in the complex and often arduous processes of immigration. On the other hand, even though the new immigrants offer considerable benefits to the host country and its economy, they might also contribute to unemployment by working for lower wages than their counterparts in their newly adopted country.

In some countries, moreover, there is a shortage of people ready to take on menial jobs such as taxi drivers and hotel maids. Often such shortages are offset by open immigration policies that do not require high levels of education and training. In Washington, D.C., for example, a preponderance of taxi drivers is from Africa and many of those who work in hotels as maids, desk clerks, or janitors come from countries that were once part of the Soviet Union. Similarly, by 2000 the population of the state of Iowa was undergoing such a decline ("If Iowa retains every single one of its graduating high school students between now and 2005, we'll have a decrease of 3 percent of the available work force") that it undertook luring immigrants by rendering the state into an "immigration recruitment zone" and thereby creating a viable workforce.[18]

Unlike the long-standing readiness of the United States to accept immigrants, Europe has adhered to an official policy of "zero immigration." Statistics, however, indicate that increasingly Europe will need to surmount its antipathy to immigrants and allow—even recruit—them to enter the workforce in various capacities. From just over 15 percent at present, the proportion of people over sixty-five in the European Union (EU) was projected to rise to nearly 23 percent by 2025, a change that suggests pension systems face collapse unless immigration is increased: the EU estimated that some 75 million new immigrants would be needed by 2050.[19]

As will be seen in Chapter 6, immigration policies that allow for the enrichment of a society's skills can be a mixed blessing. Yes, the skill level is enriched or supplemented, but in more than a few countries the presence of outsiders can be the source of prejudice and group conflicts.

The Brain Drain and Its Reversal

For the societies from which people emigrate, however, the consequences can be quite serious. Often it means either that those who leave are already highly skilled or that they are very bright and go abroad for advanced education, never to return. This "brain drain," as it has come to be called, lowers the overall skill level of the departed society and thereby deprives it of rich and irreplaceable resources. In some cases, such as Canada, bright graduate students who are awarded Canadian fellowships to study abroad receive the award on the condition that they return to Canada for their professional careers.

In other cases, a pattern has emerged wherein the drain is reversed as some of those who emigrated return to their home countries after receiving their training abroad. They do so for a variety of reasons. Some come back because their sense of loyalty leads them to recognize that their skills can be of use to their country of origin. Some return because their home economy has picked up and offers opportunities not available in the country where they acquired their advanced training. Still others contribute to the reversed brain drain because they are, in effect, homesick—that is, although they benefited from their training abroad, they never came to feel at home in the host country and are led by their earlier loyalties and beckoning opportunities to return to their families, friends, and cultures where they are appreciated and comfortable.

In some cases the dynamics of the brain drain and its reversal give rise to dramatic personal stories. When the apartheid regime was overthrown in South Africa, for instance, more than a few expatriates who had settled abroad and established a good middle-class life for themselves and their children were beseeched to return to their ancestral home and help it construct a new, race-free society. Doctors, educational administrators, and a host of others went through anguish deciding whether to uproot their families on behalf of their loyalties to their country of origin. Or consider the plight of Ali Shaker, a lawyer who had to flee Iraq in 1991 as a consequence of leading an uprising against Saddam Hussein and who settled in the United States to start a new life after being reunited with his wife and young daughter. Even though his family became more comfortable in their new home, he confronted an agonizing dilemma when Saddam's Iraq fell, and he entered a program run by the State Department to train prosecutors and judges to return to post-Saddam Iraq. On the one hand, he could not imagine declining to return to Iraq, but on the other, he could not imagine leaving his family again—a choice created by his daughter's insistence on staying in her new school and the need for both his wife and daughter to remain in order to qualify for permanent residency. These circumstances led to a complex line of reasoning: "Maybe he could commute back and forth every couple of months.... Maybe he could go for two years, three at the most. 'To be honest, it will still be painful,' he said. 'But I'd be doing something bigger than myself; something for my country, for my people, for my blood. It's going to be worth it.'"[20]

Conclusion

The science of demography is designed to trace shifts in the composition of large populations. It is about the counting of many people, their movement and their stability. Embedded in the huge quantities of data that demographers examine, however, are compelling stories of individuals who occupy a variety of roles but are essentially ignorant of the society-wide statistics and patterns to which their role behavior contributes. No less important, the data subsume a variety of troubling problems both within societies and across the world, as will be seen in subsequent chapters.

PART I

People on the Move

CHAPTER FIVE

Citizens

The role of citizen is crucial to the conduct of world affairs because states act on their behalf, or at least claim they have their support for their foreign policies. Until recent years this support was taken for granted. Citizens were compliant and supportive of any goals their country might seek to realize abroad. Today, however, their support cannot be taken for granted. The role of citizen is changing. People are more attentive to world affairs and more ready to criticize the policies pursued by their governments. More than that, they have more contacts abroad and may seek, either individually or collectively through their nongovernmental organizations, to act contrary to their government's policies, a pattern that is likely to accelerate with the passage of time.

In their long-standing, more conventional role, one of the most important ways in which people count is when they are counted in their political roles as citizens. This occurs in a variety of settings and perhaps the most conspicuous setting is Election Day and the votes citizens do or do not cast. Votes not only determine who wins and who loses, but they also provide data on the engagement of citizens in the political processes of their country. Viewed from this perspective, the proportion of a population that votes in national elections—the so-called turnout rate—is a measure of how involved a citizenry is in the affairs of its society, at least for those countries that neither require nor prohibit voting.[1] Turnout rates provide over time a picture of how the citizenry relates to its government. An increasing rate may suggest growing involvement, though a rate that turns sharply upward in one election might be interpreted as reflecting public agitation over the course of events. On the other hand, a declining rate implies that the public may be increasingly apathetic, alienated, or suspicious toward the world of officials. In short, people are counted even when they are inactive, and their inaction is often as meaningful as their counted actions.

The turnout rate varies considerably among democracies. Among most European countries the rate exceeds 70 percent, whereas elections for presidents of the United States peaked at 63 percent in 1960 and subsequently traced a slowly declining rate that hovered around 50 percent and then fell below half the eligible electorate in 1996. This decline in U.S. turnout has been interpreted as reflective of growing apathy and cynicism toward the political arena and the policies pursued therein.[2] The turnout rates for elections in political entities below the national government often fall below 30 percent and are even more strikingly suggestive of disinterest on the part of the public.

Yet, interpreting the turnout rate requires caution. Low rates could be interpreted not as apathy or cynicism, but as satisfaction and a readiness to accept whatever policies governments pursue—a stable consensus. Likewise, a sudden and sharp upturn in the turnout rate could well be a sign of distress among people, or at least sufficient involvement to warrant concern over the potential consequences of a highly agitated public. Caution is also in order because the practices of citizenship are not in abeyance between elections. On the contrary, there are other ways of engaging in political action that may, in fact, be more consequential than voting and that suggest conclusions quite contrary to those inferable from declines in the turnout rate.

Quite aside from the meaning of the turnout rate, Election Day is a moment in the life of a democratic society when people count in an extraordinary way. For at that moment when the campaign is over, the polls are open, and the outcome is unknown, there is nothing anyone can do to affect the results (aside from fraud). Democratic societies between elections are dominated by only a small portion of their citizens—those selected to govern—and subject to the whim or avarice of that portion. But Election Day is an exquisite moment in the sense that it is a moment dominated by society in its entirety. All concerned can only sit back and wait for the tallied result.[3] And as they wait, calmly or impatiently, one can only hope they are in awe of the fact that at that moment the people really do count!

Citizenship between Elections

But elections are by no means the only way in which people as citizens are counted. Pollsters periodically survey representative groups of citizens on whatever issues may comprise the political agenda of the day. There is no one-to-one correlation between the polling data and the actions of officials, but the latter are usually attentive to the former, and on occasion they may well tailor their actions to conform with the central findings of the polls. But as in the case of nonvoters, the alienation of some people sometimes reaches the point where they refuse to cooperate with pollsters, not only because they are tired of phone calls asking for their opinions but also because prevailing policies upset them so much as to alienate them from participating in this informal dimension of the political process. During the war against Saddam Hussein, for example, one American resigned from the public:

> Please don't ask me about the war. Don't ask if I strongly approve or partly approve or strongly disapprove; I'll cut you off. And don't ask my demographic stand-ins either. I don't trust their answers in this matter, and I refuse to vouch for their ability to communicate anything but their own confusion, particularly if they feel anything like I do: gung-ho at breakfast time, heartsick by lunch hour, angry at supper, all played out

by bedtime and disembodied in the middle of the night when I wake up to check the cable news scrolls. If I'm the American public, and it is I, then no opinion poll, however probing, can drill down into the tar pit of emotions churning and steaming at my core and dredge up a representative sample of anything.... The "numbers," as pollsters like to call them (thereby exposing their insulting working premise that human behavior is a digital affair), have been all over the place since the war started.[4]

In addition to unofficial polls, individual politicians employ other techniques to count the sentiments of their constituents. In the United States the tradition of writing your representatives, or of signing and sending them a postcard written by an organization to which you belong, results in a large flow of mail and e-mail that both the White House and many congressional offices tabulate in order to keep abreast of the drift of opinion on diverse issues.[5] The actions of some politicians are often inconsistent with the themes of their tabulated mail, but at the same time they are eager to know what their constituents are thinking. Others ignore the themes expressed in organization-generated correspondence, but most will take seriously a heartfelt, handwritten letter, a nearly identical message. Even more important are letters or messages from constituents who contribute money to political campaigns.

Elections and letter writing, however, are only the most conventional and institutionalized means of counting people in their political roles. Equally important, and certainly more salient, are the times when crowds gather and march in protest over one or another situation. With the advent of the Internet and e-mail, various social movements have become ever-more conspicuous features of public affairs around the world. In these cases the literal counting of people who participate in protest marches can be a source of considerable controversy, however, with those favoring the purpose of a march tending to exaggerate the number and with those opposing it tending to underestimate the turnout, and with the police usually coming up with estimates that fall between the high and low figures of the proponents and opponents. In order to reduce the discrepancies in crowd counts, the *San Francisco Chronicle* devised a systematic, if not a scientific, technique for estimating the number of people marching and attending a rally: using a photograph of the crowd taken from a plane that flew directly over an antiwar demonstration held on February 16, 2003, it subdivided the photo into rectangles and then counted the number of people (564) in the most densely crowded rectangle. That figure was then used to estimate the number in all the other rectangles. The result was a count of not more than 65,000, a figure considerably less than the 200,000 to 250,000 estimated by the police and the event sponsors.[6]

The Making of Citizens

Whether people are born in a country or emigrate to it, they are not automatically citizens. Legally they may be regarded as occupants of this role, but a lot of effort on the part of governments and other societal agencies has to be expended to move them beyond the legal to the social and political dimensions of citizenship. It is tempting to believe that citizenship is a natural role based on instinctive orientations. Such is not the case, however. On the contrary, citizenship is a constructed role. Individuals have to be taught the requirements of the role. In the United States, the Pledge of Allegiance and other flag-worship activities at sporting events, in schools, and in other settings that involve large numbers of people exemplify processes of making citizens. To the extent that these processes are ineffective, as is the case in many countries, it is a measure of the growing importance of other roles people occupy as well as of weaknesses in the state's machinery for producing citizens.

The Transformation of Citizenship

Depending on the evidence cited, there are good reasons to presume that citizenship is undergoing both diminution and expansion. If turnout rates during elections are examined, the evidence points to a clear-cut conclusion that diminution is occurring. But if data on less conventional forms of political participation are considered, and if the continued increase of persons with dual citizenship is appreciated, one is led to conclude that the practices of citizenship are expanding, especially in the industrialized world. To some degree the expansion involves people abandoning the traditional role of citizens—by not voting—in favor of other means of political engagement or by more fully taking on the role of consumer.

In short, like most everything else in an era of pervasive and accelerating globalization, the nature of citizenship, of having societal rights in exchange for performing national obligations, is undergoing transformation. Not only is the concept becoming increasingly ambiguous, but some analysts also contend that citizens are being marginalized by elites as well as by their own actions. These analysts argue that the decline of turnout rates to record levels is illustrative in this regard, that norms have changed such that personal action has replaced collective action as the means of fulfilling the tasks and responsibilities of citizenship, and that therefore "the era of the modern citizen, which began with a bang, is quietly slipping away."[7] Today, this line of reasoning asserts, "governments can fight wars, collect revenues, and administer programs without having to rely much upon the collective and active support of millions of ordinary people."[8]

Such a conclusion, however, is profoundly misleading, even erroneous, if attention turns to citizenship between elections—to signing petitions; participating in demonstrations, consumer boycotts, unofficial strikes; and occupying buildings—activities once described as "unconventional" but subsequently labeled "elite-challenging" as their frequency increasingly rendered them conventional.[9] As can be seen in the several parts of Table 5.1, the net percentage shift in virtually all these activities increased between 1974 and 2000 for seven European countries and the United States. The contradiction between these findings and those for voter turnout has been convincingly resolved by those who gathered the between-election data: describing the distributions in Table 5.1 as "dramatic evidence of rising mass political activism," the authors concluded that the "confusion over whether participation is rising or falling arises from the fact that we are dealing with two distinct processes: elite-directed participation [i.e., voting turnout] is eroding, but more autonomous and active forms of participation are rising. This decline in voter turnout reflects a long-term intergenerational decline in party loyalty."[10] Stated in terms of the perspective advanced in Chapter 2, Table 5.1 affirms the notion that the world has entered the age of the individual.

Table 5-1. The Rise of "Unconventional" Participation, 1974—2000

Table 5-1a. Percentage who have signed a petition

Country	1974	1981	1990	1995	2000	Net Shift:
Britain	23	63	75		81	+58
W. Germany	31	47	57	66	47	+16
Italy	17	42	48		55	+38
Netherlands	22	35	51		61	+39
U.S.	60	64	72	71	81	+21
Finland	20	30	41	39	51	+31
Switzerland	46		63	68		+22
Austria	39		48		56	+17
Mean:	*32*	*42*	*57*	*58*	*63*	+30

Note: In case a cell is empty, the mean for each column is calculated by inputting the figure for the last available year for that country.

Table 5-1b. Percentage who have taken part in a demonstration

Country	1974	1981	1990	1995	2000	Net Shift:
Britain	6	10	14		13	+ 7
W. Germany	9	15	21	26	22	+13
Italy	19	27	36		35	+16
Netherlands	7	13	25		32	+25
U.S.	12	13	16	16	21	+ 9
Finland	6	14	14	13	15	+ 9
Switzerland	8		16	17		+ 9
Austria	7		10	16		+ 9
Mean:	9	13	19	20	21	+12

Note: In case a cell is empty, the mean for each column is calculated by inputting the figure for the last available year for that country.

Table 5-1c. Percentage who have taken part in a consumer boycott

Country	1974	1981	1990	1995	2000	Net Shift:
Britain	6	7	14		17	+11
W. Germany	5	8	10	18	10	+ 5
Italy	2	6	11		10	+ 2
Netherlands	6	7	9		22	+16
U.S.	16	15	18	19	25	+ 9
Finland	1	9	14	12	15	+14
Switzerland	5			11		+ 6
Austria	3		5		10	+ 7
Mean:	6	8	11	12	15	+ 9

Note: In case a cell is empty, the mean for each column is calculated by inputting the figure for the last available year for that country.

Table 5-1d. Percentage who have taken part in an unofficial strike

Country	1974	1981	1990	1995	2000	Net Shift:
Britain	5	7	10		9	+4
W. Germany	1	2	2	4	2	+1
Italy	1	3	6		5	+4
Netherlands	2	2	3		5	+3
U.S.	2	3	5	4	6	+4
Finland	5	6	8	5	3	−2
Switzerland	1		2	2		+1
Austria	1		1		2	+1
Mean:	2	3	5	4	4	+2

Note: In case a cell is empty, the mean for each column is calculated by inputting the figure for the last available year for that country.

Table 5-1e. Percentage who have occupied buildings

Country	1974	1981	1990	1995	2000	Net Shift:
Britain	1	3	2		2	+1
W. Germany	1	2	1	2	1	0
Italy	5	6	8		8	+3
Netherlands	2	2	3		6	+4
U.S.	2	2	2	2	4	+2
Finland	0	1	2	1	1	+1
Switzerland	1			1		0
Austria	1		1		1	0
Mean:	2	2	3	3	3	+l

Note: In case a cell is empty, the mean for each column is calculated by inputting the figure for the last available year for that country.
Source: "1974" figures are from the Political Action surveys (actual fieldwork was carried out in 1973–1976); the figures for 1981–2000 are from the World Values Surveys /European Values Surveys. The "1990" surveys were carried out in 1990 and 1991; the "1995" surveys in 1995 and 1996; and the "2000" surveys in 1999-2000.

Counting Citizens in a Transnational Context

As the world becomes more intimate and national boundaries more porous, the notion of citizenship has become more problematic for more than a few people. With protest marches that coordinate like-minded people in different countries, with extensive international travel and migratory flows accelerating other than in interludes marked by war or epidemic diseases, with the notion of a global civil society increasingly viewed as emergent, and with globalization having become a pervasive preoccupation, the idea that national loyalties can be superceded by attachment to transnational entities and ideals appears to be attractive to more and more people. The numbers of people so attracted are not large, but neither are they inconspicuous. Indeed, some trend data indicate that their ranks are likely to grow as generations change. In one study based on attitudes in seventy countries, for example, it was found that "almost one-fifth of the baby boomers born after World War II see themselves as cosmopolitan citizens of the globe, identifying with their continent or the world as a whole, but this is true of only one in ten of the group brought up in the interwar years, and of even fewer of the prewar generation."[11] Thus has the concept of cosmopolitans—citizens of the world—reentered the analytic literature, just as the surge of concern over a person's identity has highlighted questions about what it means to be a citizen in a globalizing world. Some analysts have recently become increasingly inclined to speak of "personhood" as a characterization of individuals rather than referring to their citizenship.

In short, citizenship is an ambiguous concept. In a sense it always has been, but the complexities of globalization have made it more so. Some have even argued that the complexities are such as to have created a "crisis of citizenship," that "the context for a citizenship based on belonging to a single nation is being eroded."[12] Such generalizations refer to the question of who is included and who is excluded from becoming a citizen of a country, of what rights and obligations are held by or denied to resident aliens and immigrants, of whether a universal conception of citizenship is evolving and superceding long-standing particularistic conceptions, of the ways in which the concept of citizenship is undergoing change in different parts of the world, and so on across a wide range of specific issues. In recent years, for example, more and more countries permit resident aliens to vote in their national or local elections.[13] In Japan a native American citizen born in Brooklyn ran for elective office in the city council of Inuyama, a right accorded him by virtue of having a Japanese wife.[14] Needless to say, such ambiguities make it very difficult to count and compare the number of people that are recognized as citizens by different countries. Indeed, if the number of foreigners in a country at the time a census is taken is included, the practice in most censuses, the task of obtaining accurate counts becomes especially difficult.

At the opposite extreme from loosening conceptions of citizenship is a perspective rooted in patriotism, a view that equates citizenship with love of country and the land and boundaries that set it apart from other countries. During wars or natural disasters, love of country and a sense of belonging to it increase substantially, and the emphasis on being patriotic becomes intense. At such times individuals whose ties to the bounded land have yielded to cosmopolitan tendencies face harsh criticism or, worse, harassment and even incarceration in some instances. "You are either with us or against us," say the patriots to the cosmopolitans, an attitude that can tear societies apart, thus introducing further ambiguity into the concept of citizenship. Indeed, the crisis of citizenship becomes increasingly salient as the tensions between inclusivity and exclusivity reach a peak when wars are launched and fought.

It is a crisis that is profoundly fragmegrative, a conclusion that is further illustrated by conflicts over the processes whereby people acquire citizenship. In France some lawmakers seek to end "birthright citizenship" because they believe it is abused by efforts to acquire access to French healthcare and welfare systems.[15] Likewise, some in the United States, including members of Congress, want to overturn a similar rule that accords citizenship to those born in the country because they view the birthright rule as providing too much of an incentive to illegal immigrants.[16] But the central tendency in the United States is toward leniency and not only in granting posthumous citizenship to foreign-born soldiers.[17] In fact, there is a broad array of nonprofit groups that help immigrants assimilate, adapt, and ultimately prepare for citizenship. Moreover, the naturalization exam itself is undergoing changes, with revisions aimed toward producing more engaged citizens.[18] In short, the challenges embedded in global changes and fragmegration are generating widespread attention to the nature and rights of what it means to be a citizen. Clearly, the citizen role is deeply ensconced in a period of transformation.

The fragmegration of citizenship has become even more extensive as more and more countries allow for dual citizenship—literally fragmenting citizens. The swelling trend toward dual citizenship stems primarily from countries fearing the loss of "good people"[19]—but is nevertheless controversial. At subnational levels too, political attachments and affiliations can also serve as the focus of intense controversy. The movement for independence in Quebec, for example, experienced upheaval when two of its distinguished followers, a playwright and a director, announced they no longer believed in sovereignty for Quebec. The playwright, Robert Lesage, stated his problem succinctly: "When I'm here in Quebec, even in Ottawa, I don't feel Canadian. But when I travel abroad, I don't know what happens, I feel that Canada is a reality, and I'm part of it."[20]

Conclusion

Clearly, the citizen role is undergoing a period of transformation as the challenges of global change and fragmegration generate widespread ambiguities as to the nature and rights of what it means to be a citizen. Given the ambiguities in the nature of citizenship and the migratory flows fostered by the dynamics of globalization, the task of counting immigrants, legal and illegal, temporary and permanent, and assessing their circumstances as well as the problems they pose for societies calls for special consideration. Such is the purpose of the next chapter.

Chapter Six

Immigrants and Diaspora

Like many second-generation immigrants, I have two identities, an outside face for my Danish friends, and an inside one for my family. I cannot give up one or the other. With my name, my religion and my appearance, I will never satisfy people here that I'm a Dane. And I know these calls to become Danish are dishonest because we are always presented with a moving target.

—Bunyamin Simsek[1]

As those born in a country have been counted for a number of reasons for decades and centuries, for many of the same reasons so have those who were born abroad and the minority social groupings they form. Censuses include outsiders, be they legal or illegal, but there are also less formal ways of assessing them—by their native tongues or their foreign accents; by their dress, skin color, mannerisms; and by their tendency to cluster in the same communities. Put more succinctly, naturalized citizens, residential aliens, and other kinds of immigrants are often strangers from the perspective of the host cultures, outsiders whose different ways and looks can often be the focus of prejudice and discrimination. As one observer puts it, we know our friends and we know our enemies, but we are often ignorant and thus fearful of the strangers among us.[2]

As the world has gotten smaller through the erosion of boundaries and the shrinkage induced by new electronic and transportation technologies, migratory flows have accelerated in numerous directions. These flows are a major dimension of the mobility upheaval noted in Chapter 3 and are therefore singled out here for extended analysis. Even more, they are singled out because migrants reside alongside citizens and pose a number of opportunities and problems for their newly adopted countries as well as for the migrants themselves.

People migrate for a variety of reasons. Many seek to overcome the poverty of their situation at home by finding work and a better life elsewhere. Others flee political persecution. Still others move to be with family established in another country. Although these motives tend to result in most of the migration flows moving from the South and East to the North and West, from the developing to the developed world, there are also meaningful flows within the South, such as the movement of Bangladeshi young men to work in the oil fields of Saudi Arabia and the movement of Philippine young women to work as maids in Hong Kong.

Immigrants in a Fragmegrative World

Given their roots in their countries of origin and their ties to their newly adopted countries, immigrants and the groups they form are bound to be caught up in fragmegrative dynamics. No matter how much they may feel at home in their new circumstances and irrespective of how much they may reject their original culture, their dual affiliations are bound to render them both the bearers and foci of tensions between integrative and fragmenting forces. This is less the case for those that assimilate well into their new home countries, but all of them have to confront the tensions and challenges of fitting into their new homes. In effect, they are the carriers of some crucial fragmegrative dynamics, and as such, they have to shoulder responsibilities that are not trivial even if they are not particularly conscious of the burdens that accompanied their migration.

The question arises as to the impact of globalization on the ties of immigrants to both their newly adopted countries and those they left behind. Presumably the new communications and transportation technologies are making it easier for them to maintain their ties and loyalties to their countries of origin, but is it also the case for their capacity to assimilate to their new societies? Are the tensions surrounding immigrant issues heightened by the fact that previously their role was to assimilate as quickly as possible, whereas today the ease with which they can maintain ties to their countries of origin complicates their assimilation into their new communities? Solid data relevant to these questions are not available, but it seems likely that today's immigrant is torn between the old and new for a much longer time than was the case prior to the advent of globalizing dynamics.

In sum, immigrants and the networks they form may not be easily counted, but they certainly count a great deal inasmuch as they often foment change at both the societal and global levels. They count as a powerful dynamism in world affairs, as sources of opportunities and problems wherever their travels may take them. Given the likelihood of continued globalization, moreover, they seem bound to count as far as one can see into the future. Indeed, immigrants and their networks are quintessential examples of fragmegrative dynamics. They integrate into the communities of their host societies even as their presence fosters fragmentation within those communities. As the immigrant quoted in the above epigraph put it, they are always presented with a moving target.

The Counting Problem

Because the migratory flows are so extensive and marked by a great deal of variability and change, it is difficult to develop accurate quantitative data on them, their scope, and direction. Illegal immigrants, for example, are likely to avoid being counted out of fear that they will be incarcerated or returned to their country of origin. Similarly, if the skills of legal or illegal immigrants in using the language of the host country are, at best, rudimentary, they may try to avoid responding to the census. The data in Table 6.1 must thus be treated as closer to rough estimates than exact counts; nevertheless the figures for selected Organization for Economic Cooperation and Development (OECD) countries indicate that every country other than France and Belgium experienced an increase in its foreign population between 1983 and 1995.[3] Equally noteworthy, however, is the size of the increases. In many (though not all) cases the percentage increases at that time were quite small, reflecting the ambivalence of members of the European Union toward the presence of immigrants and thereby contributing to the problems noted in Chapter 4 fostered by an incipient decline in population size. The United States has offset these problems by a much more open immigration policy that has resulted in a doubling of its foreign-born population.[4]

Another dimension of the counting problem involves the secretive routes through which migrants without legal entry papers flee poverty or political persecution. Their desperation to find a new home often leads them to undertake hazardous, furtive, and circuitous journeys that end in capture or tragedy as frequently as they do in success. Illegal immigrants from China, South Asia, and the Middle East try to make it to the Balkans and then across the Adriatic to Italy and other parts of Europe, having previously developed a route through Central America and then to the United States that became increasingly dangerous when the United States clamped down on illegal immigration.[5] Although less circuitous, large numbers of Albanians have also sought work in Italy by crossing the Adriatic in makeshift vessels that often do not make it.[6] Africans traverse a no less dangerous route across the Sahara desert from countries south of the desert trying to get to Libya and beyond.[7] Still others try to get to the European Union via Istanbul, where forged papers and passports are available for prices that vary according to the ultimate destination.[8] Another route to the EU is through Belarus to Poland.[9] Then there are the dangerous land and water routes traversed by a continual flow of Central and South Americans through Mexico[10] and Haitians through Florida hoping to find a better life in the United States.[11] Similarly, poor Asian and Middle East refugees have boarded ill-fated ships that were not allowed to leave their passengers off at Australian ports.[12] And difficult and precarious as the diverse flows of illegal immigrants can be, perhaps none are worse off than the Gypsies, most of whom are located in central Europe and all of whom are unwanted wherever they go and are often violently abused by police and citizens alike.[13]

Table 6-1. Foreign or Immigrant Population
in Selected OECD Countries

| | Foreign population[1] | | | |
| | Thousands | | % of total population | |
	1983	1995[2]	1983	1995[2]
Austria	297	724	3.9	9.0
Belgium	891	910	9.0	9.0
Denmark	104	223	2.0	4.2
Finland	16	69	0.3	1.3
France	3 714	3 597	6.8	6.3
Germany[3]	4 535	7 174	7.4	8.8
Ireland	83	94	2.4	2.7
Italy	381	991	0.7	1.7
Japan				
Luxembourg	96	138	26.3	33.4
Netherlands	552	728	3.8	5.0
Norway	95	161	2.3	3.7
Portugal	na	168	na	1.7
Spain	210	500	0.5	1.2
Sweden	397	484	4.8	5.2
Switzerland	926	1 331	14.4	18.9
UK	1 601	2 060	2.8	3.4
TOTAL	14 715	20 714		

| | Foreign population[1] | | | |
| | Thousands | | % of total population | |
	1981	1996	1981	1996
Australia	3 004	3 908	20.6	22.8
Canada	3 843	4 971	16.1	17.4
USA	14 080	24 600	4.7	9.3

Source: OECD 1997 1998.

Notes: na = not available.

1. Data for the foreign population are from population registers except for France (census), the UK (labour force survey), and Japan and Switzerland (register of foreigners). These figures refer to foreign citizens and include neither immigrants who have the citizenship of the immigration country nor immigrants who have been naturalized.

2. 1990 for France.

3. Data for 1983 refer to the area of the "old *Länder*" prior to reunification. 1995 figures cover Germany in its present borders.

4. Census data (1980 for the USA), except the 1996 figure for the USA, which is an official estimate.

Diverse Host Reactions

No less diverse than the flow of illegal immigration are the reactions of the countries that receive both those that are illegal and those with official papers. Even though some of the percentage changes as of the mid-1990s listed in Table 6.1 were conspicuously small, subsequent years have witnessed a greater appreciation of the need for immigrants to offset the incipient declines in population and the need for special skills created by the flourishing of information technologies. One place where changing attitudes have begun to flourish is Ireland, a country that for decades lost its population to emigration in large numbers, mostly to New York and elsewhere in the United States, but that has recently undergone an economic boom and been required as a member of the EU to admit unwanted Africans, Chechens, Poles, and Romanians seeking asylum and employment. What had been a homogeneous country is now increasingly heterogeneous; what had been a net outflow by 2000 was a net inflow, with some 1,000 immigrants applying for admission every month (in 1992 only 39 people applied for asylum).[14] The reaction of the Irish to the influx had been mixed, with some people seeking to make up for past injustices visited on the Irish abroad by offering friendship while others experience bewilderment and animosity. A man who runs a tractor-trailer business doubted he had ever previously seen more than a single dark-skinned person at a time, but he turned against them when he began to see them in groups even though he did not know where they came from. "Either Romanians or Nigerians," he explained. "We don't know the difference. They're all the same. They're all black and we've never been used to colored people here."[15]

The opening up of Germany to outsiders also met with opposition and continued anti-immigrant violence, intensified by the 1998 election that brought a coalition of Social Democrats and Greens to power who were committed to adopting legislation that reformed restrictive immigration laws and allowed for the legalization of a multiethnic society. Previously some 2.2 million Turks, more than 800,000 people from the former Yugoslavia, some 600,000 Italians, and roughly 350,000 Greeks lived in Germany without citizenship, but the proposed new law sought to make it possible for about 3 million foreign residents to become German citizens.[16] The reasons underlying the shift toward legalizing the presence of more than 40 percent of the foreigners residing in Germany were numerous. Some had to do with a revulsion against anti-immigrant violence[17] and fears that the enlargement of the European Union would result in a huge influx of foreigners from Poland and other newly admitted EU member countries.[18] Coping with the fears and the violence they fostered invigorated efforts to replace traces of Germany's Nazi past with a self-image of Germany as a more open society, one thereby capable of exercising a powerful voice in the EU. Another source of the shift focused on the move of the central government to Berlin and the sense that the leadership potential inherent in the move required the legalization of a multicultural society. Still others stemmed from a realization the population was aging and a need for personnel with skills appropriate to the information age was an imperative.

Nor were Germany and Ireland the only European countries that experienced upheavals over the arrival of growing numbers of immigrants from the developing world. Periodic anti-immigrant violence in British communities and a flood of people seeking asylum (70,000 in 1999 compared to 5,000 just prior to the fall of the Berlin Wall in 1989) led to the adoption of a new Immigration and Asylum Act explicitly designed to make it more difficult to take up residence in the United Kingdom.[19] The surge of an anti-immigrant party in the Netherlands fostered tensions over multiculturalism that led to the 2002 assassination of its leader, Pim Fortuyn, who had publicly claimed that Islam was a backward culture.[20] The electoral success of a nativist party in Austria led the European Union to warn it would isolate Austria if the party's leader, Jörg Haider, were to enter a coalition government.[21] Tensions have also surfaced in Denmark and Sweden over the presence of immigrants. Throughout Europe, in short, the arrival of poor, former colonial subjects from Africa, Asia, and the Caribbean; of "guest workers" from the former Yugoslavia, Turkey, and Morocco; and of people fleeing wars in Afghanistan and the Balkans is transforming the norms and politics of the region.[22]

The United States, where virtually everyone's ancestors were immigrants,[23] exemplifies a more unqualified and long-standing acceptance of outsiders, though hardly one entirely free of animosity and violence. During the 1990s the percentage of foreign-born persons in the country increased almost four times as fast as did the native-born population, reaching 9.3 percent of the total in 1998, a figure roughly the same as that recorded in 1850, the first year the Census Bureau asked people their place of birth.[24] Moreover, today's immigrants come from more countries and speak more languages than the last great wave of European immigrants. They are more economically varied, with highly educated and skilled people among their ranks. And more than their predecessors, they are eschewing homogeneous enclaves, scattering to neighborhoods across the city. Fractured and dispersed, they have proved more difficult to unite into political movements. In New York, no group approaches the influence of Cuban immigrants in Miami, Mexican immigrants in San Antonio, or even Asian Americans in San Francisco, whose political power has been amplified by their more concentrated numbers.[25]

But the need for outside labor is not confined to persons with advanced technological skills. Personnel for menial tasks can also be in short supply and lead to the employment of illegal immigrants, who tend to be poor and uneducated. The U.S. agricultural community is especially needy in this respect. There are simply not enough legal workers to pick the fruit and harvest the crops that U.S. farmers grow. Hence it has been estimated that 52 percent of the 1.6 million farm workers in the United States openly violate the prevailing laws by not having the necessary legal documents. As apple farmer Mark Rice explained his hiring of illegal Mexican workers, "There's no way I could get my crop picked if I was legal.... I'm an honest person, but if I want to stay in business, the only option I have is to follow an illegal course."[26]

Although immigrants are viewed as critical to economic growth in much of the country,[27] tensions over their presence—in jobs and schools—are high in states such as California, Texas, and Florida that border Mexico and the Caribbean. And throughout the country many immigrants tend to be slighted, even shunned, when they get home from work or over weekends, and their presence as strangers is often discomforting for the communities in which they live.[28] It is as if many in the white population know that immigration is changing their society in profound ways and they resent it even as they benefit from the changes.[29] Anti-immigrant sentiment reached new heights in 2005 when the House of Representatives voted to build 698 miles of fences along the U.S.-Mexican border,[30] an action that contrasted sharply with an earlier discovery that parts of the U.S. border with Canada could no longer be traced.[31]

The tensions generated by the presence of immigrants do not prevail, however, in certain occupations. A shortage of nurses in the United States, for example, has led to legislative proposals to give preferences to persons abroad trained as nurses, a proposal that threatens to increase the critical need for nurses in the Philippines and Africa, since salaries for nurses in the United States are considerably higher than in the developing world and attract many immigrants in that profession.[32]

Whatever may be the consequences of immigrants in their host societies, and aside from the way they are treated by their host communities, they can have enormous consequences for the original countries from which they emigrated. Most notably, the volume of money they send to their families they left behind is considerable. Indeed, the flow of $80 billion in remittances to developing countries in 2002 from the United States exceeded the amount provided by official development assistance and was not much behind foreign direct investment. Mexico is illustrative: nearly one out of every five Mexicans receives money from a relative in the United States.[33] Moreover, these statistics underplay the situation, as they do not include unofficial remittances or anticipate the greater amount that will occur with continued immigration. The average remittance sent home by immigrants in 2003 ranged between $100 and $200.[34] The sum of these individual remittances composed a not trivial proportion of the gross domestic product (GDP) of twenty developing countries. Indeed, some countries adopt innovative policies to attract more remittances from their nationals abroad[35] or to entice them to return to their native land.[36] On the other hand, the inflow of remittance money can cause a variety of problems for the receiving society.[37] It is noteworthy, for example, that the Philippines withdrew from the military operation in Iraq because they worried that their workers in the Middle East might face repercussions and no longer be a stable source of remittances.

The Question of Identity

The westward flow of immigrants has resulted in an "increased hybridization at the level of individuals,"[38] thereby pushing the issue of identity high on the political agendas of the countries where their travels culminate. This is especially the case in countries where the proportion of immigrants approaches 10 percent, and it is further intensified by the growing authority of the EU that for some people has posed the question of whether their national identity is superceded by a continental identity. The politics of identity can lead to virulent conflict as well as mere questioning of where highest loyalties lie. At the very least it poses the question of what it means to be, say, German, or Dutch, or Danish. More important, it has fomented the rise of crime, of religious sensitivities, and of right-wing, nationalist political parties that seek new adherents by appealing to anti-immigrant sentiment. Some countries have carried this sentiment to the point of adopting news laws designed to dissuade foreigners from taking up residence in the host country. In Denmark, for example, new legislation prohibits any immigrants under twenty-five years old from bringing in a spouse from abroad.[39]

The tensions inherent in the resurgence of identity politics are especially poignant when it is understood that the Netherlands and Denmark, the two countries that ranked as highest on a scale that measures helpfulness to the poor around the world, are among those experiencing the most severe problems over the presence of immigrants.[40] It would seem that scoring high on a Commitment to Development Index reflects values about situations abroad that do not obtain when people from the developing world move into the developed world. Put differently, when distant proximities become too proximate in this period of "collapsing certainties, of exponential change,"[41] some elements of the host countries press choices on immigrants and asylum seekers that force them to adapt to their new circumstances.

Mobilizing Immigrants

As crossings into the United States from Mexico became a highly salient issue on the U.S. political agenda in the spring of 2006, organizations of the immigrant community convened and concluded the time had arrived to engage in extensive mobilization.[42] Drawn by the imminent advent of an off-year congressional election, protest marches by immigrants, both legal and illegal, occurred simultaneously across the United States in more than 100 large and small cities.[43] Large numbers of protesters called for an extension of their rights and a chance for many to gain citizenship, actions that led some businesses to fire their workers who took the day off to march.[44] Despite such setbacks, however, the fact of widespread protests proved to be a landmark for the immigrant community, an event that highlighted the potential for political action even in the absence of an immediate compliance by the Congress. It is reasonable to assert that the issue and the numbers involved transformed the immigrant community into a movement that is likely to continue to be active on behalf of its members irrespective of the provisions of any legislation that is passed.

The Adaptation of Immigrants

The way in which an outsider adapts to the host culture can vary, depending on both the person and the culture's receptivity to immigrants. Four alternatives seem plausible. Immigrants can adapt by becoming assimilationists, integrationists, or separationists or by being marginalized, depending on the values they attach to their heritage and host cultures.[45] In addition, the high degrees of mobility facilitated by transportation and electronic technologies have opened up new transnational spaces in which increasing numbers of people cannot readily be classified as any of these four types. Cross-cultural marriages, reassignments in their jobs, the travel and resettlement of their families, and the pervasiveness of global television and the Internet have created a space apart from the four parts that seems best located somewhere in the middle of them and that is occupied by what Table 6.2 refers to as "hybrids," by persons who see themselves as belonging to several cultures and having several identities[46] or, as noted in the next chapter, who are confused about their identities.

These new transnational spaces have also provided new opportunities for diasporas to form and flourish. The counting of diaspora memberships, however, is not easily accomplished and the figures are thus not reliable, since "we need to know better than we do today how diaspora communities placed in different host environments voluntarily form, or are constrained to form, spatial and social enclave communities; how they coalesce to resist discrimination and prejudice when they face it; how they develop their economic niches and specialize in the businesses and services in which are competitive; and how in time they become effective voting blocks when they become eligible to participate in local,

Table 6-2. Immigrant Acculturation Model with Spaces for Movement

	Devalue Host/ Majority Culture		Value Host/Majority Culture
Devalue Heritage/ Minority Culture	Marginalized		Assimilationist
		Hybrids	
Value Heritage/ Minority Culture	Separationist		Integrationist

state, and national politics and generate their own politicians, mediators, and political bosses."[47]

Conclusion

Thus far the foregoing analysis has been on people who are territorially oriented as they move across borders and take up residence in a new country. Some proportion (not a large one) of those who move, however, are not territorially oriented and develop identities that are not linked to a homeland. Such individuals are the focus of the next chapter.

CHAPTER SEVEN

Hybrids and Cosmopolitans

In a world of increasing globalization, many people find they are not comfortable as either citizens or immigrants, a discomfort linked to their decreasing sense of territoriality. Citizens and immigrants who view the world as organized along territorial lines are quite willing, even pleased, to be seen as citizens of the country in which they were born or naturalized, but some of those who were also born in or immigrated into the same country do not share that sense of territoriality or are confused about their affiliations, and so they are left to search endlessly for an appropriate identity. Regardless of the degree of their confusion, I find it useful to call them "hybrids"—people who do not have meaningful ties to any country. Hybrids are legally citizens of a country, but their legal status has no personal meaning for them. Much the same can be said about those who view the world as the territory of which they are citizens. Such individuals are usually called "cosmopolitans."

This is another way of saying that people are on the move as new technologies have fostered the collapse of time and distance that, in turn, has shrunk the world and rendered the boundaries of countries more porous; that the shrinking has led to a restless search for identity on the part of those whose relocations have undermined any earlier sense of territoriality they may have had. They are not nomads like Gypsies, who know who they are and do not seek a national identity, but they are nomads in the sense of an inability to retain their national identity as they move around the world or otherwise develop cosmopolitan impulses. The following observations are illustrative of the modern-day hybrid:[1]

> I was born in Argentina, my entire family is Argentinean and culturally, I have been raised Argentinean. Yet, at age four I moved out of Argentina and only returned on vacations. I grew up in Panama until I was thirteen and then moved to California. So where does that leave me? I speak perfect English and Spanish. Physically, I can pass as Californian, Panamanian or Argentinean. I know many people that are in my same situation. In a sense, we identify with each other. We have created our own territory, imagined, but a territory nonetheless. [2]

I see myself as a citizen of the world, and someone who is unmistakably American and Chinese. My parents are Chinese but I grew up in a small town in the Midwest. I have no attachment to a place, but I wish I had one. I am a scientist but I like philosophy. I am a social psychologist but I read a lot of anthropology, sociology, mythology, and political science. I am a shifting person of multicolored hues. I can disguise myself very well, and make it very difficult for others to know exactly where I come from. There are probably more people like me now than at any other time in human history.[3]

I feel equally at home dancing with sherpas on the slopes of the Himalayas as I do at dinner parties in Hong Kong. I have never lived in my country of citizenship. I bow to Hindu deities and kneel at the Cross. Air stewardesses greet me by my first name and in my address book Steve Green, the American Ambassador to Singapore, is listed next to Raya Gunung, a rice farmer in Thailand. Who am I? I am a global nomad, a third culture kid. And what's more, I'm not alone. I come from a growing class of upwardly mobile people whose allegiance has shifted from countries to corporations and who have to think for a minute if you ask them where they're from.[4]

[Woods said it bothers him when people label him as African American since he is one-quarter black, one-quarter Thai, one-quarter Chinese, one-eighth white, and one-eighth American Indian] Growing up, I came up with this name. I'm a Cablinasian.[5]

Although an accurate count of the number of hybrids and cosmopolitans that presently populate the world is not possible, and although their number is probably infinitesimal in comparison to the number of citizens, these observations suggest that their number is growing as the mobility of people increases, as new global issues and situations intensify questions of identity, and as transnational social movements proliferate through the Internet and other technologies. Indeed, both Virginia Barreiro and James Liu explicitly assert a conviction that the ranks of hybrids are growing.

Cosmopolitans

Whether or not they spent their early lives in two or more cultures, cosmopolitans tend to be secure with their identity as people who view the world as their home and thus have minimal attachments to particular countries. Although they may not parade their conviction that they are citizens of the world, both their attitudes and their actions are marked by the absence of territorial orientations. For them, the world is their home in the sense that they care about its well-being and the major economic, political, and cultural issues that comprise the global agenda. Family and friends at "home" are important to cosmopolitans, but they organize their perspectives and activities in terms of a more encompassing worldview. This is perhaps especially the case for those who live the life of the mind:

We may describe as transnational those intellectuals who are at home in the cultures of other peoples as well as their own. They keep track of what is happening in various places. They have special ties to those countries where they have lived, they have friends all over the world, they hop across the sea to discuss something with their colleagues; they fly to visit one another as easily as their counterparts two hundred years ago rode over to the next town to exchange ideas.[6]

Stated more generally, cosmopolitans derive their orientations from their education and experience: their parents may have emphasized territorial concerns; their education may have included study abroad or otherwise have fostered concerns about remote situations; their careers may require extensive foreign travel or prolonged residence abroad; or they may be active in transnational social issues such as human rights or environmental degradation.

Unsurprisingly, therefore, cosmopolitans tend to be well-off and to have college degrees. Many may even have earned advanced degrees or become accomplished in the arts. In numerous instances their careers trace paths into that stratum of people regarded as elites, as leaders responsible for developments not confined by local or national boundaries. Individuals may well develop the foundations of cosmopolitan orientations before they join the elite ranks, but it is reasonable to presume that by the time most cosmopolitans reach the age of, say, thirty-five or forty, they will have become leaders in their fields.[7] And irrespective of whether they attain elite status, it seems likely that the trend line for the number of cosmopolitans is a gentle upward slope. They may not be numerous in absolute terms, but increases in their number do seem likely as the world shrinks and transnational issues become more predominant, thereby creating a need for aid givers, peacekeepers, business executives, technical specialists, and a host of other occupations that involve movement around the world and a concern for circumstances in distant locales. Indeed, even though the history of cosmopolitanism extends back across centuries, today the ranks of cosmopolitans are more diverse than ever before: "Commercial pilots, computer programmers, film directors, international bankers, media specialists, oil riggers, entertainment celebrities, ecology experts, movie producers, demographers, accountants, professors, lawyers, athletes—these comprise a new breed of men and women.... "[8] Interestingly, moreover, cosmopolitans are likely to have an attitude toward their own diversity:

> The perspective of the cosmopolitan must entail relationships to a plurality of cultures understood as distinctive entities.... But furthermore, cosmopolitanism in a stricter sense includes a stance toward diversity itself, toward the coexistence of cultures in the individual experience. A more genuine cosmopolitanism is first of all an orientation, a willingness to engage with the Other. It is an intellectual and aesthetic stance of openness toward divergent cultural experiences, a search for contrasts rather than uniformity.[9]

Because of their diversity, however, it seems highly unlikely that cosmopolitans will ever acquire coherence as a transnational class. In the words of one observer, "since they embrace a wide variety of occupations—brokers, bankers, real estate promoters and developers, engineers, consultants of all kinds, systems analysts, scientists, doctors, publicists, publishers, editors, advertising executives, art directors, moviemakers, entertainers, journalists, television producers and directors, artists, writers, university professors—and since they lack a common political outlook, it is ... inappropriate to characterize managerial and professional elites as a new ruling class."[10] Segments of cosmopolitans, however, may well be or become an interactive and coordinated subclass of elites, or at least a subculture. Such a tendency, for example, is said to mark those who attend the annual meetings of the World Economic Forum in Davos, Switzerland:

> Participants in this culture know how to deal with computers, cellular phones, airline schedules, currency exchange, and the like. But they also dress alike, exhibit the same amicable informality, relieve tensions by similar attempts at humor, and of course most of them interact in English. Since most of these cultural traits are of Western (and mostly American) provenance, individuals coming from different backgrounds must go through a process of socialization that will allow them to engage in this behavior with seemingly effortless spontaneity. ... But it would be a mistake to think that the "Davos culture" operates only in the offices, boardrooms, and hotel suites in which international business is transacted. It carries over into the lifestyles and presumably also the values of those who participate in it. Thus, for example, the frenetic pace of contemporary business is carried over into the leisure activities and the family life of business people. There is a yuppie style in the corporation, but also in the body-building studio and in the bedroom. And notions of costs, benefits, and maximization spill over from work into private life. The "Davos culture" is a culture of the elite and ... of those aspiring to join the elite. Its principal social location is in the business world, but since elites intermingle, it also affects at least the political elites. There is, as it were, a yuppie internationale.[11]

It should also be noted that although the number of cosmopolitans may not be increasing at anywhere close to the same rate as many populations, globalization and the advent of new information technologies, particularly e-mail and the Internet, would appear to be quickening the pace of growth. The new technologies allow for the formation of networks that are not dependent on face-to-face interactions and that even afford cosmopolitans time to participate in the routines of their families and hometowns:

> Cosmopolitans are usually somewhat footloose, on the move in the world. Among the several cultures with which they are engaged, at least one is presumably of the territorial kind, a culture encompassing the round of everyday life in a community. The perspective of the cosmopolitan may indeed be composed only from experiences of different cultures of this kind, as his biography includes periods of stays in

different places. But he may also be involved with one culture, and possibly but not usually more, of that other kind which is carried by a transnational network rather than by a territory. It is really the growth and proliferation of such transnational cultures and social networks in the present period that generates more cosmopolitans now than there have been at any other time.[12]

Finally, the question arises as to the consequences for national loyalties induced by cosmopolitan orientations. Most commentators argue that the two are incompatible, that national loyalties yield as cosmopolitan perspectives develop. One observer, for example, concluded that "patriotism, certainly, does not rank very high in [cosmopolitans'] hierarchy of virtues,"[13] that "their loyalties ... are international rather than regional, national, or local. They have more in common with their counterparts in Brussels or Hong Kong than with the masses of Americans not yet plugged into the network of global communications."[14] Another commentator, focusing on the world of commerce, perceived that cosmopolitans are "a new breed of men and women for whom religion, culture, and ethnic nationality are marginal elements in a working identity,"[15] that "the word foreign has no meaning to the ambitious global businessperson.... How can the physical distinction between domestic and foreign have any resonance in a virtual world defined by electronic communications and intrinsically unbounded markets?"[16]

Some analysts view the shifting loyalties of cosmopolitans as worrisome. Where one contends that without national attachments, cosmopolitans are seen as having "little inclination to make sacrifices or to accept responsibility for their actions,"[17] another ponders

> whether the habits of citizenship are sufficiently strong to withstand the centrifugal forces of the new global economy. Is there enough of simple loyalty to place—of civic obligation, even when unadorned by enlightened self-interest—to elicit sacrifice nonetheless? We are, after all, citizens as well as economic actors; we may work in markets, but we live in societies. How tight is the social and political bond when the economic bond unravels?[18]

The same analyst subsequently recurred to essentially the same questions and posited troubling answers to them:

> But will the cosmopolitan with a global perspective choose to act fairly and compassionately? Will our current and future symbolic analysts—lacking any special sense of responsibility toward a particular nation and its citizens—share their wealth with the less fortunate of the world and devote their resources and energies to improving the chances that others may contribute to the world's wealth? Here we find the darker side of cosmopolitanism. For without strong attachments and loyalties extending beyond family and friends, symbolic analysts may never develop the habits and attitudes of social responsibility. They will be world citizens, but without accepting or even acknowledging any of the obligations that citizenship in a polity normally implies.[19]

Hybrids and Cosmopolitans in a Fragmegrative World

Unlike immigrants for whom the conflicting dynamics of integration and fragmentation can be confusing and even distressing, hybrids and cosmopolitans are accustomed to the tensions sustained by fragmegration. They appreciate that communities break down even as they seek to facilitate their coherence. This is especially the case for cosmopolitans, as they devote considerable energy to sustaining broad perspectives in which people and groups are encouraged to cooperate. Since hybrids have come to terms with having affiliations in more than one country and by definition have resolved the tensions that accompany multiple loyalties, they too are likely to understand and accept fragmegrative dynamics.

Conclusion

Although the aforementioned experience of hybrids who spent their early years in more than one culture renders them especially sensitive to their identity, the stresses and strains of modern, complex societies have posed identity questions for cosmopolitans and typical citizens as well. The expansion of multicultural societies, ethnic rivalries, religious tensions, the intensity of localism, the persistence of racism, the tendencies of many polities to fragment and of others to coalesce at a regional level, the teaching of foreign languages in schools, the revival of traditions, the rejuvenated reach of diasporas, the arrival of "strangers" who manage to obtain entry visas, the weakening of states, the vigor of social movements, and a host of other dynamics at work on a global scale today have contributed to the rise of identity issues on the agendas of local, national, and transnational systems. More than that, often such issues are divisive and foster conflicts as questions of identity become pervasive at every level of community. Some even argue that such questions amount to a "crisis of identity" that consists of "the weakening of former national identities and the emergence of new identities—especially the dissolution of a kind of membership known as 'citizenship,' in the abstract meaning of membership in a territorially defined and state-governed society, and its replacement by an identity based on 'primordial loyalties,' ethnicity, 'race,' local community, language and other culturally concrete forms."[20]

And if such questions are stressful and confusing for ordinary citizens, they also involve matters with which cosmopolitans must contend as they engage in transnational activities:

> Cosmopolitanism is, in identity terms, betwixt and between without being liminal. It is shifting, participating in many worlds, without becoming part of them. It is the position and identity of an intellectual self situated outside of the local arenas among which s/he moves. The practice of cosmopolitanism ... is predicated on maintaining distance, often a superiority to the local. By this very self-definition,

the cosmopolitan is unauthentic and quintessentially 'modern.' ... By means of the installation of a continuous alterity with respect to other identities, cosmopolitans can only play roles, participate superficially in other people's realities, but can have no reality of his or her [sic] own other than alterity itself.[21]

Once again there are no reliable figures on the diverse identities that people claim. Censuses do count people of different nationalities and religions, but the point here is that there are numerous identities that people try to fashion out of their circumstances and to which they then cling or aspire that do not lend themselves to being counted. It is thus not far-fetched to conceive of the present era as pervaded by a restless search for identity. It is a search that has fostered the emergence of political parties, led to violence and even genocide, facilitated the organization of indigenous peoples, energized social movements, and served to place issues of justice and equity on the agendas of communities. And given the accelerated pace at which events unfold today, identities are endlessly in flux, some being revised, others abandoned, and still others created.

CHAPTER EIGHT

Travelers

A knowledge of the Globe and its various inhabitants, however slight ... has a kindred
effect with that of seeing them as travelers, which never fails, in uncorrupted minds,
to weaken local prejudices, and enlarge the sphere of benevolent feelings.

—*James Madison (1812)*

As technologies shrink the world, more people experience an impulse to travel.
It is an impulse that stems from a wide variety of sources, especially as television,
the Internet, and other media offer glimpses from all corners and crannies of the
globe. Travel itself takes many forms: businesspeople interact with counterparts
abroad; students study in foreign universities; legal and illegal immigrants flee
persecution or seek work and a more satisfying lifestyle; tourists explore new
places; artists perform and exhibit abroad; athletic teams compete with foreign
challengers; and so on across a broad spectrum of human activities. In short, with
jet aircraft able to transport ever-greater numbers of passengers, people are on
the move—so much so that, as indicated in Chapter 3, a mobility upheaval is a
major source of globalization. The upheaval can also be a source of conflicts that
are inherently fragmegrative.

Counting Travelers

The statistics on travel across national boundaries provide a good measure of the
scope of the mobility upheaval. In the United States, for instance, more than
46 million persons entered the country in 1998, a figure that fell to 41 million
in 2003 after the September 11, 2001, terrorist attacks but that was expected to
rebound to 52 million in 2006, which is the equivalent of nearly one-sixth of the
U.S. population, or 125,000 jumbo jets full of passengers.[1] And the outward flow
was more than matched by the inward flow, with an excess of 56 million who
left the country in 2003[2] and 61.7 million who did so in 2004.[3] Similarly striking
numbers, more than 11 million, were recorded for those who left Europe and

came to the United States in 2000, but this number shrank after the September 11 terrorist attacks to 9.6 million in 2004.[4] In 2005 the World Tourism Organization (WTO) anticipated that international tourist arrivals would grow by an average of 4.1 percent annually until 2020.[5] Even people in countries known more as destinations are now turning to tourism: for example, in 1995, only 4.5 million Chinese went abroad, a figure that increased to 31 million in 2005 and was expected to grow to 50 million by 2010 and 100 million by 2020.[6]

If travel within continents is added to these statistics, the scale of the mobility upheaval is even more stunning. In North America, for example, 1.52 billion passengers traveled through its airports, even counting connecting passengers only once.[7] Driven largely by a search for jobs, the flow of people among the countries of Europe is also considerable. Although the growth rates of Central European countries are much greater than is the case for the richer countries of Western Europe, most of the flow is from the former to the latter. Indeed, the flow of people in Europe has "created a hierarchy, with Western Europeans like the French or Germans at the top, Eastern Europeans in the middle, working mainly in construction, and Africans and Asians at the bottom of the labor heap, working in restaurant kitchens, or in garbage removal."[8]

Given the scale of the mobility upheaval, it is hardly surprising that travel has been institutionalized. Not only do travel agencies abound throughout the world, but they have also long banded together to sustain an international organization devoted to protecting their interests and those of travelers. In 1924 the International Congress of Tourism Associations was founded and succeeded in 1974 by the World Tourist Organization. In 2001 the General Assembly of the UN adopted the Global Code of Ethics for Tourism (GCET), and in 2003 the WTO was converted to a specialized agency of the UN. In 2005 the WTO had a membership that consisted of 145 countries, seven territories, and 300 affiliate members who represented the private sector, educational institutions, tourism associations, and tourism authorities. Nor is the institutionalization of travel confined to the international level. Universities now have tourism programs or departments that offer advanced degrees in tourism. In fact, tourism has become the world's largest industry.[9]

Tourism and Territoriality

For some people, perhaps especially those among the ranks of elites, the statistics only tell a small part of the story. The impact of travel on a person's sense of territoriality offers an insight into the potential consequences of travel. Some travelers, although surely not a majority, undergo a shift in their national loyalties. Experience in different parts of the world unties their links to their hometown and the society in which they grew up. They become cosmopolitans, people for whom the world feels like home. Consider, for example, this observation by Esther Dyson, an entrepreneur and former chairwoman of the Internet Corporation for Assigned Names and Numbers (ICANN):

> For now, I like the feeling of being at home in a lot of places. I am rooted in myself, not in some place. I like the feeling that there are lots of places where I belong, that are familiar.... On New Year's Eve, my brother counted the stamps in my passport. There were 385. Since 1995. A lot of exotic ones like the Ukraine and Macedonia. There's a certain pride you take in the wealth of experience. That's kind of nice. That you belong all over the world rather than a little part. You're proud of the world, not just proud of your neighborhood. Proud to be part of it. It's not like you're saying, "Go Bronx." It's "Go World."[10]

Although most people retain their ties to home even as they travel widely, many of them can nevertheless share in Dyson's excitement over what she experienced abroad. Such persons become what have been called "rooted cosmopolitans,"[11] individuals who do not feel a necessity to choose among the possible objects of their loyalty and who thus are able to sustain a constructive balance between their local and global orientations.[12] There are no reliable data on their numbers, but it seems likely that increasingly their ranks will grow, that the experience of moving around the world will incline more and more people to share in the values of rooted cosmopolitanism. The cosmopolitanism of some individuals is continent-wide in scope. Consider, for example, this observation of Marc Routier, a French businessman: "I definitely describe myself as a European. I may get sentimental when they play the Marseillaise, but for all the practical things, I see myself as a citizen of Europe. I like the lifestyle in France, but I don't make my living there."[13]

It should be noted, however, that some travelers remain deeply ensconced in their home communities even as they travel, an orientation that can lead them to find fault with foreign cultures and may thus result in behaviors abroad that offend the people with whom they come into contact during their travels. Even more likely, such travelers do not fully immerse themselves in the communities they visit abroad, preferring to eat in restaurants that serve dishes with which they are accustomed and otherwise finding fault with the unfamiliar local practices they encounter. Travelers from the United States who yield to these impulses are often called "Ugly Americans."

To a large extent, however, people abroad put up with pompous and insensitive travelers such as the Ugly American. Visiting tourists tend to spend substantial sums of money as they move around the world. In the case of developing societies, the spending of tourists is a major source of revenue, along with the remittances that those in developing societies who take up residence abroad send back to their families and friends at home.

Multicultural Societies

But not all travelers return to their original homes. Some stay in the countries they visit and then gather in the same neighborhoods with others from their home country. As a result, an increasing number of societies can be characterized as multicultural in their makeup, countries distinguished by enclaves of people from another country who develop their own newspapers, churches, radio stations, and schools. It takes two or three generations for those in the enclaves to make the transition to their new communities and become fluent in its languages. As previously noted, the periods of transition may well be marked by a variety of fragmegrative tensions, periods in which the one-time travelers have to become accustomed to their new cultures and in which their new communities have to become adjusted to their presence. The local prejudices that Madison noted long ago in the chapter epigraph may not yield readily to benevolent feelings.

Conclusion

Moving around the world is not a trivial experience. For most people travel is eye opening, broadening in the best sense of the word. It fosters person-to-person relationships that span national boundaries and expands our understanding of the world. Corners of the world that were once distant mysteries increasingly come into focus, with the foreigner becoming less and less foreign and the routines of other cultures less and less strange. The fact that jet aircraft narrow the distance to what once seemed impossibly far away promotes the sense that problems elsewhere in the world are quite near at hand.

To be sure, cultural and linguistic differences continue to separate peoples and to sustain long-standing animosities. Yet, it seems clear, or at least likely, that the various forms of travel will narrow the distances in the long run. Already much of the world speaks some form of English, thus serving to narrow the gaps that once so fully kept people apart. Stereotypes of people elsewhere are bound to fray in the face of the mobility upheaval.

In sum, the fact that national and local loyalties continue to prevail among the vast majority of people does not diminish the consequences of the mobility upheaval. Widespread foreign travel and electronic contacts are rendering the distant very proximate, spanning long-standing gulfs of misunderstanding and promoting degrees of empathy with foreigners that once seemed impossible. The thrust of Madison's observation is sound even if the dynamic he described may be slow moving and erratic.

CHAPTER NINE

Activists

Although all the roles considered in previous and subsequent chapters matter in world politics, the fact is that some people count more than others. Most notably, activists who persuade other people to act count much more than those they mobilize. U.S. activists direct civic participation toward particular goals, and without them their fellow citizens would be considerably less active and less organized. Thus activists tend to energize communities, and without that energy the course of events would be sustained solely by public officials and their governments. Indeed, activists tend to serve as the glue that holds communities together and enables them to remain cohesive.

Every activity in the reservoir of human endeavor attracts committed persons who are active on behalf of one or another of its dimensions. A Google search in 2006 returned 94,600,000 entries under "activists," a number that nicely conveys the range of concerns that provoke people to engage in intense and sustained behavior to preserve or alter arrangements in the public arena. Some of the entries focus on activists who achieved luminary status because of the issue for which they fought—Martin Luther King Jr., Mahatma Gandhi, and Nelson Mandela are recurring examples—but the vast majority of entries are about diverse issues and the communities in which activists are controversial.

Activists are not the only people who mobilize others. Politicians, educators, and organizational leaders also devote considerable energy seeking to get others to act on behalf of their goals. What distinguishes activists from other mobilizers is their lack of professional affiliations. Professional activists—such as politicians or lobbyists—receive a salary for their work but may not even be deeply committed to the goals they promote. Amateur activists, on the other hand, tend not to be paid for their activity. Most earn their living in other occupations and are, in effect, part-time volunteers who care so much about an issue that they promote it without concern for remuneration. Stated differently, activists are distinguished by intense commitments to one or more political issue, commitments that lead them to work alone or through nongovernmental organizations to get others involved in the issues that concern them and thereby to promote those issues in a wider audience.

Viewed in this way, we can draw a distinction between single-issue and multi-issue activists, between those who are interested in only a single area and those whose interests are not confined to one area. Multi-issue activists are likely to be involved in most of the issues on a community's political agenda at any one time, whereas single-issue activists are selective in their concerns and may go for long stretches of time before their activist impulses are aroused. For the former, in other words, activism tends to be a way of life, an unending readiness to get involved in the course of events, whereas their single-issue counterparts may have occupations far removed from the issues that arrest their attention. Furthermore, given their diverse concerns, multi-issue activists are much more likely to contribute to the processes of fragmegration than are their single-issue counterparts. The former may even personally experience the tensions inherent in a fragmegrative society as they seek to promote two or more issues that are marked by contradictory concerns.

Of course, for activists to be successful, there has to be a readiness in their community to respond. More accurately, there have to be sufficient members of the community who have been affected by an issue for the mobilizing efforts of activists to produce results. But activists are not deterred by the unwillingness of others to follow their lead or by tepid support for their goals; as a way of life, activism is sustained by much more than the immediate responses of others. Activists do not demand immediate responses as a test of their success. They understand that the obstacles to mobilizing others are considerable, and thus their commitments tend to be accompanied by patience, and an awareness that their message may have to be repeated numerous times and in numerous settings for the people to develop a readiness to follow their lead.

Open, democratic societies are most receptive to nongovernmental activism, inasmuch as the warp and woof of their politics is sustained by different groups articulating their needs and pressing their demands. Indeed, on occasion activists and mobilized publics can become a transnational movement. In anticipation of the U.S. decision to attack Iraq in 2003, for example, protests circled the globe in what were called "rolling demonstrations" that broke out "not only in the great capitals but also in provincial cities and even small towns."[1]

On the other hand, the leaders of closed, authoritarian systems view as threatening mobilization on behalf of private goals, and it is thus unwanted and unwelcome. The importance of this distinction is plainly manifest in China today. Still an authoritarian society, but ever more open to a modicum of dissent and pressures to redress wrongs, China has lately witnessed an increase in the ranks of its activists as its system undergoes a loosening of controls.[2]

Sources of Activism

Many activists have at least one politically active parent who serves as a model for their children early in their lives. For such activists, political education begins at a young age and continues into and through adulthood. The issues that galvanize them into action may change, but the impulses to do something about whatever issues arrest their attention tend to be constant. They may go off in political directions contrary to those of their parents, but the activist inclinations acquired as children and adolescents do not waver with the passage of time.

Another source of activism is a unique and searing experience—contact with an issue that leaves a person committed to promoting alternative solutions to the problem. Those active in the civil rights arena are a good example in this respect; many of them suffered the indignities and deprivations that followed a denial of their rights, experiences that served to motivate their subsequent efforts to energize others on behalf of civil rights causes.

A concern for their community, coupled with an ability to envision its future, is still another source that sustains activists. They worry that one or another group or institution prevents their community from moving in desired directions, a worry that may serve to activate them on a number of issues. Put differently, successful activists think on large scales; they understand the political dynamics with which they must cope to turn their community in desired directions.

It follows that multi-issue activists are likely to be knowledgeable about their communities, to know its leaders, its pockets of apathy, and the obstacles that need to be overcome to mobilize effectively on particular problems. They are likely to have at least a passing acquaintance with each other and with the community's officials, contacts that may serve them well when they undertake to mobilize support for their goals.

The Skills of Activists

Activists have a variety of skills and temperaments. The good ones—those who more often than not get followers to follow—tend to be dogmatic in their convictions and yet diplomatic in their appeals for support. They are disinclined to yield on the issues they champion, but at the same time their patience and sense of the long-run goals to which they aspire can lead them to move slowly in their pressures for change. Most notably perhaps, they are familiar with all the arguments that need to be answered and overcome in order to mobilize any individuals who may be reluctant to follow their lead. They know that by being articulate and energetic they improve their chances of prevailing over those who doubt their goals or strategies.

Whatever may be their skills, of course, activists have innumerable obstacles to overcome. People are not easily persuaded to adopt new perspectives, however skillful an activist may be in demonstrating the gains to be enjoyed by altering perspectives and adhering to new ones. Activists' success depends on their ability to overcome the habits and attitudes of those they seek to mobilize. But habits can be deeply engrained and do not change readily; thus activists are called on to be especially imaginative and patient in their efforts to generate support. Indeed, the resilience of habits can lead mobilizers to exaggerate, even to distort the underpinnings of situations, thereby leading them to run the risk of undermining rather than enhancing the readiness of their potential followers to yield to their mobilizing efforts.

Although the skill sets of activists are thus highly similar to those of politicians, their tasks are in important ways more difficult. The ultimate goal of politicians is to persuade voters to vote for them, whereas the goal of nongovernmental activists is to lead people to new perspectives in order to obtain their cooperation. More than that, they must sustain the support of their followers across long stretches of time, whereas election campaigns and voting occur only periodically and occasionally.

Another skill that activists and politicians share is that of maintaining a wide (and widening) set of acquaintances in their community. The more people in the community with whom an activist or politician is acquainted, the easier it is to generate support on behalf of specific goals, whether they are a particular interest of the mobilizer or the votes needed by a politician. In this respect activists, especially multi-issue activists, are politicians even though they do not take on the role of public officials or occupy positions in political parties.[3]

Conclusion

Since they serve as significant links between publics and the policy world, activists clearly are important. Indeed, since their efforts to press their perspectives on policymakers and publics occur at all times of the year and during all the years between elections, activists are central actors in the political process of democratic societies. Without them and spokespersons for nongovernmental organizations, the critical voice of citizens and publics would hardly be audible between elections. In effect, activists go a long way toward making people count!

Chapter Ten

Terrorists

In recent years no role has provoked as much attention or concern than has that of "terrorist." People who commit atrocities against civilians for political or ideological reasons have become a central problem of the twenty-first century, especially in Western and democratic societies. The fears they evoke and the damage they cause are pervasive, not only because they bring death and destruction but also because some are willing to die doing so. Whether the terrorists are suicide bombers or assassins, governments and societies have yet to devise effective means for reducing their number. In short, they are an infinitesimal minority of the world's population, but terrorists count!

Terrorism before Fragmegration

Terrorism is not the brainchild of Muslim fanatics, as recent events might lead one to think. There are examples in history of groups using terrorist tactics, the names of which have percolated into modern usage, such as the Zealots of ancient Israel or the Hashashin (Assassins) of Persia. These groups were internal organizations, focusing their violence on imperial or occupying forces. Given the limitations of ancient weaponry, that violence tended to be very specific, often confined to the assassinations of political leaders. Mass casualty attacks were unheard of.

The birth of modern terrorism can be attributed to the Russian anarchist movement at the turn of the twentieth century. In their unsuccessful efforts to destroy the Russian state, the anarchists were among the first to employ explosives. Although there was some concern that the anarchist movement would spread to other countries—notably expressed in Joseph Conrad's *The Secret Agent*—it never became a serious problem. Furthermore, anarchists tended to direct their activities at their own governments, not at other nations. Terrorists did not interact with the world polity, and terrorism was not a problem of world politics.

One notable act of terrorism did affect world politics, namely, the assassination of Archduke Ferdinand by a Serbian nationalist, Gavrilo Princip. This death is widely understood as the first shot in World War I. Yet, it would be a mistake to attribute the war solely or even primarily to Princip's action. Whatever his motives, there is no way that Princip could have imagined the subsequent events of that incident. In this case, world politics was already deeply dysfunctional, and Ferdinand's death was simply the trigger.

Terrorism Today

Since then, and especially since the end of World War II, terrorists have become the major problem of world politics, at least in some analyses. Even in recent times, as terrorism has emerged as a problem for world politics, it has often been so as a tool of sponsoring nations. The attack on Pan Am 103—also known as the Lockerbie bombing—was the work of Libyan agents in retaliation against the United States and the UK for the bombing of Tripoli by U.S. warplanes. Various other nations have sponsored terrorism or have been accused of doing so, such as Iran, Iraq, Pakistan, India, Cuba, and even the United States. This phenomenon, however, is little different from the prior era of nation-based politics, as nations are ultimately behind these sorts of acts.

The break with the past has come with those persons engaged in terrorist campaigns without state sponsorship or affiliation. These people are what many have called "super-empowered" terrorists—people with the desire and ability to bring devastation anywhere around the world, thanks to the technologies and processes of globalization. Al Qaeda is perhaps the best example of this, with a global network able to reach from caves in Afghanistan to Saudi Arabia, Yemen, Kenya, Tanzania, the United States, and elsewhere. The network has used a wide array of the technologies that are emblematic of globalization to accomplish its goals, including laptop computers, satellite phones, and—of course—jet airliners.

The change is not just in the terrorists' reach, but in their targets. They are no longer directing their violence toward their own governments but are reaching out to attack foreign governments. Terrorists are able to formulate and implement their own foreign policy, often to the consternation of states that might otherwise be sympathetic. For example, Iranian leaders worried after the attacks of September 11, 2001, that their nation might become a target for retribution, despite a history of "Death to America" antagonism. Because they are independent of state sponsorship, the terrorists' agenda often include goals or ideas that are antithetical to established world politics, such as the coalition of Muslim people into an Islamic caliphate.

There are a number of reasons why individuals choose the role of a terrorist. Despair over particular circumstances in world affairs induces others to engage in terrorist acts directed toward governments and whole populations. Born out of hatred of the United States and its policies toward the Arab world, the September 11 attacks on the World Trade Center and Pentagon are a dramatic case of terrorist actions generated by this pervasive despair, as are the numerous instances of terrorism derived from Israeli-Palestinian tensions. Deep-seated ideological and religious convictions are still another source of terrorist acts, a set of motivations illustrated by individuals enamored of the perspectives articulated by radical Islam philosophies.

Less grandiose purposes have also been cited as reasons why terrorists are led to engage in murderous violence. One researcher found that "95 percent of attacks worldwide were motivated by resentment of the presence of foreign combat troops."[1] To view Islamist terrorism as global, the analyst contended, is to "overplay religion in contrast to political objectives." Terrorist groups may share money and information, "but what motivates them primarily is independent, local issues. At its core, it's about political control of territory that the terrorists prize."[2]

Organizational Contexts

With few exceptions, and whatever may be the personal bases of their conduct, most terrorists belong to organizations that recruit, train, and fund them as well as pick their targets. Few terrorists act alone. Most of their acts derive from decisions made by terrorist organizations, some of which are private and secretive, whereas others are governments. Al Qaeda, the most effective and notorious terrorist organization of the modern era, was behind seventy-one suicide bombers between 1995 and 2004. Although a compilation of data on the nationality of these suicide bombers revealed that all of them came from the Middle East, they also "show that Al Qaeda is today less a product of Islamic fundamentalism than of a simple strategic goal to compel the United States and its Western allies to withdraw combat forces from the Arabian Peninsula and other Muslim countries."[3]

Some analysts perceive a move away from terrorist organizations that are structured along military lines. As one expert put it,

> We've moved into a realm where we are obliged to speak of universes of like-minded fanatics, from which have emerged small galaxies of conspirators, or in some cases, simply individuals who mentally incorporate the belief systems, whether it is racism or anti-Semitism or religious fanaticism, of the broader universe, but are not receiving orders in any formal sense of the term.[4]

This nonorganizational route to religious fanaticism was also evident in the young South Asian men in England who bombed the London subways. Indeed, they found their way into an extreme form of Islam not through the mosques but rather "through Islamic bookshops, the Internet, and university societies."[5]

Suicide Bombers

Obviously, the personalities and prior experiences of terrorists are also a source of their behavior. Many Muslims, for example, share hatred for the United States without becoming terrorists. They may or may not condone such behavior, but their orientations are such that they do not engage in it. Likewise, most Japanese were hostile toward the United States during World War II, but only a few became kamikaze pilots. What generalizations, then, can be made about the personality and personal histories of terrorists? More specifically, what characteristics do suicide bombers have in common? Why have 200 Palestinians since 1995 and more than 500 individuals in Iraq since 2003 engaged in suicide attacks?[6]

It is erroneous to view the modern surge of suicide bombings as a phenomenon of Muslims in the Middle East. Its origins can be traced to the early 1980s in Sri Lanka and its Tamil Tigers. Although composed predominantly of Hindus, the Tigers are avowedly a secular movement, marked by ethnic and nationalist outlooks in which religion does not play a significant role. Between 1980 and 2003 the Tigers accounted for 76 of 315 suicide attacks carried out around the world, whereas only 54 resulted from actions by Hamas and 27 by Islamic Jihad during the same period.[7]

It is clear that popular stereotypes of suicide bombers are profoundly flawed. Neither the bombers nor those who train and support them are unintelligent or crazy people. Rather, diverse researchers who probed different groups of suicide terrorists have converged around the same findings: they tend to come from middle-class homes and have education and income that is above the average for their societies. In one study it was found that "a surprising number have graduate degrees," that although one-third of Palestinians live in poverty, only 13 percent of the Palestinian bombers are under the poverty line; compared to 15 percent of the population at a comparable age, 57 percent of the suicide bombers went beyond high school for their education.[8] In 2003, moreover, a nineteen-year-old woman who wanted to earn a doctorate in English became the first of a series of Palestinian women to blow themselves up.[9] Another fallacy of the popular stereotype is that Muslims comprise the ranks of suicide bombers.

Conclusion

The attacks in Madrid, Bali, London, New York, and Washington, D.C., have proven a dramatic and lethal demonstration of the expanded scale and scope of terrorism in recent years. Terrorists have been so fully woven into the fabric of societies that governments have created bureaucracies to attempt to cope with them and residents of potentially vulnerable cities have been unsettled by the potential of attacks at any time in any place. Often, moreover, the anxieties of publics have fostered hostile actions directed at people with backgrounds presumed to be similar to those of terrorists. The specter of terrorism, in short, has undermined civil rights and had significant consequences for international travelers and immigrants seeking to cross borders. It has also led to a conflict known as the War on Terror, thereby generating a seemingly endless series of fragmegrative situations, with people of goodwill arguing against scapegoating even as frightened publics nonetheless focus their anger and anxieties on innocent people. So terrorists count in a whole variety of important ways.

PART II

People at Work

CHAPTER ELEVEN

Soldiers

Counting military personnel is relatively easy, as governments usually announce the figures, but assessing the ways in which they count—their roles, capabilities, and morale—is another story. The number of men and women in uniform is no more crucial than the training and equipment they receive and the attitudes they bring to war-fighting and peacekeeping tasks. Before this fragmegrative era, soldiers could be counted on as instruments of their government's policies. Even when they went to extremes by contesting the policies and toppling the government in a coup d'état, the consequences were largely domestic and minimal for world politics. This is changing, however, as soldiers are finding themselves able to act outside the confines of their native government, either as private military companies, as bloggers and amateur journalists, or as dissidents and protesters. Ironclad discipline is no longer pivotal to the role of soldier; instead fragmegration has allowed for expansion and more flexibility in this role, so that soldiers can engage in world politics themselves, apart from their armies or governments.[1]

Volunteers and Draftees

One of the major developments in the soldier role has come with the emergence of an all-volunteer professional military. A volunteer army and an army of draftees are not the same in a number of ways. Most notably, a high proportion of those who volunteer see themselves as making a career choice,[2] whereas draftees have no choice unless they are ready to flee and take up residence in another country. Of course, a certain number of professionals are essential to any army, but previously this careerism was confined to the officer corps and general staffs, whereas the enlisted ranks were fleshed out with conscripts. Although many armies still rely on draftees, some—that of the United States being a prime example—rely on volunteers. Among the consequences of this difference is that most volunteers become, through extensive and rigorous training, professionals and experts at whatever aspects of military operations in which they specialize, whereas draftees are not likely to be as motivated to perfect their specialties and are thus less reliable on the battlefield. The technology of modern warfare requires a cadre of expert soldiers capable of operating and maintaining complex electronics and computers; a volunteer, career-oriented military can better cultivate these skills in its ranks. Conscripts may not be unreliable, but their capacity for learning new skills is limited by their focus on returning to civilian life rather than on how they can build their careers and extend their competencies as soldiers. A professional army, in short, has numerous advantages over its drafted counterpart.

This is not to simplify the motivations of drafted soldiers. A number of other considerations besides length of service are relevant to their conduct. It has been found, for example, that the main reasons drafted soldiers fight—and fight hard and creatively—is not so much perfecting skills relevant to their postservice lives. Nor is it just the perquisites due them upon receiving a discharge from the services. Nor is it ideology and the causes for which they were drafted to fight. Rather, a major source of their motivations on the battlefield is concern for their comrades, their sense of camaraderie with those in their platoon, or in their squadron, or on their ship.[3]

Recruitment

In the absence of a military draft, however, it has become increasingly difficult for armed forces to replenish themselves through recruitment of new personnel. Wars have become ever-more fierce and people have become ever-more sensitive to the risks and loss of life involved. As a result, armies that do rely on volunteer and professional soldiers find themselves hamstrung when they are unable to entice enough recruits to fill their ranks. The absence of sufficient soldiers then becomes a factor in world politics. For example, many analysts have suggested that the United States might not have the military strength to intervene in places such as Darfur or North Korea, assuming it wanted to, because of the strain Iraq and Afghanistan have put on the military. In recent years it has thus been difficult for armed forces to maintain their desired force levels, whether it be in Russia, where the war in Chechnya has taken a heavy toll on both sides and increased the rate of desertion on the part of Russian soldiers, or in the United States, where the continuing rise of Americans killed in Iraq has reduced the voluntary enlistment rate. The case for military service in both countries is not so clear-cut that potential enlistees are able to overcome their doubts and join up at rates comparable to those of the past. In an effort to reverse the decline in enlistees, the U.S. Army has published a *School Recruiting Program Handbook*. Designed to guide recruiters when they go into high schools to sign up new enlistees, the text is marked by a "palpable . . . sense of desperation."[4]

At some level, would-be soldiers must view their country's war (or wars) as being fought for just reasons if the recruitment and retention of soldiers are to occur. Many volunteers enlist for this reason, but even though the threshold for a just-war definition is usually somewhat flexible, there are limits. In contrast to World War II, for example, the U.S. war in Vietnam quickly reached the point where it was no longer seen as sufficiently just to warrant obedience to the draft, much less volunteerism. A similar pattern is increasingly evident with respect to the second U.S. war in Iraq. Patriotism has its limits and these are revealed by the extent to which the purposes and successes of a war are realized. As of this writing in fall 2007, it seems clear that the United States is either at or near the verge of exceeding this limit.[5]

On the other hand, military recruiters can reinforce considerations of patriotism with a range of incentives. In the United States, for example, the new technologies used to fight wars are so advanced that new recruits can anticipate having marketable skills when they eventually return to the civilian world. They can train in a wide variety of technologies that have relevance for a host of jobs in the private economy, a fact that increases their readiness to enlist. Put differently, much of today's warfare is fought with complex technologies that are not readily mastered. Many of today's soldiers thus possess technical skills that they would not have otherwise obtained. For the most part, those with specialized skills view them more as useful to their postservice careers and their future livelihoods than as aspects of their time in the military. In addition, draftees do not anticipate long careers in the military and thus, unlike their career counterparts, do not have strong incentives to expand their knowledge base.

Morale

The commitment of military establishments to their societies can vary considerably, depending on a variety of circumstances. Most notably, the key to high morale lies in the support a society accords its military. Such support cannot be taken for granted. Much depends on whether the military has a reputation for efficiency, resisting corruption, respecting civilian authority, and openness to organizational reforms. If it does, then it earns the respect of the larger society, and morale in its ranks is likely to be high. If it does not, if its reputation has been sullied by instances of self-serving actions, violence, and undue intrusions into the society's civilian realm, then the military is likely to be feared and not respected, circumstances that do not conduce to high morale. The Indonesian military is illustrative in these regards. After the fall of the Suharto regime in the late 1990s, the Indonesian military sought to demonstrate that it was "not the enemy of society" even as its middle-level officers resisted reforms that would undermine their privileges, tensions that eventually improved its reputation and morale.[6] Quite different circumstances marked the Russian army after the end of the Cold War and its retreat from Eastern Europe and the Baltics: "It is an understrength, over-officered army with enormous problems of money and morale, ranging from corruption and draft-dodging to delayed salaries and poor housing. And it is becoming more disillusioned with politicians of all stripes, wanting to stay out of their squabbling at nearly any cost."[7]

The advent of the Internet and satellite phone has served to improve morale in the military. Soldiers can now talk, e-mail, and blog about their service abroad with families and friends at little expense and with a fair amount of ease. Home does not seem so distant to the present-day soldier serving abroad.

Women, Children, Gays, and Lesbians

A vast majority of the world's soldiers are men, but increasingly armies and militia include women and young children. In many countries the presence of women and children in the armed serves is controversial. On a host of grounds, their service is seen as inappropriate and just plain wrong, even as other militaries seek to enlarge their ranks beyond the population of adult males. Several international organizations and treaties prohibit the recruitment into military service of people younger than eighteen, yet many developing. countries and some guerrilla groups engage in such practices despite these prohibitions. The recruitment of children is made possible by the global proliferation of lightweight automatic weapons such as the AK–47 and M–16, which are lethal even in the hands of preadolescents. Especially in guerrilla movements, children are recruited or forced into service as front-line infantry. As Amnesty International reported in 2002, "more than 300,000 children under the age of 18 are thought to be fighting in conflicts around the world, and hundreds of thousands more are members of armed forces who could be sent into combat at any time. Although most child soldiers are between 15 and 18 years old, significant recruitment starts at the age of 10 and the use of even younger children has been recorded."[8] In addition, roughly 40 percent of the 300,000 child soldiers are girls.[9]

Notwithstanding lingering controversies over the appropriateness of women serving in the military, their presence in the militaries of a number of countries is not trivial. As can be seen in Table 11.1, which lists the proportion of women in the armed services of twenty-one selected countries, women comprise at least 8 percent of the ranks in seven countries and in another ten they exceed 5 percent.[10] The role played by women in combat situations has changed as the nature of combat has changed. Until the second U.S. war in Iraq, women were assigned to units not likely to be caught up in fighting, but the advent of an insurgency in Iraq has obscured the line between combat and noncombat situations, with the result that U.S. women serving in that conflict have fought, died, been wounded, and received medals for bravery in Iraq. In 2005, for example, U.S. forces in Iraq included some 15,000 female troops, a few of whom received medals for bravery under fire despite a 1994 Pentagon policy that prohibits women from serving in direct combat ground units smaller than brigades.[11] Accordingly, the controversy over women in the military roles has revived in the United States. Some critics, both in and out of the military, argue that the battlefield is a place for men only, partly because women are seen as not strong enough to perform a variety of tasks that effective performance in combat require and partly out of traditional conceptions of the nature of war.[12]

Although the recruitment of women into the military has become increasingly legitimate, the same cannot be said of gays and lesbians in the armed forces. Their presence is widely considered a threat to the stability of combat units. This issue has been especially intense in the United States, which has adopted a "don't ask, don't tell" policy as a basis for permitting their inclusion in the ranks of soldiers. The policy is a source of continuing controversy, with its advocates arguing that it enhances military effectiveness while preserving inclusivity and its opponents insisting that it is deleterious in a number of ways, including a loss of talent, money, and reputation as well as undermining unit cohesion and fostering increased violence against women. The opponents also call attention to the fact that twenty-four foreign militaries have lifted the ban on gays and lesbians without incurring a diminution of unit cohesiveness.[13]

Table 11-1. Selected Countries Where Women Serve In the Military

Country	Total Number	Total Women	Percentage Women
Australia	52,245	6,947	13.3
Belarus	79,940	4,000	5.0
Belgium	41,077	3,393	8.3
Brunei	7,000	400	5.7
Canada	99,156	16,136	16.3
China	2,200,000	136,000	6.2
Czech Republic	23,455	2,885	12.3
Denmark	21,564	1,054	4.9
France	350,447	44,829	12.8
Germany	190,570	10,030	5.2
Netherlands	24,150	3,181	13.2
New Zealand	8,610	1,290	15.0
Norway	11,110	700	6.3
Portugal	35,747	2,988	8.3
Poland	75,220	346	4.5
Romania	19,520	779	4.0
Russia	960,000	100,000	10.4
Slovenia	6,642	1,069	16.0
South Africa	75,913	16,437	21.7
Spain	130,660	12,444	9.5
United Kingdom	207,680	18,338	8.8

Sources: The Military Balance 2003–2004, The International Institute for Strategic Studies (London: Oxford University Press), 2003. Women in NATO Forces Year-in-Review 2004 NATO HQ Aug. 2004. Australian Defence Force Annual Report 2003–2004 of 30 June 2004. Defense Analytical Service Agency Statistics TSP 1 UK Regular Forces End Strength as of February 2004. Compiled by the Women's Research & Education Institute, April 2005.

Tasks and Training

Although traditionally soldiers are trained for and have engaged in warfare on battlefields, in recent decades they have also had to shoulder new responsibilities that are not usually associated with military service. Most notably, they have been assigned to serve as peacekeepers in areas of the world that are prone to violence among factions and that lack local police establishments capable of maintaining order. In some cases—most notably, U.S. forces in Iraq after 2003—these tasks involve training local military units to shoulder control of a country in disarray. Combating urban guerrilla movements and the production and circulation of drugs are other unwelcome tasks that have fallen to military troops.[14] In effect, increasingly soldiers have taken on tasks that are normally performed by police, a shift of responsibility that top military officers regret and tend to resist on the grounds that their job is to prepare for and fight wars rather than criminals. Their resistance, however, has been to no avail, as the line between military and police functions has been obscured in many of the situations that mark our complex, fragmegrative world.

More often than not, young recruits in the military are not trained to manage the new tasks subsumed by expansion of their roles. Yet, whether they are officers educated in special schools such as West Point in the United States and the Royal Military Academy at Sandhurst in the United Kingdom or enlisted personnel put through basic training, the expanded tasks of "state building" have not been incorporated as units in their training programs. Learning these tasks tends to occur when the need arises on the ground and the military are called upon to reconstruct civilian institutions.

Rank in a Large, Hierarchical Organization

To understand the attitudes and behavior of enlisted men and officers it is crucial to grasp that militaries in developed countries, if not everywhere, are large, complex bureaucracies in which the flow of commands moves from the top to the bottom. But the hierarchies of armies do not free them from the constraints that any large organization imposes on its personnel. To be sure, the hierarchical character of military organizations renders them different from other types of organizations in the sense that orders have to be obeyed and implemented at all levels of their command structures, else official reprimands or dishonorable discharges can follow.[15] In the lower reaches of the structure the orders tend to be obeyed without discussion, but in the upper reaches of the officer corps decisions tend to be made after some deliberation, even though once they are made it is expected they will be followed.[16] These expectations, however, often fall prey to all the tensions, delays, and stalemate that mark any large bureaucracy. From the very start of their training, officers are inculcated with the values and goals of their services, with the result that they often put loyalties to their services ahead of those to the larger military organization of which their service is a part. The rivalries that first find expression in, say, the annual football games between the army and navy academies in the United States tend to get carried forward as officers advance in the ranks. They become rivalries over prestige, power, and money. As such, rivalries are as much a feature of the interactions among high-level command officers as are those that accompany the sports competitions of the service academies.

Not only are military establishments complex, bureaucratic organizations, they are also part of more encompassing bureaucracies—their governments—which further complicates the challenges that soldiers face. Indeed, in the United States the even more encompassing politics of the country had consequences for the assignments of top generals. For example, a plan to appoint Lt. Gen. Ricardo S. Sanchez as head of the Southern Command was considered desirable for several reasons, among them the fact that he was the highest ranking Hispanic officer and thus a role model for young Hispanics who were being more successfully recruited than those in other socioeconomic groups. As one army officer put it, "The Army sells growth, opportunity and development. We cannot ignore what our population's makeup is."[17] On the other hand, General Sanchez was the top commander in Iraq during the Abu Ghraib scandal and thus became the focus of much concern and criticism. Even though an official inquiry cleared him of wrongdoing, his proximity to that scandal posed the problem of whether he would win sufficient societal and congressional approval to justify offering him the post.

Civil-Military Relations

The role of military establishments also has to be considered in a larger context. A long-standing value in democratic societies asserts that military establishments and their personnel are subordinate to their civilian agencies and officials. The notion of "civilian supremacy" is even embedded at several points in the U.S. Constitution. Given the technological nature of modern warfare, however, often the military are more knowledgeable about certain kinds of issues (such as weapons, strategy, and tactics) than their civilian superiors, with the result that the practice of civilian supremacy frequently takes the form of "civilian ratification." On the other hand, occasionally military officers openly criticize their civilian superiors. This happened in 2006 in the United States when several retired generals publicly criticized then secretary of defense Donald H. Rumsfeld and his handling of the war in Iraq. A subsequent survey revealed that the criticisms were shared by junior officers on active duty, a finding that some officers criticized as inappropriate and a threat to the value and practices of civilian supremacy,[18] while a number of officers were sufficiently distressed by Rumsfeld to consider giving up their military careers.[19] Notwithstanding this unique series of events, the value of civilian supremacy remains intact. Indeed, it is widely viewed as a crucial value, as is demonstrated by the histories of those circumstances in other countries—dictatorships and coups d'état—in which a commitment to civilian supremacy is either nonexistent or weak.

Where the commitment to civilian supremacy is weak or nonexistent, of course, the military can give rise to fragmegrative tensions. Even when they remain on the sidelines rather than taking over the reins of government, soldiers intent upon guiding the course of a society's life can be the source of considerable fragmegration. This is especially the case when they divide into factions, with some seeking to protect and preserve the civilian government and others aspiring to giving it direction and rendering it subordinate to them. In these circumstances those in the armed service who seek to defend and preserve civilian supremacy contribute to the integration of their society, whereas those who aspire to commanding the civilian scene foster fragmentation. In democratic societies that maintain the precepts of civilian supremacy, on the other hand, the military serve as a source of stability and rarely engage in actions that are fragmegrative.

Conclusion

Soldiers are key people in the life of societies, but in democratic systems their centrality is sporadic. Only when war is threatened or underway does their importance become salient. At these times questions about their coherence, training, competence, and loyalty climb high on the agenda. But achieving armed forces that are coherent, well trained, highly competent, and deeply loyal cannot be taken for granted. All concerned, both within and outside the military structures, have to work diligently to maintain combat readiness and then prevail when hostilities break out. This is especially the case when casualties are high and the probability of victory is not clear in a fragmegrative era, circumstances that intensify the restlessness of publics and widen the gap between citizens and governments, with the former questioning the policies of the latter and pressing for clarity as to when the troops can be brought home. Such problems are further compounded because it is usually far from clear what victory means and when it is achieved. The enemy can succumb and its government can crumble, but guerrilla wars and insurgencies can continue. The history of the United States in Vietnam and in Iraq after 2003 offers poignant evidence of how vulnerable and frayed the links between publics and their governments can become when wars drag on and the adequacy of the military establishment is questioned.

That soldiers count when war looms is obvious from a basic military perspective, but there are two other ways that the extent to which they count is important. One occurs when families and towns suffer a combat loss of a loved one and undergo intense anguish and painful disruption; under these circumstances soldiers count in a very personal as well as a societal sense. The other involves the call-up of reserve units to active duty. Reserve units are precisely what their label implies:

clusters of citizens soldiers who live at home and periodically engage in military exercises even as they maintain their civilian pursuits. This reserve arrangement can last for years, except during wartime when their services are needed as combatants and they are called to active duty. Much anguish and painful disruption can also follow these call-ups, depending on how long and under what conditions the reserves are used. At those times soldiers count in terms of the war effort, the daily life of communities, and the course of world politics.

Chapter Twelve

Workers

People are still dangling, ever so precariously, on the edge of the labor market. They are still filing job applications, but they acknowledge that their searches have slowed over the months, and even years. Many have begun to talk about giving up on the traditional job path. The question is where they will go.

—*Monica Davey and David Leonhardt*[1]

Immigrant workers are now a critical part of the labor force across the board. We are into a new world of immigrants basically spreading throughout the economy. This is something that is going to continue and intensify.

—*Demetrious Papademetriou*[2]

We are the target market of a lot of these brands and they want a positive image on campus because they want consumers for life. We also have the moral and ethical argument being on the side of a university, so we can pressure the university to use their leverage in society to change the policies of the brands.

—*Molly McGrath*[3]

Much like soldiers in armies, the worker was once limited in his role as such; any concerns he or she might have outside the company were addressed by the union, and perhaps by elected representatives. At the level of world politics, workers did not matter; they were part of the economic calculus of international trade only as employees of their respective companies.

With fragmegration, the role of the worker has changed dramatically. Workers and their unions have been profoundly affected by the advent of pervasive information technologies and robotic machinery. Assembly lines still exist, but humans no longer carry out many of the tasks that accompany an ever-greater automation of labor. Consequently, counting workers no longer tells as much, given the difficulty of assessing the quality of work and the extent to which workers are trained to perform highly skilled jobs. Indeed, quantitative analyses of the workforce are relatively easy compared to tracing its qualitative trends. Ample quantitative data descriptive of the workplace are available for many countries on the web sites of the OECD, the International Labour Organization (ILO), the World Bank, and the U.S. Bureau of Labor Statistics. These data do not present a clear picture, however, of how workers matter in a fragmegrated world. Workers count in different ways if they are employed, unemployed, or no longer seek jobs; if their skills are adequate to the jobs available; if their jobs migrate abroad; if they join or avoid unions; and if they strike against employers or rally against the labor and welfare policies of their governments. These dynamics are often the source of considerable tension within and between countries.

Employed and Unemployed Workers

Taken overall, the data on the labor force depict a huge number of unemployed or underemployed people as well as many who have dropped out of the workforce and no longer seek a job. According to a 1996 ILO estimate, the number of persons throughout the world needing work amounted to roughly one billion people. Although this figure disguises substantial differences among regions and countries, in no country or region do the data show a workforce close to being fully employed.[4] On the contrary, the same ILO report observed that "the global outlook on unemployment is grim," and the subsequent slowing of economic growth around the world has probably rendered the situation even grimmer. Diverse reasons account for the large number of people who are either out of work or who have given up looking for work: among the most oft-cited of the many reasons are the downsizing of companies, a sense of futility over the scarcity of jobs, the migration of jobs to locales where labor is cheap, the advent of laborsaving technologies, a pervasive illiteracy and uncontrolled population growth in the developing world, the aging of populations and a resulting increase in the number of retirees, a slowing of the global economy, the downturn of national economies, and the insufficiency of governmental policies to offset the downturns.

Although different analysts get committed to one or another of these explanations, each of these is at root a problem of conditions changing faster than people are able to adapt. In effect, those hours of the day devoted to work have been increasingly difficult and tension ridden for most people in every occupation and in every part of the world, leaving many of them struggling to keep up and worrying about their plight.

The inability of able people who were laid off from good jobs in the economic downturn—and who subsequently were unable to find a new position in the so-called jobless recovery—offers a compelling insight into these tensions. The stories of individuals who opted out of the labor market during the twenty-six months following January 2001 are expressions of pain and disappointment far more telling than the quantitative picture represented by the fact that the percentage of, say, Americans neither working nor looking for work increased in nineteen of the twenty-six months. Mike Guido, for example, held a job for nearly twenty years as an engineer developing products for a Pittsburgh company that makes safety and industrial equipment. Some nine months after losing the job and looking unsuccessfully for a new one, "it started to dawn on me" that "it wasn't happening. It wasn't going to." So at age forty-eight, with a ten-year-old daughter, a mortgage, a shrinking retirement account, and new student loans, he enrolled in a PhD program. "This is definitely not easy financially," he said. "The economy has sideswiped me." Similarly, at age fifty-six, Janis M. Leftridge lost her job as a human resources manager charged with handling other peoples' problems. After two years of failing to find another position, she had used up her savings and was trying to sort out how she would pay the monthly rent. "I'll figure something out, it'll happen," she said. "But it's funny how, when you're younger, you don't think you'll find yourself in a position like this. I didn't think I'd ever be here."[5]

Nor are the pains accompanying unemployment confined to the United States. In Canada, which has long welcomed immigrants in order to compensate for an aging population and labor shortages, it has become increasingly difficult for even the most highly skilled immigrants to find suitable positions. This is due partly to a decline in jobs appropriate to workers with advanced skills, but to some extent the problem is also rooted in the success of Canada's efforts to resolve its shortages by encouraging people from all over the world to immigrate to Canada. Positions requiring advanced skills have become increasingly scarce, making it increasingly difficult for immigrants to locate jobs for which they were trained. Consider the plight of Gian S. Sangha: an environmental scientist from India, the holder of a German doctorate, the author of two books, he could not find a position that enabled him to draw upon his expertise and was forced to cut lawns until he found a clerical position. Indeed, "nearly half of the [highly skilled immigrants in Canada] are driving taxis and trucks, working in factories or as security guards, hoping their children will do better." Sangha ascribed his difficulties to "a hidden discrimination," adding that "it's a painful life. I'm angry and frustrated. I never thought it would be like this in Canada."[6]

Skills in the Skill Revolution

In sum, there are limits to the current wisdom that the acquisition of advanced skills is the key to employment today. The service sector may have replaced the assembly line as a large pool of available jobs, but the pool can dry up when an economy turns down. The advice that one observer says should be given to young people—that "you have to constantly upgrade your skills"[7]—may not yield immediate results in the absence of a thriving economy. Put differently, it is doubtless the case that today the route to job security involves having a skill that allows one to move from employer to employer, that today it matters less "whom you work for than what you can do."[8] Having a secure job is not, however, the same as having a good job. The best-paying jobs tend to require workers of substantial and particular skills, but these workers find themselves unable to apply those specialized skills in other occupations. As these jobs become scarcer, people are left with jobs that accommodate general skills and that tend to pay less.

The increasing disparity between highly skilled and unskilled trades contributes to the gap between rich and poor. Discrepancies in employment, pension arrangements, and transnational processes also contribute, each in its own way, to a gap between the rich and poor within and between societies. And it is a gap that has grown over time, resisting efforts at reduction and poised for continual growth. The sources of this growth are numerous: technological advances are resulting in jobs being performed by machines; many routine jobs are being transferred to developing societies where wage rates are low relative to comparable positions in developed societies; positions that sustain the information revolution involve highly technical skills—what one observer calls the skills of symbolic analysts[9]—that only relatively few are able to obtain; more and more people are getting at least some education, but oftentimes the scarcity of jobs for the well educated raises questions about the value of the education and fosters a sense of malaise; the availability of new entrants in developed societies who are desperate for work lowers wage rates and often leads to the exploitation of immigrant populations; salaries for top managers and executives in the United States have soared in recent years even as real wages have been stagnant; and a variety of other sources in particular countries is contributing to the widening of the rich-poor gap.

Whatever the appropriate explanation for the burgeoning rich-poor gap—and doubtless different combinations of the foregoing reasons obtain in different communities in different parts of the world—contrary interpretations of the gap are a major source of tension between workers and their managers, between the same industries in different countries, between unions and corporations, between wealthy and poor countries, and between publics and governments. Sometimes the tensions foster violence and sometimes they are addressed by leaders who seek to narrow the gap through peaceful means. There is no reason to believe, however, that the gap is going to diminish in the near future.

Outsourcing and Migrants

Like so much else, work is caught up in the shrinking of time and distance that has rendered national boundaries increasingly porous. In a number of ways transnational processes are shaping the lives and activities of workers. Most notably, both jobs and workers have moved long distances to meet personnel and financial needs. The movement of jobs, often referred to as "outsourcing," stems from the calculation of businesses that they can keep their labor costs down by moving their operations to low-wage countries and then selling the products that result at home for a larger profit. This practice has been the source of considerable controversy in high-wage countries such as the United States, where worker protests against the practice have been frequent and intense. In some instances the protests have been effective and resulted in the reversal of outsourced work.[10]

Although jobs tend to flow from developed to developing countries, the opposite is the case for workers. As indicated in the chapter's second epigraph, the flow of foreign workers into developed countries has been extensive, partly because the incentives to immigrate are considerable and partly because host companies and countries seek to enhance their labor pool by recruiting both low-skilled, low-wage workers and high-skilled technicians from abroad. At the present time, for example, the United States admits some 800,000 legal immigrants a year and another 300,000 are estimated to enter illegally each year. All together, immigrants comprise some 12 percent of the workforce in the United States. Some of them are high-paid software developers from India, but most of the legal and illegal immigrants have low-paid menial jobs—such as hotel and restaurant workers, taxi drivers, and fruit pickers—that even unemployed Americans are loath to take. One consequence of immigrant laborers is that they drive down wages of U.S.-born workers with little education in those occupations where they are competitive.[11] Needless to say, tensions surrounding the presence of immigrant workers rise whenever the receiving economy enters periods of difficulty.

Some of the initiative underlying the flow of immigrants stems from labor shortages in developed countries that governments and companies seek to offset by recruiting in the developing world. There is, for example, an acute shortage of nurses in the United States—it is estimated that the country will have 800,000 fewer nurses than it needs by 2020—that has led to vigorous and successful recruitment efforts in the Philippines and India.[12] An equally serious shortage involves surgeons. For a variety of reasons, with perhaps the main one being the high coast of malpractice insurance, a decline is underway in the number of medical students who choose to specialize in surgery. "If this trend continues, less than 5 percent of medical school graduates will choose a career in surgery by 2005, and only 75 percent of general surgery residency positions will be filled by graduates of medical schools in the United States."[13]

One particularly repugnant aspect of the incentive of illegal immigrants to move into the West and the reluctance of unscrupulous employers to not even pay minimum wages is the smuggling rings that traffic in people. All too often incidents are reported of injury and death in unventilated and overheated vehicles used by smugglers to move their human cargo.

Unions and Fragmegration

Workers have been affected by fragmegration, perhaps more so than is the case for most roles. But in what ways might they count as sources of fragmegration? The most obvious way involves their membership in trade unions. Committed to improving the well-being of their members, unions are integrative in the sense that they bring together workers in the same industry to engage in collective action. Even as such integration occurs, however, it contributes to fragmentation when the members are called out on strike. The long-term consequences of labor strife may be beneficial to the larger community, but it can also tear the community apart as it unfolds. Workers and unions are not inherently fragmegrative. Their conduct can serve to improve the well-being of their communities even as at other times they can inflame passions and division among groups.

Workers and unions were most famously engaged in world politics with the rise of Solidarity in Poland, and the eventual ascension of the union's founder, former shipyard worker Lech Walensa, to the presidency of that country. His efforts affected not only Poland but also the entire Soviet bloc. More recently, Luiz Inacio da Silva ("Lula") has risen from steelworker to president of Brazil, and his union-informed politics have affected Latin American politics. In a similar vein, President Evo Morales of Bolivia has become a champion of the coca farmers in his country, with potentially dire implications for U.S. narcotics policy in the Andes. In each case these men fill the role of "public official" (see Chapter 14), but in a manner very much informed by their previous roles as workers, farmers, and organizers.

The instability of fragmegrative conditions has also led workers to demand more from their governments, particularly in the form of social welfare programs, often called "safety nets." The skilled workers who find themselves stranded when no suitable jobs are available fall back on such programs in order to retrain and adjust to new circumstances. In fact, such programs may be necessary to encourage workers to develop such skills in the first place; albeit the presence of social welfare programs ameliorates some of the risk involved in investing in specialized training and education.[14]

Resistance

Still another, somewhat more circuitous transnational process is sustained by activists in developed societies who employ boycotts and other forms of indirect pressure in an attempt to alleviate the working conditions of those who labor under sweatshop situations for very low wages. As indicated in the chapter's third epigraph, a current example of this process is the pressure that students and labor activists on campuses in the United States bring to bear on university administrators not to purchase athletic equipment (with their schools' logos) that is made in such sweatshop-type factories of the developing world. And their combined efforts have not been in vain. Unions have been allowed to form in, among other places, the Caribbean and Mexico, and subsequently working conditions as well as salaries have been improved.[15]

Perhaps the most manifest tensions are those that ensue when companies and governments seek to alter their pension systems. The problem is most acute in

Europe, where many of the governments are seeking to overhaul the public employee systems that have become increasingly out of phase with the aging of their populations. In France, for example, four workers financed each pensioner in 1960, but by 2000 the figure dropped to two workers, and demographic trends pointed to each pensioner being supported by only one worker in 2020, a pattern that seems destined to shrink the size of pensions and eventually to bankrupt the system entirely. It was forecast that without alteration of the law, France's pension fund would fall about $50 billion short in 2020 and would lack more than $100 billion to pay retirees in 2040. In 2003 the French government decided to confront these projections directly with a proposal to overhaul the system by lengthening the period of years workers had to contribute to the pension system from thirty-seven-and-a-half years to forty years in 2008 and to forty-two years in 2020. A series of strikes led by employee unions followed, along with increased acrimony as the government refused to back down and the strikers refused to get off the streets. Similar projections and proposals, which also provoked widespread strikes, occurred at the same time in Austria, Germany, and Italy.[16]

The same problem obtains in the United States, but despite the efforts of President George W. Bush to press the Congress for new Social Security policies attuned to demographic realities, the legislative branch has yet to confront the realities of demographic trends. Unable to think in terms of their grandchildren, politicians keep postponing the day of reckoning, aware that they will not be around when aging of the society results in the funds deposited in the Social Security system being insufficient to pay its obligations. A sign of the problem has already surfaced in the case of company pension funds, which are also vulnerable to the aging of workers and an increasing pace of withdrawals from the funds. Such funds have thus been defaulting at a greatly accelerated rate, leading to proposed legislation that would allow businesses with union workers to greatly reduce their pension obligations on the grounds of an actuarial finding that blue-collar and the poorly paid workers do not live as long as their white-collar and well-paid counterparts.[17] A harsh perspective, to be sure, but nonetheless one that has been advanced and transformed into policy.

Conclusion

The conditions of work would appear to be increasingly difficult around the world. These conditions and the issues and processes that sustain them vary in different countries and regions, and so do the degrees of union organization in different locales. Yet, without workers and their diverse skills, production would grind to a halt and economies would not function. Technological innovations have and will continue to supplant jobs in many industries, but there remain lots of both simple and complex tasks that only people can perform. In short, workers count!

CHAPTER THIRTEEN

Business Executives

Although only relatively few members of the world's population head up large multinational corporations, business executives count. Their influence far exceeds their number because their activities and those of their firms are important to the well-being of the economies—local, national, and international—in which they are active. As chief executive officers (CEOs) of powerful organizations that have numerous employees and that provide goods and services for many thousands of persons in diverse parts of the world, they are conspicuous members of the global elite. Their influence is extensive not only within their companies but also in the distant markets where their products are available. Indeed, their influence is such that many critics view them as culprits, as individuals who create and sustain the large gaps between the rich and the poor within and among countries.

Whatever the validity of this criticism, it is clear that business executives tend to favor free trade, globalization, and the liberalization of national economies. A recent study provides considerable evidence that CEOs—at least in the United States—are considerably more in favor of such policies than elites from other walks of life. It also demonstrates that they are considerably more involved in global affairs than their counterparts whose leadership is not located in the world of business.[1]

Prior to the Asian financial crisis, the bursting of the dot-com bubble, and the Enron and other scandals at the turn of the century, CEOs were highly and widely regarded, with much of the credit for the boom years of the 1980s and 1990s going to them. More recently, however, their celebrity has declined. This is perhaps especially the case in Europe, where there is little respect for business executives among the public at large (except in Denmark). "Most Europeans believe top executives are dishonest, overpaid and place their own personal interests ahead of the interests of company shareholders, employees, and customers."[2]

Much the same can be said about the United States, where "the role of business leaders has been enormously diminished" since the terrorist attacks of September 11, 2001.[3] Subsequently this diminution was quickly accelerated in response to a rash of corporate scandals. As they piled up, with jury trials consistently finding enough evidence of fraud and mismanagement to convict the top leaders of En-ron, Worldcom, Adelphia Communications, Tyco, HealthSouth—to mention only the more conspicuous cases—so did attitudes of disrespect for CEOs spread and deepen. Juries and others in the larger public could not accept the argument of some of the CEOs that they were ignorant of the transgressions committed under their leadership. As a former federal prosecutor put it, "Most people on juries aren't business owners. They are employees, and their bosses would never tolerate those excuses. To have someone making millions and millions of dollars saying 'I was disorganized; I wasn't paying attention' is something that jurors just can't understand."[4] Another former federal prosecutor expressed a similar reaction: "There is an inconsistency between someone who takes the position that he built a company from scratch but forgets certain things that jurors find important and material. They are going to wonder how anyone could have risen to the top of the world, earned justifiably the pay and not known what was going on."[5] Stated more succinctly, "a defense that you were more cheerleader than ringleader is going to be very difficult for a jury to buy."[6]

Criticism of CEOs has been further stimulated by reports of corporate boards rewarding them with astronomical salaries, lavish bonuses, generous expense ac-counts, and perks such as the use of their company's jet planes for private trips.[7] A typical example is provided by the General Dynamics Corporation: the total compensation of its CEO, Nicholas D. Chabraja, was estimated to be $13.7 million in 2004, an amount that served as a basis for an annual retirement pay projected at $2.1 million. In addition, his contract stipulated that the company would buy his Virginia home after he retired.[8] Even more conspicuous, after thirteen years as chairman and chief executive of Exxon Mobil, Lee R. Raymond retired after receiving a total of $686 million, or $144,573 a day during his chairmanship.[9] Stated more generally, "the median compensation for chief executives at roughly 200 large companies rose modestly to $8.4 million" in 2005 from $8.2 million in 2004.[10]

Training and the Skill Revolution

The path to the top of the business world in the United States is traversed mainly by white men, but increasingly diversity marks the education and social back-grounds of top business leaders. Where most used to attend Ivy League universi-ties, this pattern is much less conspicuous today. To a large extent it is also a path that takes the leaders through schools of business and the acquisition of a Master of Business Administration (MBA) degree.[11] The essential training provided by the schools involves preparing their graduates to run profitable organizations. Although most of the schools do a good job in this respect, they tend to fall short in terms of preparing their graduates to think on a global scale, to view their responsibilities to include involvement in shaping the global economy such that equity as well as prosperity prevails. Or at least there is little evidence that CEOs see themselves as tasked to do more than insure profitability for their firms.[12] One business educator put it this way:

> There was a time when leaders of big multinational companies were thinking about supporting some governance of the global economy. The idea was that there was no such thing as world government and that national governments were much too focused on their own jurisdictions to create the rules of trade or finance or environmental protection or labor. Companies were going to move into this vacuum, gingerly, but the world would be run more according to business and market principles. Over the past decade, most C.E.O.'s decided this was not for them. They created a vacuum into which governments are moving, for better or worse.[13]

Whatever the weakness of formal MBA programs, relevant training continues after graduation from business school. A variety of courses, such as game theory and scenario planning workshops, is offered that enables business executives to tool up on the latest techniques of analysis, thereby adding to the analytic skills of those who sit in on them.[14] It would appear that the skill revolution has roots in the business as well as the academic community.

Mobility

As globalization has increasingly organized the course of events, so have more and more midsize and large companies sent executives abroad to manage their overseas operations. In fact, in 2000 some 80 percent of U.S. businesses assigned some of their personnel to foreign posts and 45 percent reported plans to increase the number of overseas assignments. Although this practice might be expected to compensate for the inward orientation of MBA programs, apparently it has also led to unanticipated consequences. One survey found that coming home from foreign assignments was difficult for the returnees: 75 percent of those surveyed felt that the position to which they returned was a demotion, 61 percent reported that they lacked opportunities to use their foreign experience upon taking up new duties at home, and 25 percent left the company within a year of returning from their foreign assignments.[15] These findings suggest that there may be a downside to the mobility upheaval noted in Chapter 3 as well as the upside claimed for it. Moving around the world may not always be experienced as enlarging for business executives whose careers include foreign assignments.

On the other hand, the aforementioned findings relative to the involvement of business executives in global affairs revealed that those who lived and/or studied abroad as younger persons were more likely to be extensively involved than those whose early experiences did not include living in a foreign country.[16] Viewed in this context, the lack of emphasis in schools of business on assuming global responsibility is perhaps less crucial than it might otherwise seem. Enduring commitments along this global dimension appear to be set well before people move on to study for their MBAs.

Needless to say, advanced education is not the only source of commitments on a global scale. The global commitments of certain individuals—such as Bill Gates, George Soros, and Ted Turner—stand out as exemplars of responsible business executives. Their contribution of significant amounts of their wealth to charity or service organizations has had meaningful consequences for the recipients: health in underdeveloped countries on the part of Gates, a variety of organizations and institutions in eastern Europe on the part of George Soros, and the United Nations on the part of Ted Turner. It would seem that success in business is as important a source of responsible behavior on the part of chief executives as are foreign travel and exposure to advanced education.

Conclusion

A central finding of the aforementioned inquiry into leaders on the cutting edge of globalization is that business executives are not readily differentiable from leaders in other walks of life. The former do travel more and are more extensively connected to global affairs, and as a consequence they are also more committed to policies that promote globalization. Nevertheless, there are also a number of ways in which the activities and orientations of leaders in the world of business are similar to counterparts engaged in other pursuits.

Chapter Fourteen

Public Officials

Public officials—those individuals who are responsible for the day-to-day functioning of government—are increasingly visible in this era of fragmegration. At one time they were invisible cogs in the machinery of their governments, and if they mattered in world politics, it was only as part of that government. In the present era of networked individuals and innovative technologies that allow for tracing their activities, however, the roles public officials occupy in world affairs have become increasingly salient and discernible.

In many, if not most, countries, public officials at every level of government are maligned and lack the respect of the public that they serve. In a profound sense, however, they are either unaware of or dismiss the public's negative attitudes. The reasons for this discrepancy are several. First, public officials work hard and long hours because they have a sense of service and commitment to the publics they serve. Second, they know they cannot please all segments of the public and thus view the criticism as part of their jobs. Third, many do not associate themselves with the antagonism with which the entire public service is viewed. Individually they know they are doing their jobs as best they can and thus presume the criticisms are not directed at them. Fourth, they tend to presume that the criticism originates with feelings about elected policymakers at the top of the government.

Nonetheless, the discrepancy between the long hours and tireless commitments that mark the lives of many public officials on the one hand, and the attitudes of citizenries on the other, is huge. Or at least they do not enjoy the respect on the part of the public that they deserve. Why then, it might be asked, do they stay on the job and continue to maintain the long hours and deep commitments? The answer probably varies from person to person, but it is likely that most public officials believe in what they are doing and the goals toward which they are working, an attitude that makes it much easier to absorb the lack of respect with which they must cope.

Of course, there are two major types of officials: the civil servant whose tenure in the government is secure and long term on the one hand, and on the other those who are elected or appointed to their positions for as long as their political superiors or the electorate want them to remain in their jobs. The previous two paragraphs and the remainder of the chapter are descriptive of the former, whereas elected or appointed officials know that their policymaking responsibilities are bound to create controversy and disrespect in some quarters of the public. Lacking tenure and always subject to the whims of the electorate, most of them do not view their political positions as a lifetime job. Indeed, in open, democratic societies few, perhaps none, of the elected or appointed officials would be able to keep their positions even if they wanted to. The tides of politics periodically rise sufficiently to sweep officeholders out of their posts.

Modest Remuneration

Civil servants do not invest large amounts of time and energy in order to make a lot of money. They earn much less than their counterparts in the private sectors of society. On the other hand, they tend to be secure in their positions and enjoy tenure as long as they do not engage in corrupt practices or otherwise violate societal norms. Although the tenure system encourages loyalty and commitment, one of its negative consequences is that those who perform poorly cannot easily be removed from their positions. Relatively few take advantage of that reality by not working hard, but that is not relevant to the vast numbers whose dedication leads them to work long and intense hours. For the latter there is satisfaction in their work and compensation in knowing that they are contributing to the well-being of their society, and it probably never occurs to them to slack off. For most civil servants the rewards of public service are intangible and not readily measured in monetary terms.

Whatever their salaries, civil servants receive annual increments that are determined by a scale for each type of position. In addition, there is always the possibility of a promotion to a different scale that ultimately will take them higher on the income ladder. More often then not, movement up a scale is accompanied by greater responsibilities, which for many civil servants may be no less important than the salary increment that accompanies a move up to a new location on the scale. On the other hand, if they do not want to shoulder the responsibilities of the new position, they can turn it down and continue in their present line of work.

Mobility

Individuals who enter the civil service after college or in their early twenties and then stay on for a lifetime are not necessarily bound to the same position for the entire period. In the course of performing their duties, of serving on interagency committees, they may well establish links to counterparts in other agencies who then seek to have them transferred. Mobility within the government can thus be high, and few civil servants remain in the same position for an entire career. Some perquisites attach to seniority in an agency, but this does not mean a lifetime of service in that agency. Mobility within the civil service can involve what is called "lateral entry," which means one can enter an agency at the same level for which he or she was previously qualified. Indeed, the idea of serving in the same position for an entire career is explicitly contrary to the philosophy that guides the British civil service and is frowned on in other civil services, the reasoning being that developing generalists who can fit into any position is preferable to training specialists whose expertise is narrow and who lack, in effect, the skills to move around the government. Specialists on any issue can always be found and recruited, but competent generalists tend to be in short supply.

Neutrality

In exchange for the tenure that attaches to their positions, civil servants are obliged to remain neutral in the positions they advance in public. Partisan actions on behalf of their beliefs are prohibited under all circumstances, even when their superiors seek to get them to support their policies in public. Indeed, even if they disagree vehemently with a particular policy, they cannot take their case to the public. More accurately, if they do not remain silent, they are likely to be reprimanded at least and fired at most. The tradition of neutrality on the part of civil servants is central to the notion of public service. The tradition enables civil servants to serve with equal loyalty and commitment to superiors of different political parties. To be sure, they are not ciphers. They do have policy positions that they press on their superiors, but doing so in public is not permitted. If the policies of their superiors are so abhorrent to them that they cannot remain quiet, then they are obliged to resign from their position in order to take their case to the public. Some may try to leak their alternative perspectives to the press, but such efforts can often be traced to them and lead to their being dismissed from their positions.

Bureaucratic Challenges

Perhaps the most frustrating part of life as a civil servant is getting your ideas through the layers of decision above you. Usually recommendations move upward through memorandums that may or may not be followed up by phone calls, but it is a treacherous and complex route, as each pair of eyes that passes over a memorandum may lead to a modification of a word, a phrase, or even paragraphs. The document that finally forms the basis of decision may thus be a far cry from the initial input, the alterations being the result of bureaucratic procedures. Such outcomes are the bane of a civil servant's life, as he or she may not get credit for having been the document's originator and, even worse, may no longer be pleased with its contents.

Stated more generally, civil servants work in large bureaucratic organizations, virtually all of which have procedures that militate against creativity and clear-cut conclusions. More than that, organizational theory tells us that people in bureaucracies tend to get overly attached to their bureaucratic unit, with the result that the memorandum may well pass through hands that are inclined to alter it to fit somewhat different purposes. Even worse, those in other units of the bureaucracy may recommend not sending the memorandum on or, at least, drastically changing it. This is not to imply that bureaucratic procedures are designed to make things difficult for those they encompass. Quite to the contrary, they are designed to ensure that certain standards are met and certain goals are achieved, even though the resulting procedures may prove frustrating for some of the personnel caught up in the process. Such is the price that has to be paid for the maintenance of large policymaking organizations.

Whistle-Blowers

On occasion the policymaking processes of bureaucracies may go so far astray as to violate regulations or result in outrageous recommendations. Such circumstances are likely to be ignored by most civil servants, but some may be led to call attention to the irregularities by talking to their superiors or, if that avenue proves to be blocked, by talking to the press. Individuals who do so, known as "whistle-blowers," run substantial risks, as those who initiated the recommendations or those who equate whistle-blowing with disloyalty may well seek to punish or otherwise harm the whistle-blower in one way or another. Indeed, even though many regard whistle-blowers as engaging in brave and loyal actions, often they are chastised by colleagues and reassigned by their superiors. In short, it takes courage to be a whistle-blower.

Whistle-blowing can often launch government personnel to worldwide prominence. Such was the case for Joseph Wilson, the U.S. Foreign Service officer who criticized the president for including in a State of the Union address inaccurate intelligence about Iraqi imports of uranium ore from Niger. Along the same lines, Dr. David Kelly, a Foreign Service officer in the United Kingdom, assisted journalists criticizing the British government's preparation of intelligence for the war in Iraq. When his assistance was revealed, he became very prominent, and his suicide led to an inquiry by the British government into its handling of the matter.[1] In both cases the actions of public officials undermined their government's foreign policy, contrary to what would be their expected loyalty and goals. Perhaps less well known is James Hansen, a climatologist for the National Aeronautics and Space Administration (NASA), who has emerged as one of the world's most respected scientists of global warming, to the U.S. government's dismay.[2]

Mobilizing Capacities

Most bureaucratic units and those affiliated with them have one or more constituencies, members or segments of the public who support their goals and rely on them for desired policies. Often their constituents will align themselves with the units whose policies have served them well in the past and, presumably, will continue to do so in the future. It follows that the mobilizing capacity of civil servants is no less than the size of their constituencies and the support their constituencies can, in turn, mobilize from their followers. In some cases, especially in the field of agriculture, these mobilizing capacities are considerable, whereas they are likely to be limited in scope in most instances.

Conclusion

In sum, for all their hard work and unqualified commitments to the public welfare, civil servants confront innumerable obstacles and often fall short of their goals. Whether the obstacles can be overcome and the goals met depends crucially on the support civil servants get from their political superiors as well as their skills at moving around in the bureaucracy. It also depends importantly on whether or not a civil service has a reputation for engaging in corrupt practices. Most civil services of Western democracies do not have such a reputation, but this is less so for other parts of the world.

Chapter Fifteen

Consumers

The ultimate purpose of economic activity is to entice consumers to make purchases. The goal is best served by having an attractive product that is well constructed, readily available, compellingly advertised, and carefully designed to meet the needs and tastes of possible buyers. People are not by nature consumers of any product. Rather, consumers must be created, so to speak, persuaded that purchases serve their needs, interests, and values. On the other hand, nearly all people, wherever they may be, are consumers. They need to acquire food, clothing, and housing in order to survive, and to meet these needs they perforce must move into the consumer role. Thus, whether they are viewed as selective or compulsive buyers, they count, and they count a lot!

But counting consumers is complicated. It is not sufficient simply to assert that the number of consumers in any population is exactly equivalent to the size of the population. Much depends on the goods and services that are being marketed, and just as the products have to be produced, so do the consumers. That is, people have to be persuaded that they can use a product, a task to which an entire industry—advertising—is devoted. Since the same product is offered by different producers, advertisers have to compete for the attention and loyalty of buyers. In a profound sense advertising is a form of engineering: it engineers consent through the production of consumers. And once the consumers have been produced, they have to be transformed into customers, a task that also falls to a large degree to advertisers. For many consumers their preferences and purchases eventually become habitual, but even then their buying habits have to be serviced by advertisers because competitors are ever ready to entice them into new purchasing impulses.[1]

Advertisers reach out to consumers through several channels. Most notably they do so through print and electronic media, and the money they spend to advertise in newspapers or on the radio or television is the prime source of revenue for these media. More recently, advertisers have turned to the Internet, to mass mailings called "spam," and to pop-up ads that seem to come out of nowhere. Publishers of print media are increasingly concerned that they are losing their business to the Internet, and their concern is well-founded: in 2005, spending on Internet advertising was found to be growing in double digits compared to single-digit growth in the traditional print and electronic media.[2] Indeed, Internet advertising was up by 26 percent in 2005 to $14.7 billion (the total spent on all forms of advertising in 2005 was $278 billion). In the same year Google alone sold $6.1 billion in advertising.[3]

Consumer Protection

Whether consumers are aware of the efforts to procure their loyalty to products, or whether they are oblivious to the numerous ways in which advertisers and merchants seek to persuade them, they are the focus of numerous private and public agencies devoted to protecting them from fraud and false advertising. These agencies often provide a seal of approval that reassures consumers as to the worth of any product they may be inclined to buy. They are also the focus of a variety of specialists who seek to comprehend how they make decisions.

Consumers International (CI) is one such agency. It seeks "to defend the rights of all consumers, particularly the poor and marginalized, through empowering national consumer groups and campaigning at the international level. CI represents 234 organizations in 113 countries."[4] It has offices in four continents. Similarly, recognizing that "every citizen is a consumer," the European Union also "takes great care to protect their health, safety and economic well-being. It promotes their rights to information and education, takes steps to help them safeguard their interests and encourages them to set up and run self-help consumer associations."[5] An example in this regard is the EU's opposition to genetically modified foodstuffs.

Although consumers are protected from fraud and false advertising, these protections do not shield them from research techniques that explore their feelings, reasoning, brand loyalties, biases, needs, desires, habits, beliefs, and a host of other personal qualities that are not likely to be explicitly identified in the research instruments advertisers employ. A well-known and widely practiced research instrument for such purposes is the focus group, in which people who fit the characteristics of interest to the advertiser gather for a discussion of an agenda set by the investigators. As often as not, the researchers' agenda is not explicit; rather it is embedded in the seemingly extraneous questions posed by the researchers.

To the array of instruments designed to protect the consumer from unwanted advertisements should be added mechanisms that sift spam out of a consumer's in-box on the computer. It is a mechanism that falls short of working perfectly, as some spam does get through the protective wall.

The Psychology of Consumers

Treatises on the sources of consumer behavior are both lengthy and sophisticated. Rooted in both the precepts of psychological behavior and experience in attempting to sell goods and services to unknown people, numerous dos and don'ts are offered to those who work to generate buyers. An example makes the point: "Several factors influence the extent to which stimuli will be noticed. One obvious issue is *relevance*. Consumers, when they have a choice, are also more likely to attend to *pleasant* stimuli but when the consumer can't escape, very unpleasant stimuli are also likely to get attention—thus, many very irritating advertisements are remarkably effective."[6]

But the preoccupation of consumer research with material goods is not without limits. In another study designed "to provide insight into the extent to which the consumption of goods and service factors into perceptions of how life should be," it was found that "satisfying relationships with family and friends dominate perceptions of an ideal life, with products and possessions being of significance second only to these relationships." This finding was quite contrary to what the researchers anticipated: "Given the emphasis that is often placed on the Western world's insatiable appetite for consumer goods, it was unexpected that greater ownership of possessions should not feature to any great extent in interviewees' accounts of their ideal lives."[7] Even though everyone is a consumer, clearly people do not occupy this role at all times.

Nor are consumers lacking in a capacity to keep their exposure to advertising to a minimum. To the regret of advertisers, people use the remote control to watch television selectively—to change channels and mute sound, especially as a means of avoiding advertisements. No less relevant, it is also used to "fast forward" through advertising. Still another technique to keep advertising to a minimum is to register with the Mail Preference Service (MPS), an organization "designed to assist those consumers in decreasing the amount of national nonprofit or commercial mail they receive at home."[8] At the other extreme is the wide attention paid to the advertising on special broadcasts such as the Super Bowl, with many commentators subsequently assessing which were the most clever and irresistible advertisements.

Consumer Production as a Transnational Activity

Although most consumers purchase local products, substantial numbers of consumers and producers are active abroad. A number of companies and states, for example, purchased exhibition booths at the 2005 Paris Air Show for the purpose of generating customers at some later date.[9] Then there are the innumerable foreign travelers who purchase artwork as well as trinkets. Likewise, as indicated by the increasing reach of products such as Coca-Cola and other global brands angling for consumer loyalty, mass-market products have infiltrated traditional lifestyles. In short, consumption and consumers are not confined to conventional boundaries. The data on foreign trade are testimony to the large degree to which the whole world has become a vast marketplace.

Nor is it far-fetched to suggest that the whole world has found its way into the supermarket. It was not long ago that consumers had to buy domestic-made versions of foreign products, but today most stores carry the authentic, foreign version of the products. To cite but one example, it used to be that the only Mexican food product one could buy were brands like Old El Paso, made in the United States, whereas now most supermarkets have an extensive Mexican section, along with many other ethnic specialties. Thailand, Japan, and India, for example, are major sources of foreign foods available in Western supermarkets.

Conclusion

Irrespective of the tensions between the efforts to protect and produce consumers, people in industrial societies are bombarded with attempts to get them to buy goods and services, so much so that the consumer role is for most people a central concern, one they occupy at all times of the day and night, either actively on buying sprees or thinking about what they need. More accurately, such is the case in affluent societies that are awash with stores that sell a variety of items that people may want. And with the advent of the Internet, consumers now have access to an endless array of commodities to ponder, a fact that is reflected in the rising figures on e-commerce. In short, sales figures may lead advertisers to pat themselves on the back, but their successes are due less to their efforts and more to the number of consumers and the needs and wants they bring to their roles.

PART III

People in Society and Culture

Chapter Sixteen

Networkers

It can be highly misleading to explore the ways in which people count by treating them as autonomous individuals whose actions and attitudes are self-generated. They act alone, to be sure, but their actions are normally in the context of the relationships they sustain or contest with others. Whether they are citizens, immigrants, hybrids, or cosmopolitans, people conduct their affairs through their relationship with others—through the networks of family, friends, acquaintances, associates, colleagues, and competitors that they have acquired or constructed. They are, in short, embedded in a number of networks that vary in size, purpose, scope, coherence, intensity, location, and duration, but that nonetheless share at least one common feature: all networks contribute to the way in which the individuals who participate in them spend their time and conduct their affairs.

Counting the number of networks in which a person participates or the number in a community is nearly impossible. They are not recorded in censuses, and few studies attempt to trace the connections that individuals maintain. To be sure, formal networks can be tabulated in the sense that their organizations are active in the public arena, but most networks are informal and often ephemeral and mostly imperceptible. Commuters on the same train, book-reading clubs, and Internet chat rooms are illustrative of informal and virtually untraceable networks. In the words of two analysts, it is not an easy task to "simply 'add up' all these different forms to produce a single sensible summary of the social capital in a given community, much less in a nation."[1] Still, no assessment of how people count can ignore the fact that they live in world of relationships, a complex of networks that matter in a huge variety of ways.[2] Hence this chapter seeks to suggest the range of networks to which they are linked and the relevance of some networks to public affairs.

Networks as Micro Foundations of Macro Aggregates

Although the focus here is on individuals as micro actors, the networks that they form in the various capacities delineated by each chapter are usually the basis of macro organizations (hybrids and travelers may be exceptions). Citizen groups, immigrant associations, clubs of cosmopolitan elites, unions, churches, armies and navies, student organizations, and pressure groups that represent the poor, aged, and other marginal people are macro expressions of the networks traced in the various chapters.

The informal networks themselves are not organizations in the sense that certain of their members are authorized to act on behalf of all the persons who comprise a network. Rather, such networks encompass people who are connected to each other through shared concerns and purposes that serve as the basis for recurrent interaction. The interactions may be sporadic or continuous, but they do not become the basis for organizational structures until efforts are made to mobilize the members of a network, what one analyst calls "institutionalized relationships of mutual acquaintance and recognition."[3]

Social Capital

Perhaps the most systematic way to assess networks is through the concept of social capital, by which is meant the connective tissues of civil society and "the norms of reciprocity associated with them."[4] In other words, social capital involves ties among persons in a social unit that enrich both the persons and the unit by virtue of being founded on goodwill, shared values, and interactions that are frequent enough to give expression to the shared values. Thus families have social capital, as do businesses, sports clubs, professional associations, and a wide variety of other groupings founded on cooperative and interactive networks. In some circumstances interaction within a network may be frequent and face-to-face, as is the case with most families and college fraternities, or the interaction can be periodic and sustained by correspondence as much as by direct personal contacts, as is the case with extended families or fraternity members who have become alumni. In addition, networks can vary in their density, in the extent and depth of the ties that bind them together.

From the perspective of both individuals and communities, social capital is for the most part an asset, one that enriches the former and facilitates the smooth functioning of the latter. The more dense a network of social interaction is—that is, the greater the number of persons involved, the greater the number of nodes they form, and the more extensive the interaction among the nodes—the more will its individual participants be enriched and the more effective will be the communities in which such networks are located. Dense networks tend to contribute to reciprocity in societies and to their viability, to the lessening of crime in communities, to the spread of information, to the resolution of disputes in families, and a host of other types of situations. It has been found, for example, that communities that have numerous and vigorous associations are more likely to have a strong and democratic political culture than those that do not.[5] Not all dense networks, however, foster constructive outcomes for the larger communities in which they are embedded. The mafia and the Baath party in Iraq are illustrative of dense networks that have had largely negative effects for their communities and that are, in effect, prime sources of fragmegration.

Networks in Cyberspace

One increasingly important way that people count is through their actions and interactions as networkers in cyberspace. More accurately, e-mail, web pages, message boards, and other uses of the Internet have become major channels through which individuals give voice to their opinions and commitments. Even though the collective impact of this solitary communicative behavior can be difficult to assess, there are myriad data that depict the extensive resort of individuals to diverse electronic channels. Indeed, year-by-year and overall the data are staggering. For example, more than 200 million users worldwide were connected to the Internet in its first ten years of commercial availability after 1989. "By 1999 almost 40 percent of U.S. households were connected; 20 percent in the European Union; and 10 percent in Japan."[6] And the figures depicting growth in subsequent years are equally arresting. In August 2001, for instance, it was estimated that "approximately 513 million people, or 8 percent of the world's population, had accessed the Internet at least once during the previous three months."[7] Five years later, in 2006, comparable estimates cited more than one billion people as using the Internet.[8]

Anecdotally, too, the data are impressive. A newspaper analyst wrote a column in which he asked his readers to e-mail their reactions to him. Six days later, after receiving more than 8,000 messages from the United States and around the world, he wrote, "I'll never do that again."[9] Even more disconcerting was the experience of Shannon Syfrett, a fifteen-year-old ninth grader in Macon, Mississippi, who sought to find out where and how fast information travels by sending an e-mail message to twenty-three people and asking them to respond and also pass her message along to others. Her request generated 200 replies the next day, an average of one every 7.2 minutes. Two days later she received messages from forty-seven states and twenty-five countries. Ten days after her original message, 8,768 e-mails arrived, and three days later the figure rose to 12,013, or one every 7.2 seconds. In another two weeks the flow reached 37,854 messages, or one every 2.3 seconds. Subsequently, after Shannon felt compelled to close down her e-mail address, she totaled up the messages she had received in thirteen days: 160,478 messages had come in from 189 countries and 50 states.[10]

Or consider what happened on the first day that the U.S. Federal Trade Commission sponsored a new do-not-call list on which citizens could avoid telemarketing calls by registering their phone numbers either online or by phone: more than 735,000 numbers were called in for inclusion on the list. At one point 108 people per second were registering their numbers, a rate that soon overwhelmed the system and slowed to a halt the procedure of acknowledging each registration with an e-mailed response.[11]

A vast proportion of the myriad connections fashioned in cyberspace by e-mail and the Internet do not culminate in viable and dense—or even in fragile and shallow—networks. The recipients of mass e-mailings normally do not respond to the messages they receive. And since unanswered messages cannot serve as the basis for a network, most of the connections that pervade cyberspace are momentary and transitory. Only when the solitary behavior at the computer terminal results in recurring interactions is the action no longer private and potentially becomes part of a network. So numerous are the connections in cyberspace, however, that even if relatively few of them are sufficiently interactive and recurring to become networks, the absolute number of viable networks is nonetheless sufficient to render them crucial to the ways in which people count (see Chapter 17).

But the importance of a network does not depend on its evolving into face-to-face interactions among some or most of its members. A preponderance of the networks in cyberspace are sustained by online aliases and do not undergo transformation into face-to-face connections.[12] Still, it is arguable that cyberspace networks have a potential for affecting the course of events that is at least as much as, if not greater than, those based on large rallies, conferences, or other types of face-to-face gatherings.[13] This potential increases as some in the network get together and plan to utilize and apply the cyberspace network's shared values on behalf of policies in the public arena. Short of its transformation into an action network with leaders advancing its goals, however, the consequences of a network's formation are not trivial. Among the possible consequences are the diverse ways in which people experience a sense of civic competence through participation in cyberspace networks, the possibility of participating no matter what time of the day or what day of the week, the sense of safety one feels through the anonymity of the Internet and thus the ability to alter one's opinions through sustained and challenging e-mail interactions, the ability to find out what others think about an issue of concern, and so on across a wide range of emotional and intellectual foundations out of which civil societies can emerge. In short, cyberspace networks may well be the prime precursors of the direct organizations that mobilize their participants through signed petitions, street protests, and public meetings.

Of course, it is difficult, perhaps impossible, to ascertain the extent to which street demonstrations or any other mobilized crowd actions are the result of net-worked interactions in cyberspace on the one hand, and face-to-face interactions in political space on the other. Doubtless both underlie the dramatic protests that have marked recent years. In the spring of 2006, for example, the issue of immigration and the status of illegal aliens climbed high on the U.S. political agenda, and it was accompanied by a series of huge protests in a number of U.S. cities.[14] Most of the protesters were illegally in the United States and many were Latinos, presumably constituting crowds that were not adept at moving in cyberspace and thus were mobilized by word of mouth in political space. Yet, it is hard to imagine that so many were activated in several cities in a brief span of time simply through word of mouth. Or at least it seems likely that in each city a few were reached in cyberspace and they, in turn, used word of mouth, telephones, and other organizational channels to alert and mobilize others. To repeat, however, it is a near impossible task to calculate the extent to which the outpouring of protesters was fomented in cyberspace even as it seems certain that some were.

Whatever the potential whereby networks in cyberspace underlie collective action in political space, there would appear to be a downside to involvement in cyberspace networks, namely, sadness and loneliness. A major study revealed that "people who spend even a few hours a week on line experience higher levels of depression and loneliness than if they used the computer network less frequently," a finding that "shocked" the researchers who conducted the inquiry. Although some observers noted the study was not definitive and was subject to alternative interpretations, many agreed with the researchers' conclusions that "relationships maintained over long distances without face-to-face contact ultimately do not provide the kind of support and reciprocity that typically contribute to a sense of psychological security and happiness, like being able to baby-sit in a pinch for a friend, or to grab a cup of coffee."[15] The lead researcher added, "Our hypothesis is there are more cases where you're building shallow relationships, leading to an overall decline in feeling of connection to other people."[16]

Another possible downside can be at least partially attributed to the expansion of cyberspace and the blogosphere to which it has given rise. There is considerable evidence that newspapers are losing some of their buyers as more and more people turn to the Internet for foreign news, local developments, and other kinds of information. In response, many newspapers are opening up their web sites to participation by their readers, resulting in "a transformation taking place across the country, where top-down, voice-of-God journalism is being challenged by what is called participatory journalism or civic or citizen journalism."[17]

Conclusion

In sum, networking is not only pervasive and of paramount importance to the ways in which people count, but it is also increasingly easy to undertake and sustain. Although there have always been networks, today they are distinguished by a potential for being massive in scale and, as such, for reorganizing the practices and processes of politics. Counting the number of networks, or even closely estimating their number, is extremely difficult, but we know enough about their nature and the functions they perform to be confident they have become a central feature of the world scene. As one observer put it:

> As an historical trend, dominant functions and processes in the information age are increasingly organized around networks. Networks constitute the new social

morphology of our societies, and the diffusion of networking logic substantially modifies the operation and outcomes in processes of production, experience, power and culture. While the networking form of social organization has existed in other times and places, the new information technology paradigm provides the material basis for its pervasive expansion throughout the entire social structure.[18]

It follows that networkers are not only familiar with the processes of fragmegration but are also key players in those processes. Collectively they can contribute to both the integration of communities and their breakdown. Indeed, since most networkers are likely to be involved in more than one network, they may be helping to foster integration with respect to some issues while simultaneously serving to advance fragmentation on other issues.

Chapter Seventeen

Journalists and Bloggers

The circulation of ideas is undergoing vast changes. Journalists and others who work for the media are still central figures in the communications system, but the advent of the Internet has opened up participation to vast numbers of other people. So although this chapter is mostly about journalists and others for whom circulating ideas is a full-time occupation, it also notes the growing numbers of people who use the Internet to voice their opinions about whatever issues may interest them. Many of these people put their ideas on the Internet by posting blogs, a word that has evolved to mean the practice of expressing private perspectives in the public spaces of the Internet on whatever may be on a blogger's mind. Despite hype to the contrary, the blogosphere is unlikely to replace the conventional (and commercial) media of communication, but its usage is spreading widely in the United States. Indeed, it is anticipated that "the Internet will quickly surpass television as the primary medium for communicating political ideas."[1] There are 110 million Google entries for bloggers. The first entry describes them and their activities as follows:

> A blog is a personal diary. A daily pulpit. A collaborative space. A political soapbox.
>
> A breaking-news outlet. A collection of links. Your own private thoughts. Memos to the world.
>
> Your blog is whatever you want it to be. There are millions of them, in all shapes and sizes, and there are no real rules.
>
> In simple terms, a blog is a web site, where you write stuff on an ongoing basis.
>
> New stuff shows up at the top, so your visitors can read what's new. Then they comment on it or link to it or email you. Or not....
>
> Blogs have reshaped the web, impacted politics, shaken up journalism, and enabled millions of people to have a voice and connect with others.[2]

Not much is known about persons who turn to blogging. They share an inclination, perhaps a need, to express themselves through communications with unknown others, but otherwise it is difficult to generalize about their common characteristics. In all probability they are young in the sense that they are likely to be members of the Internet generation, and the chances are high that they have also graduated from high school, if not from college.[3] It takes a fair amount of education to have the confidence to share ideas with unknown others.

Journalists

Notwithstanding the importance and pervasiveness of the Internet, journalism is still very much a central feature of communities, whether it takes the form of newspapers, magazines, radio, television, or the Internet—and here *journalists* refers to all those who circulate ideas through these media.[4] Those who write regularly for news-papers—i.e., reporters—have a long history and lore that attaches to their efforts. Books and plays are written about them and about journalists whose work has been especially noteworthy, with the result that stereotypes have emerged that picture the journalist as working in his shirt sleeves, a hat tilted on his head, and a lit cigarette dangling from his mouth. Indeed, journalism is regarded to be of such importance and sustained by long-established practices, rules, and regulations that increasing numbers of schools of journalism have been founded in U.S. universities.

But the stereotypical image of journalists has become outmoded as the mass media have become more diverse and required a greater variety of skills. It is noteworthy, for example, that the stereotype has yet to catch up to the increasing numbers of women journalists and others who write for the mass media. Nor does it embrace those who are stationed in foreign countries and report from abroad, often serving as the prime source of understanding that people acquire about foreign situations.

Perhaps no situation was more revealing of the role journalists can play as sources of fragmegration than the war the United States fought in Vietnam. Every night's news reports on television depicted the horrors of war for both the soldiers who fight and the civilians on the ground who experience it. Most analysts regard the coverage of the war in such realistic detail as a major reason why the U.S. public turned against the war and eventually forced a U.S. retreat from Vietnam. Indeed, it was for this reason that the U.S. government prohibited unfettered coverage of combat situations in Iraq more than thirty years later.

Whether they are assigned to wartime or peacetime situations, journalists carry out their assignments by observing situations and interviewing those who participate in the situations. For the most part they are impelled to meet deadlines set by their editors as well as to keep their eyes open to new situations that are not perceived by those in the home office. Good journalists are those who discern a story—either a single incident or an underlying and recurring pattern—that may not be calamitous but that is unique enough to be of interest to their readers or listeners. Whatever may be their specific assignments, they have leeway to pursue developments of which the home office is unaware. Thus journalists are both reporters and, so to speak, pattern recognizers, ever alert for unexpected and surprising developments at work in the communities they are assigned to cover. In this sense they are social scientists, even though many of them are quick to look down on academics dedicated to uncovering and explaining the underlying dynamics at work in communities. The bridge between those in journalism and those in the academy is far from sturdy.

Some journalists move beyond their role as journalists to that of columnists who foster fragmegration by pushing one or another value-laden perspective on various policy issues. Thomas Friedman, for example, has long been a champion of globalization in both his columns and on television. Likewise, Seymour Hersh published stories on torture in *The New Yorker* that served to galvanize world opinion and fomented a lot of opposition to the U.S. "War on Terror." More recently, Lou Dobbs has used his program on CNN to express a preoccupation with illegal immigrants crossing into the United States from Mexico.

Code of Ethics

Like most professionals, journalists are often confronted with ethical questions that have not been formally codified but that are very much a part of their training as rules to which they must adhere. Some are procedural rules and some are more general principles that need to be followed regardless of what procedures are in place. The former category includes, for example, the need to have an event confirmed by more than one source. During the *Washington Post*'s coverage of the breaking Watergate story in 1973–1974, for example, the newspaper's editor, Ben Bradlee, required two young reporters, Bob Woodward and Carl Bernstein, to obtain confirmation of the leads they uncovered from one or more source independent of their original source. "Deep Throat" provided them with leads to investigate, but they needed additional confirmation when the leads turned out to be accurate.

The general principles can be more difficult for some in the journalism field. They involve integrity and treating one's aspiration to advance as secondary to ethical standards. A conspicuous case is that of Jayson Blair, the former *New York Times* reporter who was caught plagiarizing and fabricating elements of his stories in the spring of 2003.[5] Similarly, another *New York Times* reporter, Judith Miller, went to jail in 2005 for refusing to provide evidence to a grand jury on who leaked the name of Valerie Plame as a covert Central Intelligence Agency (CIA) officer.

Journalists as Mobilizers

Unlike bloggers, and with some exceptions such as Fox News and the *Washington Times,* journalists in Western democracies are not only expected to uphold the norm of reporting unbiased accounts of the situations they observe but are also trained to avoid summarizing judgments of the actors and relationships that comprise their accounts. Editorial pages in newspapers are reserved for judgments about the course of events that the owners of the media may want to offer, but otherwise the norm against biased reporting is standard practice. The application of the norm is somewhat more lax in the electronic media, which permit, though do not encourage, anchors of news broadcasts to voice their opinions. A classic case in this regard was the reporting from Europe during World War II of Edward R. Murrow and his subsequent readiness to condemn the witch-hunting practices of Senator Joseph McCarthy.

But a caveat is in order. News reports can have consequences that some argue should have been anticipated by the journalists and therefore not published. This is especially the case during times of war or comparable situations that involve issues of patriotism and, in so doing, straddle the line between the maintenance of a free press and the preservation of national security. When the *New York Times,* the *Wall Street Journal,* and the *Los Angeles Times,* for example, disclosed the existence of a secret program the Bush administration maintained to track terrorists by monitoring Americans' banking transactions, the president, members of Congress, and other officials reacted angrily, stressing that the press was endangering the security of the U.S. public. Vice President Dick Cheney was especially irritated: "Some in the press, in particular *The New York Times,* have made the job of defending against further terrorist attacks more difficult by insisting on publishing detailed information about vital national security programs," he was quoted as saying, adding that the program provides "valuable intelligence" and "has been successful in helping break up terrorist plots." President Bush called the publication of the story "disgraceful," an action that "does great harm to the United States of America."[6] The House of Representatives voted 227 to183 to condemn the media disclosure.[7]

But the press stood its ground, elaborately explaining the pros and cons that were deemed relevant to the clash between national security concerns and free expression, and then indicated why the secret program that monitored banking transactions was not viewed as requiring the subordination of the rights of a free expression to the risks of national security.[8] Nor did they hesitate to take issue with their critics on Capitol Hill. In the words of the executive editor of the *New York Times,* Bill Keller, "if the members [of the House of Representatives] who voted for the resolution believe the press is insensitive to the risks of reporting on intelligence programs, they could not be more wrong. We take these risks very, very seriously." He said that in the past the *Times* had agreed to withhold information when lives were at stake. "However, the administration did not make a convincing case that describing our efforts to monitor international banking presented such a danger. Indeed, the administration itself has talked publicly and repeatedly about its successes in the area of financial surveillance."[9]

In short, journalists do not mobilize people in any direct sense. Their reporting can have the consequence of energizing publics and enabling activists more easily to mobilize support, but neither their motives nor their reported accounts of events involve efforts to trigger action on the part of their readers or listeners. This is not to imply that the contents of what they write or verbally report must be neutral; rather, it is only to say that for the most part they do not purposely skew their accounts and analyses with a view to influencing those who read or hear them. There are exceptions of course. Some columnists and commentators are known for their political perspectives. Rush Limbaugh, for example, sustains his reputation by taking conservative positions on all the issues discussed in his broadcasts. And often he explicitly urges action on the part of his listeners, either by writing letters or otherwise acting on behalf of the issue positions he regards as important. But such media figures are called columnists and not reporters, a distinction that is not trivial when considered from the viewpoint of individuals who regularly circulate ideas through the mass media. Most newspapers, though less so for the electronic media, designate some of their personnel as columnists explicitly expected to take value positions with respect to the issues about which they write.

Deadlines, Diversity, and Danger

The life of journalists and radio and television reporters is dominated by deadlines. They have little time for prolonged reflection on what they have observed, as most of them are expected by their editors to file their stories at certain hours on a daily basis. The immutability of deadlines thus infuses a degree of tension, competition, and challenge into the lives of journalists. Meeting the deadlines involves pleasing editors and at the same time competing with counterparts from other media to be among the first to get the story on the air or in print. Winning such competitions can result in salary increments and, in some cases, being honored by journalism societies.

Among the challenges journalists confront, perhaps none is more considerable than those that derive from the diversity of the stories they must cover. Although some journalists specialize in certain kinds of issues—such as sports, obituaries, military security—others are generalists who report on a wide variety of situations, from corporate squabbles to crime scenes, from political crises to foreign visitors, and a host of other situations whereby, in effect, they become generalists capable of probing whatever diversity may be embedded in each day's assignments.

In some parts of the world, especially in authoritarian countries with regimes that like to control what the public knows and doesn't know, the job of reporters can be dangerous. Efforts to silence them, to get them to report only what the regime regards as safe, can readily become official government policy in such countries. Such may have been the case with Anna Politkovskaya, a Russian journalist who relentlessly and critically reported on the Putin regime and who was murdered in 2006. Clearly, journalists practicing under authoritarian regimes have either to abide by their government's dictates or to devise means of bypassing the censorship when they investigate situations their government prefers not to have reported. Venezuela, for instance, "criminalizes expressions deemed disrespectful to public officials even if completely true." Nonetheless, despite the obstacles, to a limited extent "good investigative reporting exists in Latin America, even at regional newspapers."[10]

Nor is extensive and explicit bias confined to newspaper journalists. It can also be discerned in radio and television coverage of world news. Consider, for example, Al-Jazeera, an electronic medium that broadcasts throughout the Middle East and that does not hesitate to give its news accounts a Muslim bias.

Conclusion

It is journalists that enable us to appreciate the large degree to which the same circumstances generate both integration and fragmentation. They may not see the link between the two opposite processes (though often they do) in the events they cover, but their coverage of such tensions enables their readers and listeners to appreciate both the power and pervasiveness of fragmegrative dynamics. Indeed, it can readily be said that the media sustain these dynamics. With few exceptions, they do not create the dynamics, but in going about their jobs they serve to convey the diversity and intensity on which fragmegration rests throughout the world.

This is not to imply that fragmegrative situations are necessarily built into the same events that journalists report. On the contrary, many, perhaps even most, fragmegrative dynamics are sequential, with either the fragmenting or the integrating event preceding the other by a day, a week, or a month. But whatever the time difference, the reports of journalists either explicitly or implicitly serve to link the seemingly unrelated developments into fragmegrative sequences. That is not their purpose, and they may even be unaware of the nature of fragmegration, but in carrying out their work they are the conveyors of this central feature of the current era.

Chapter Eighteen

Worshippers

Before God we are equally wise—and equally foolish.

—*Albert Einstein*

This epigraph can be interpreted in at least two ways. One is to take it at face value and view it as expressing the conviction that religion can be deleterious as well as uplifting. Alternatively, perhaps Einstein had in mind that religion is essentially irrelevant, that the conduct of people occurs irrespective of their religious beliefs. The approach in this chapter falls somewhere between the two. It is an approach rooted in a definition of religion as "a set of beliefs about the ultimate ground of existence, that which is unconditioned, not itself created or caused, and the communities and practices that form around these beliefs."[1] This definition is neutral in the sense that people of all faiths can be driven by their religious commitments to engage in violent as well as charitable acts even as they might use religious rhetoric as a screen for more fundamental motives. Yet, however the commitments are articulated and activated, there can be no doubt that religion is a core feature of human existence. It provides many persons, even whole societies, guidance in answering big questions about the origins of life and the meaning of death. The pervasiveness of such concerns is evident in the fact that on April 2, 2007, the number of hits for "religion" in a search of the World Wide Web exceeded 600 million.

Gross figures, however, can be misleading and contradictory. Diverse crosscurrents are at work both within and among the world's many religions. Not only did one study find that "in recent years, trust in religious institutions and religious and spiritual leaders had declined 'by statistically significant margins' in more than two of every three nations surveyed,"[2] but other inquiries have documented that the proportion of worshipers varies considerably—both up and down—from country to country and from religion to religion. Counting the adherents of any religion, moreover, is a difficult task. Figures on church attendance may provide a clue to the extent of religious practices, but they do not come close to telling the full picture on the number of persons in any locale who attach importance to their religion. Consider, for example, the findings of a global attitudes survey of more than 38,000 people in forty-four countries conducted in 2002 by the Pew Research Center. As can be seen in Table 18.1, a majority of the respondents in a majority of the countries said they regarded religion as important, but this was not the case for sixteen countries. Indeed, a large gap separated the latter from the twenty-four countries in which a majority ascribed importance to religion.[3] In addition, the data in Table 18.1 suggest huge regional differences on the question, with substantially greater importance being attached to religion in African and most Latin American and Muslim countries, whereas secularism was prevalent in Western Europe and Canada. Since Table 18.1 does not include the Scandinavian countries, the regional gap is even greater than the data indicate. At a maximum, for example, church attendance in Denmark is estimated at 6 percent.[4] Nor do the entries in Table 18.1 include Spain, where legislation permitting gay marriages was adopted in 2005, an action consistent with the observation that in Spain "religion is rapidly losing strength and influence in politics."[5]

The survey also uncovered a noticeable correlation between wealth and religion: among those countries with a majority who ascribed importance to religion, and Vietnam among those with a minority who did so, individuals in wealthy countries (except for the United States) tended to attach less importance to religion than

Table 18-1. Importance of Religion in 44 Countries

Country	% of adults for whom religion is important	Country	% of adults for whom religion is important
Senegal	97	Turkey	65
Indonesia	95	Venezuela	61
Nigeria	92	United States	59
India	92	Mexico	57
Pakistan	91	Argentina	39
Ivory Coast	91	Poland	36
Mali	90	Ukraine	35
Philippines	88	Uzbekistan	35
Bangladesh	88	Great Britain	33
South Africa	87	Canada	30
Kenya	85	Slovakia	29
Uganda	85	Italy	27
Ghana	84	South Korea	25
Tanzania	83	Vietnam	24
Angola	80	Germany	21
Guatemala	80	Russia	14
Brazil	77	Bulgaria	13
Honduras	72	Japan	12
Peru	69	France	11
Bolivia	66	Czech Republic	11

Source: Adapted from http://religious tolerance.org/rel_impo.htm.

did those in poorer countries. Most notably, a considerably smaller proportion of persons in two countries of Asia with relatively high per capita incomes, Japan and South Korea, indicated religion was important than did those in four of the poorer counties of the region.

Although there are limits to interpreting the patterns evident in Table 18.1—especially as people can be spiritual without practicing or attaching importance to religion—its data underscore the large extent to which the tensions and conflicts of the present era are rooted in diverse religious convictions. Put differently, assuming that being a worshipper does not necessarily mean one attends church regularly or even sporadically, and knowing that *religion* means different things to different people in the same country, the proportions listed in Table 18.1 probably understate the potential for tension. In some countries, moreover, people conflict more intensely over their religious differences than they do with persons elsewhere in the world.

Changing Patterns of Worship

That crosscurrents are at work within and among the world's religions is perhaps especially evident in the changing ranks of their worshipers. Some religions have experienced a substantial diminution of their numbers, while others have undergone large increases in their adherents. In this sense the percentages in Table 18.1 are profoundly misleading. They reflect only a particular moment in time (2002), and they do not convey the shifts that are occurring in the membership, commitments, and orientations of worshipers. In Europe, for example, contrary trends are readily discernible. Although countries that were part of the Soviet Union have experienced an "explosive growth" in the Eastern Orthodox Church since 1990,[6] quite the opposite trend has unfolded in Western Europe: the number of persons committed to the Christian faiths—Catholics and mainstream Protestants—is withering, with the result that church attendance is down and the flock is engaging in other pursuits. The comments and behavior of Giampaolo Servadio, a resident of Rome, are illustrative. He used to go to Roman Catholic Mass every week and even served as an altar boy—but no longer. He began running rather than attending Mass on the grounds that it was a more relevant use of his time. "The church seems really out of step," he said. "I don't see how something like a confession and a few repetitions of the 'Hail Mary' are going to solve any problems."[7]

Numerous reasons have been cited to explain the decline of religion in Western Europe,[8] but these tend to be undermined by the opposite pattern among the people of a country, the United States, that is witnessing an increase in religious commitments, even though its socioeconomic and historical experience is quite like that of West Europeans. Among the people of Africa and Latin America, too, there appears to be a surge in religious fervor, stimulated largely by evangelical groups and Pentecostal churches that have evolved messages appealing to the many individuals whose difficult circumstances incline them to reach out for divine intervention. Indeed, Pentecostalism has attracted substantial numbers of Catholics and Muslims in the poor countries of Africa and Latin America, offering as it does a message that God can protect worshippers from the scourges of poverty and crime.[9]

These patterns highlight the anomaly of Americans. For the most part their circumstances derive from a history of economic and historical progress, and yet Table 18.1 locates the United States among the countries of the developing world in terms of the importance attached to religion by Americans. This pattern stems in part from a sizable increase in the number of evangelical churches and worshippers in the United States. For example, there are more than 7,000 such churches and about one million evangelicals in New York City alone, owing in part to a recent influx of immigrants.[10] Perhaps even more important, diverse people, collectively known as the Religious Right, have lately come to occupy significant roles in the politics of the country.

Clearly, it is erroneous to treat the experiences of West Europeans and Americans as comparable insofar as their religious orientations are concerned. Again a number of reasons can be cited to account for the differences between the two sides of the Atlantic, but there is little doubt that the differences do exist and, in fact, are widening.

Worshippers Caught Up in Fragmegrative Tensions

Since worship and God are intrinsically personal aspects of life, it is hardly surprising that religious tensions have intensified in the age of the individual and that they are sustained by fragmegration. To be sure, fragmegrative dynamics underlying religious tensions have always marked world affairs, but they appear to be founded on greater uncertainty, and as such are more pervasive than ever before. Consequently, in a time of ambiguity that seems enduring, many people in all parts of the world have become preoccupied with the large questions that religions seek to answer. It is a preoccupation that, excepting Western Europe, has heightened religiosity everywhere, with many individuals and peoples feeling a need to find a more encompassing meaning in a world that has become ever-more complex, both more proximate and more distant.

Stated differently, troubled by the uncertainties on which the pervasiveness of fragmegration rests, and often unable to comprehend its implications for themselves, numerous people in all parts of the world and in all walks of life are inclined to look for answers in spiritual outlooks that provide clarity on the large, seemingly irresolvable questions of life and death. Of course, such inclinations are hardly new. Concerns about "final events," the "end of time," the "coming of Christ," the "return of the Buddha," the "new Jerusalem," the establishment of the Kingdom of God on earth, otherworldliness, apocalyptic events, and Armageddon have a long history. What is new about such concerns is the intensity with which they are held and their spread on a global scale. Indeed, it can reasonably be observed that no other line of thought is as concerned about the well-being of humankind as those founded on spiritual sources. If the clash between the global and the local cannot be readily resolved, if the disarray that follows from the intrusion of the distant upon the proximate cannot be easily managed, many people are inclined to search for meaning in the calm that spiritual formulations can provide.

Whatever the sources of the diverse religious orientations in different regions and countries of the world, it seems clear that their intensity is generating intense rivalries that have the potential for violence. As a consequence, a host of social issues rife with religious implications—such as abortion, homosexuality, female priests, and gay marriages—have climbed ever higher on local, national, and international agendas. In the United States, for example, the United Methodist church is beset with intense divisions over worship by gays: the issue surfaced at the same time in Virginia, Pennsylvania, and California, with churches in the former two states favoring antigay rulings, whereas the opposite was the case in California.[11] The Anglican/Episcopalian church also experienced a divisive debate over the acceptance of gay bishops when six traditional Episcopalian dioceses and some individual parishes announced plans to withdraw from the denomination in the United States because they could not accept a church with openly gay bishops and ceremonies for same-sex unions.[12] In Africa, a rivalry between Christianity and Islam has mushroomed in most of its countries. Likewise, Saudis in Indonesia are seeking to spread the word about the strict precepts of Islam[13] and much the same is happening in Pakistan,[14] even as proselytizing has warranted headlines in the United States.[15] In 2006 Muslims around the world were distressed by cartoons in a Danish newspaper that depicted Mohammad in an unfavorable light; in some instances the distress led to violent reactions. And in Alexandria, Egypt, the police had to be called out to protect a Coptic Christian church against Muslim protesters, resulting in three people being killed and many injured "in what officials called the worst case of sectarian violence to strike this Mediterranean city in recent memory."[16]

Fundamentalists

The need for clarity and certainty has fostered a revival and spread of fundamentalism—of thought that leaves no room for doubt and answers all questions—in virtually every religion. In so doing it has intensified tensions both within and among the several religions, often to the point of splitting them apart.[17] The tensions are especially manifest with respect to Muslims, but they can also be discerned in a host of other religious communities. It follows that the spread of religious fundamentalism both mirrors and intensifies fragmegrative dynamics.

Whatever may be their religious commitments, fundamentalists adhere to rigid values in their search for certainty, and they do so unyieldingly, leaving little or no room for compromise with fellow religionists whose views are more open and tolerant. In some instances their fundamentalism reaches an extreme that results in violence and mayhem. For a few Muslims, for example, the certainties born of uncertainty and hatred have led them to become suicide bombers.[18] And even short of this extreme, their rigidity and intolerance tend to wreak havoc within societies where their numbers are sufficient to roil neighborhoods and communities.[19] It can fairly be said that fundamentalists of any religious stripe have a view of world order that so resolutely rejects alternative perspectives as to generate enduring fragmegrative conflicts. Illustrative in this regard are those who subscribe to Salafism, a fundamentalist school of Islam, and who constitute a radical fringe that advocates war against non-Muslims.[20] As one observer put it, referring to al Qaeda terrorists, "Their target is the entire rational, secular political universe that we instinctively—and mistakenly—turn to for explanations of their behavior and our response. They attack not to create another Arab state but to turn the existing ones into a single fanatical theocracy that will eventually extend its control over other civilizations."[21]

Qualifiers notwithstanding (such as religions of "any stripe"), it is highly misleading to cite Muslims as the only example of fundamentalists. They and their suicide bombers are very much in the news at the present time, but they are hardly the only believers whose perspectives are rigid and intolerant and whose violent actions can dominate the headlines. In the United States those known as the Religious Right are no less conspicuous and no less strident. Their interpretation of Christianity that condemns abortion and gay marriage has come to pervade much of the political scene, thereby fostering disarray even as they promote the need for order. In some rare instances devotees interpret world order as permitting the murder of doctors who perform abortions. Likewise, in Israel some fanatic Orthodox Jews have resorted to acts of violence or otherwise sought to block policies that would greatly alleviate tensions between Israelis and Palestinians: in 1994, for example, Baruch Goldstein, a well-known leader of the Jewish extremist Kach group, entered Al-Ibrahimi mosque in the West Bank town of Al-Khalil and fired two clips from an automatic rifle into Muslim worshipers during the dawn prayer, killing at least fifty people and injuring 200 others. Extremism on behalf of a religious perspective has also marred recent history in Japan. Some 500 Japanese, for example, have subscribed to the religious fanaticism of Asahara Shoko, who named his group Aum Shinrikyo. *Aum* is Sanskrit for the "powers of destruction and creation in the universe," and *Shinrikyo* is the "teaching of the supreme truth," a perspective that, among other violent acts, led to placing a deadly sarin gas in several Tokyo subway stations, resulting in the deaths of twelve people and incapacitating thousands.[22]

This is not to imply that religious fundamentalism necessarily culminates in violence. On the contrary, most fundamentalists do not engage in violent action, whereas more than a few nonfundamentalists do justify violence on religious grounds even as diverse religions advance philosophical principles that do not call for a resort to brutality. To be sure, conceptions, even paintings, of hell can be pervaded with savage barbarity.[23] Nonetheless, for every barbarous depiction, one can point to more than a few religious scenes in which peace and nonviolence predominate. Such formulations may be marked by rigid certainties as to how humankind is or ought to be ordered, but they nevertheless stop short of urging the use of violent methods to put the world on a proper path. On occasion the urgings even focus on the need to avoid violence.[24] Indeed, there is no reason "to suppose that any of the religious faiths is inherently more prone to violence than the other: the problem is not the words on the page, but how they are read."[25]

But the tensions spawned by peaceful, nonviolent forms of fundamentalism can have significant, if subtle, consequences. It has been observed, for example, that the fundamentalist resurgence in the United States is undermining its intellectual vitality. For example, compared to their counterparts in Western Europe, where fundamentalism and, indeed, religiosity are waning, the productivity of U.S. scientists no longer predominates. Consider these findings published by the *Physical Review* in May 2004:

> The number of scientific papers published by West European authors had overtaken those by U.S. authors in 2003, whereas in 1983 there were three American authors for every West European. The percentage of patents granted to American scientists has been falling since 1980, from 60.2 percent of the world total to 51.8 percent. In 1989, America trained the same number of science and engineering Ph.Ds as Britain, Germany and France put together; now the United States is 5 percent behind. The number of citations in science journals, hitherto led by American scientists is now led by Europeans.[26]

To be sure, there are other reasons why intellectual vitality in the United States is in decline. Budget deficits have limited the resources available to the country's scientists, and immigration restrictions adopted in response to the September 11 terrorist attacks has led to the denial of visas to many talented foreign students who sought to study in the United States. Yet, whatever the full panoply of reasons underlying the findings uncovered by the *Physical Review* and cited by Peter Watson,[27] it seems clear that the intellectual climate fostered by the fundamentalist resurgence—such as the constrictions on cloning and stem cell research or the continuing squabbles over the relative validity of evolution and intelligent design as explanations of the origins of modern life—has been substantial.

It is important to note that some worshippers, many progressive churches, and religious leaders such as recent popes, Desmond Tutu, and Mother Theresa are inspired by their faith to engage in supraterritorial involvement. Members of an organization called Christian Peacemaker Teams, for example, moved into the combat zones of Iraq with a view to promoting "violence-deterring, human rights work." Subsequently, one of their volunteers, Tom Fox, was captured and killed, an event that saddened the organization but did not alter its commitments.[28]

Conclusion

In counting worshippers, at least two tallies need to be made. One involves those people around the world who are concerned with their own well-being and believe that the only true faith is their own, a perspective that readily leads to exclusionary arrogance and an occasional resort to violence. The other tally consists of individuals who are tolerant and inclusionary, an outlook that easily leads them to care about the well-being of others, especially those who do not share their faith. On occasion these conflicting approaches to religion can lead to efforts to bridge the gap between them,[29] but all too often they foster tension and, in the worst instances, religious wars. Religious convictions, it can readily be said, are a profound source of fragmegration. They unify like-minded groups even as they can divide them from each other and intrude division within groups.

CHAPTER NINETEEN

Students

American high schools are obsolete. By obsolete I just don't mean that our high schools are broken, flawed and underfunded.... By obsolete I mean that our high schools—even when they are working exactly how they were designed—cannot teach our kids what they need to know today. Training the work force of tomorrow with the high schools of today is like trying to teach kids about today's computers on a 50-year-old mainframe.... Our high schools were designed 50 years ago to meet the needs of another age. Until we design them to meet the needs of the 21st century, we will keep limiting—even ruining—the lives of millions of Americans every year.

—Bill Gates[1]

Students count in a variety of ways, but perhaps their main significance is that they constitute future generations, as the epigraph suggests. The values they acquire, the training they receive, and the motivations they develop are bound to affect what a society will become with the passage of time. Educational institutions seek to prepare individuals at various stages in their youth for managing and shaping the world in which they will live in subsequent decades.

It is concern about how the future will be a reflection of the training of present-day students that underlies society-wide preoccupation with the content and practices at every level of education. Each of these levels—elementary, secondary, college, postgraduate—is marked by its own distinct processes and problems, but they all are central issues for publics and their officials because they build on each other to produce the citizens and specialists of tomorrow. Educators and analysts focus on the challenges at one or another level of education—on what curriculum innovations are most appropriate, on how to improve student performance, on how to test and measure student performance—but they are also ever mindful of how the level that concerns them contributes to the maturation of their students and generates students able to move on to the next level. In effect, the ultimate product of education—informed citizens who share the society's basic values and who may also be well-trained specialists—determines how the future will unfold. Little wonder, then, that educational issues are pervasive and the source of considerable controversy at every level of community.

On one issue, however, there is no disagreement: namely, that the ranks of students toward the bottom of the educational pyramid are huge and remain large at all levels of education. In the United States, for example, elementary and secondary school students numbered 49.6 million students in 2003, a record figure reflective of population growth and immigration.[2] The number of students also poses enormous challenges for schools and those who educate them. In addition to the substantive challenges associated with improving curricula, libraries, and specialized training, many problems derive from the need to provide adequate facilities, from classrooms to playgrounds, from textbooks to competent teachers, not to mention the challenge of maintaining the support of trustees, politicians, parents, and the community at large. In short, counting students is easy; training them to count as effective adults is hard.

Educational Philosophy

The values and procedures most appropriate to training students are contentious issues in virtually all societies at all levels of education. Linked as they are to the notions of morality, maturation, and human nature to which people subscribe, educational issues are the source of strong convictions on the part of citizens and specialists alike. Publics, faculties, and legislators can be deeply divided over the substantive content and pedagogical techniques to which students should be exposed, and these divisive issues are so crucial that they can linger across decades. Depending on historical and cultural circumstances, the philosophical differences may vary widely from country to country, with perhaps the prime distinction involving traditionalists who feel students should be taught by rote in ways that do not allow for exploration and modernists who want to avoid constraining curiosity while enabling students to be free to pursue ideas wherever they may lead without neglecting fundamentals that need to be acquired. Put differently, traditionalists tend to presume that students are not very bright and need to be motivated, whereas modernists tend to assume that students are more competent, creative, and self-sustaining than adults give them credit for. Furthermore, as indicated by the key role students play in protest movements, they know their own values and are thus unlikely to respond to philosophical perspectives with which they are not comfortable.

Such philosophical differences underpin the various issues that revolve around students and their education. The substance and the handling of the issues may differ from one society to the next, but whatever form they take, the differences between traditionalists and modernists are likely to shape how the issues are considered on the agendas of communities everywhere. Traditionalists tend to be more skeptical of electronic forms of teaching and to place more stock in test scores than do modernists, and the two groups also differ on curricula and required courses, on how learning that endures is best achieved, on the kinds of reforms that are needed at every level of education, and on problems associated with student cheating.

Learning

Like much else, students and education have benefited from the advent of new electronic technologies. Both in colleges and secondary schools in advanced industrial societies, students are offered opportunities to move around in virtual learning environments, to enroll in "laptop universities," and thereby to experience the vast resources of cyberspace. Along with computer simulations and games, these developments have the potential of greatly altering long-standing modes of education. They give students who have to write term papers and graduate students who have to submit dissertations access to much of human knowledge and thereby encourage exploration, creativity, and venturesomeness. Perhaps more significantly, the available electronic technologies allow for "long-distance" learning that bypasses the classroom and enables learning to occur in a variety of new settings. Video games provide an insightful example: as noted in Chapter 3, electronic games have been found to hone talent in such a way as to better equip people for responsibilities they shoulder as members of the workforce. It is telling that surgeons who perform laparoscopic surgery were better the more they played video games when they were young.[3]

There are, of course, downsides to these new forms of education. Perhaps most notably, they minimize the face-to-face contacts that students have with their instructors and fellow students, thus inhibiting the learning that emerges from exchanging and arguing about ideas. Viewed in this context, it is not surprising that in the United States the literacy in the English language of the average college graduate declined between 1992 and 2003: in the former year, 40 percent of the country's college graduates scored at the proficient level, whereas the comparable figure for the latter year was 31 percent.[4] Hardly less worrisome, the availability of the Internet's vast range of resources also heightens, as noted below, temptations and opportunities to cheat. A number of problems also arise in multicultural societies. Most notable perhaps, their elementary and high school students from cultures outside the dominant one in which their families have settled usually have trouble studying in a language with which they are not familiar, and training teachers to cope with such problems is difficult at best.

On the other hand, a childhood spent immersed in electronic games and computer simulations does not necessarily undermine the motivation to learn through conventional means. The deep involvement—what one observer has labeled a "ravenous hunger"[5]—of children in the United States with Harry Potter books suggests that reading and video games are not mutually exclusive sources of learning. When J. K. Rowling's fifth novel in the series was published, it sold five million copies in one day, an event that "bubbled up spontaneously from below, propelled by kids' word of mouth, rather than being imposed by synergistic browbeating from above."[6] Nor was this a one-time happening: the advance sale of the last in the series was a million and a half three weeks before its publication in 2005, and the publisher was planning to print 10 million copies to meet the anticipated demand for the book.

Whatever may be the fragmegrative repercussions of the ways in which education is undergoing transformation induced by electronic technologies, it is clear that the life of students is destined to experience huge alterations. On balance, and irrespective of their downsides, these changes seem likely to enhance and advance the benefits of education in ways still beyond calculation. Bill Gates may feel the changes are not occurring quickly enough, as he unqualifiedly asserted in this chapter's epigraph, but across the long haul they seem likely to mark the educational scene.

Activism

In addition to their long-term role as members of future generations, students in institutions of higher education can also play significant short-term roles in the issues currently on a society's political agenda. With the possible exception of workers, no group has been more collectively active in pressing for change than students. Their participation in protest marches, strikes, sit-ins, and other forms of political activism has a long history and has often become a major feature of the political landscape in most societies. Partly because they have the time, and partly because their youth fosters idealism—to mention only two of the many motives that may underlie their activism—many college and graduate students can readily be mobilized to support or oppose causes that they share or abhor, often transforming campuses into beehives of activities that then spread into the local community and beyond.

Nor is the activism of students confined to particular countries and political cultures. Student protests helped overthrow the shah in Iran; they were very much involved and in some cases killed during the Tiananmen Square protests of 1989; in France they were prominent in the street marches of 1968 and 2006; and recently more than 700,000 high school students walked out of their classes in Chile by way of demanding reforms.[7] Likewise, students in the United States played an important role in mobilizing protests against pending immigration bills in 2006, just as earlier members of the Student Non-Violent Coordinating Committee were major players in the U.S. civil rights movement in the 1950s and 1960s. Clearly, students have never been empty vessels into which educational authorities pour the values of the society.

The issues around which protests are organized can vary considerably in different countries, and on occasion they span borders and occur in several countries at the same time. Likewise, often they escalate from relatively specific issues to all-encompassing demands. In 1968, during the Vietnam War, students in the United States became so agitated that in many universities they occupied the office of the university president, often refusing to leave until their demands were met. In 1989 Chinese students played a central role in the events that culminated in standing up to tanks in Tiananmen Square, just as earlier their counterparts in Iran were active in the overthrow of the shah. In 1999 U.S. student groups on several campuses were aroused by a much narrower set of issues: they protested the scope of a code of conduct that universities framed for apparel makers who supplied clothing blazoned with the universities' names and logos, contending that the code failed to disclose the names and addresses of all factories making the clothes, thus preventing checks as to whether the sports gear was manufactured in sweatshops. In Mexico a student strike against the National Autonomous University—one of the largest in the world, with 275,000 students—began in 1999 and lasted well into 2000 as a rough, anarchic leftist movement took control of the student upheaval and transformed it from a protest seeking open admissions and the preservation of free tuition to a focus on the evils of globalization and competitive, free-market policies.[8] In 1998 the protests of an increasingly fractured student movement in Indonesia brought down the Suharto government and for months thereafter continued their protests to ensure the integrity of new governmental institutions.[9] In 2003 student rioting in Iran escalated from a small march against the issue of university privatization to demands for social, economic, and political freedom.[10] These are but a few of the more recent instances of student activism.

Another form of student activism involves their foreign travels. It has become almost standard that college students spend a year abroad. The practice is so widespread in so many countries that students can readily be regarded as a transnational class. This is perhaps especially the case for students from developing countries who come north and west to earn advanced degrees. Some then stay on in the developed world and become assimilated. Others return home, bringing with them ideas and values that may have been incidental to their formal education but nevertheless shape their interactions with their home culture.

In sum, although students count as future generations, they count very much in the present when they initiate or join protests in different parts of the world. Indeed, their occupancy of activist roles often obscures the importance of the ways in which they are trained as citizens and specialists.

Measuring Achievement

Educational systems at the primary and secondary levels have an ongoing need to ascertain how their students are performing, partly because teachers and administrators are professionals and want to know whether their efforts are succeeding and partly because they need to please their superiors on boards of education or in the political realm. Consequently, most systems have designed methods for checking up on the progress of their students and, thus, on their own success.

The issue of testing precollege students and improving their scores has surfaced with special intensity in the United States, in good part because comparisons of their achievement with counterparts in other countries have revealed a lag in the training of U.S. youth. A 2003 study of the mathematical and reading skills of fifteen-year-olds in forty countries, for example, found that teenagers in the United States ranked twenty-eighth in math and eighteenth in reading. Only 10 percent of the U.S. students were among those who scored high on the test, a proportion half as many as in Canada and a third of those in Hong Kong. On the other hand, more than a quarter of the Americans were among those who scored low, whereas one-tenth or fewer of the Finnish, South Korean, Canadian, and Hong Kong students scored in the lowest brackets.[11] Similar findings were uncovered when the comparisons were across time in the earth, physical, and life sciences: a nationwide test administered to more than 300,000 students in all fifty states, the District of Columbia, and on military bases around the world revealed that over a ten-year period the achievement scores of high school seniors declined, those of fourth graders increased, and those of eighth graders remained constant.[12] A further indication of trouble in the U.S. educational system is evident in the fact that although the country once led the world in high school graduation rates, it fell to fourteenth in 2004, with a rate much less than that of other major industrial countries.[13]

Those inclined toward a more liberal interpretation of testing procedures have difficulty with statistics such as these. They argue that measuring talent and accomplishment is complex and that the results of standardized testing can be misleading. They contend that such tests measure only the easily measurable and that they exert undue pressure on teachers and principals to conduct the classroom activities in ways—such as holding classes on Saturday and having an extra ninety minutes of instruction twice a week—that raise the scores of their students at the price of reducing the exposure of students to subjects such as art, science, and social studies that do not lend themselves to multiple-choice tests.[14] Those who are more traditional in their approach to education, on the other hand, contend that testing serves to improve performance, that "what gets measured gets done."[15]

Reform

Given the importance of society's stake in the training of students, it is hardly surprising that efforts to reform the educational system are periodically undertaken at every level. Curricula are frequently revised to account for new developments in the world, new research findings in the scientific disciplines, and lessons derived from experiments addressed to the processes of learning. Performance standards are often upgraded to enhance the motivation of both faculties and students.

Usually the reforms encounter resistance on the part of some faculty members and students who adhere to philosophical premises that run counter to the reforms or who have long been habituated to a set way of carrying out their responsibilities. Often, too, the reforms become the basis of intensely waged issues in the larger political community.

The continuing controversy over the No Child Left Behind law in the United States is a recent case in point. The law was one of several adopted in the 1990s founded on a bargain: in exchange for a share of some $50 billion annually, the states were required to raise their standards and work to improve student performance through testing as well as to recruit highly qualified teachers. The goal of the legislation was to employ information (the test scores) and shame (low scores) as means of eliminating the discrepancies in achievement between rich and poor children, between students in the inner cities and those in suburbia. For a number of reasons, however, implementation of the law lagged and heated controversy persists. The shame of low scores has not been consequential in the inner cities, but it has in suburbia, where outrage has resulted in the granting of exemptions from the law.[16] In addition, although test scores did rise in some locales and the achievement gap did narrow in some states, many states did not receive the necessary funding or otherwise failed to fulfill their responsibilities. The presumption in the United States that public education is a local matter also inhibited administration of the law and undermined efforts to get states to comply with directives. Equally important, other issues, especially the war in Iraq, lowered the salience attached to making sure that no students were left behind.

Another controversy in the United States concerns vouchers that children from low-income families who perform poorly in public schools could use to attend private and religious schools. Such proposals are supported by conservatives and religious leaders and opposed by liberal politicians and teachers unions, who point to a recent survey that compared the test scores of 700,000 fourth and eighth graders in public schools and 25,000 in private school students. The survey found, after controlling for economic, racial, family, and other background variables, that public school students did as well as or better than their private school counterparts in fourth-grade reading and math and in eighth-grade math. Private school students did better only in eighth-grade reading.[17]

In sum, although reforms at university and college levels are continuous and relatively easy to try out and revise, they encounter obstacles at lower levels in federal systems that diffuse responsibility for implementing them. The scale of public elementary and secondary education in the United States would appear to be just too great to ensure that reforms are promptly and effectively adopted. Put differently, the well-being of students is too complex and controversial an issue for adults who long since passed through the educational system to achieve a consensus on appropriate remedial actions. In short, it can readily be concluded that fragmegrative dynamics are also operative in the field of education.

Cheating

Getting through all the levels of an educational system has become so central to a student's future that the temptations to cheat are considerable, and as far as one knows, more than a few students succumb to the temptation. As noted in Chapter 2, the Internet has facilitated plagiarism in writing papers for courses at the secondary and university levels even as it has also enabled professors to more easily find the original sources from which the plagiarized passages were taken. The price for getting caught cheating varies from one university to another, but all of them have procedures for handling such cases and appealing the outcomes.

Furthermore, there is evidence that the same can be said about moving up in the fields of science, medicine, business, journalism, and drama.[18] Cheating takes different forms in the different fields, but more than a few of those entering and seeking to advance in the various fields yield to the incentive to stray outside the boundaries of probity. The rewards of success and the drive to succeed are often strong enough to override established norms of honesty.

Conclusion

Given the problems faced by educational institutions, it is perhaps astounding that so many persons in the adult world are creative and effective in their work and daily routines. This may partially be due to the maturation of people subsequent to their student days, but the maturation is founded on a base acquired in schools and colleges. To a large extent both the strengths and flaws of modern societies can be traced back to the training of students. Clearly, they count!

CHAPTER TWENTY

Artists

Just so you know, we're ashamed the president of the United States is from Texas.

—*Natalie Maines, lead singer of the Dixie Chicks*[1]

Artists find their expression in any of a number of media—be they words, paint, metal, clay, fabric, film, concrete and steel, movement, wood, pixels, or whatever else. Though their pursuits are numerous and diverse—such as poets, painters, sculptors, singers, designers, directors, photographers, choreographers, and architects—they share certain core attributes. Perhaps the most important of these is that the work of all artists is an articulation of a particular vision, a conception of how the subject of their art will reflect their own notions of beauty and ugliness, of complexity and simplicity, of persistent habits and new departures, of conventional patterns and innovative experiments, of continuity and change—to mention only a few possibilities.

This artistic concern often leads to an activist engagement with politics. It is perhaps natural that artists go so easily from interrogating and reframing their surroundings to defining for themselves an explicitly political role. In a state-centric world, this tendency most often takes one of two forms, either patriot or dissident, both ultimately focused on their own national context. Some artists have worked in service of their nation-state—e.g., Leni Riefenstahl—and some have worked against it—e.g., Nadezhda Mandelstam. Even when artists express a vision of shared humanity, their visions are limited by the boundaries and borders that divide humankind. Artists tend to represent and reproduce their own national cultures, and through their work they provide a primary means for the maintenance of those cultures.

Artists and their works may also differ in important ways. They can be differentiated in terms of their degrees of abstraction, ranging from those that are marked by realism and those that are highly abstract. They can also vary in terms of the extent to which they reflect regional and national origins as well as different eras of history. Even individual artists can be viewed as marked by different eras in their creative careers. The works of Picasso, for example, have been described as reflecting, among others, his "blue" and "cubist" periods.

The Globalization of Art

As globalization erodes and avoids those boundaries, artistic vision is no longer limited to local expression. As their art reaches across international boundaries, into distant lands and languages, so too are artists themselves reaching across the world, expanding their role and becoming activists in world politics. This is especially the case for popular culture, and even though calling its creative agents "artists" is sometimes charitable at best, there is no denying that theirs products are increasingly a global commodity. As their records, books, pictures, movies, and other works disseminate around the world, the particular visions those artists articulate—and the artists themselves —become increasingly relevant to world politics.

Art has always made its way across boundaries. Art and artifacts are frequent finds in archaeological sites wherever trading populations once lived. The colonialist conquest of the world often brought back artwork and performers, filling museums like the Louvre with antiquities and objects from faraway lands. Performance works often enjoyed popularity with foreign audiences, even those who could not speak the works' native languages; so opera in Italian, tangos in Spanish, and so on.

What is different about the modern era is the rapidity and depth of assimilation of foreign art and culture into people's day-to-day lives. The Chinese youth buying a counterfeit English-language Shakira CD in the street of Beijing is probably not making a self-conscious effort to search out Colombian art; he may well think of her as a U.S. artist, anyway. His interest in the album likely carries no overtones of nationalism or self-identity; he simply enjoys the music in its own right, and it is easy for him to obtain. A child whose parents may not have had even a record player might now be able to play CDs in a home stereo, the family computer, and even a portable player. This kind of access has greatly increased demand for art and culture—especially in electronic media—often outpacing domestic artists ability to produce it. Thus television programs such as *Baywatch* can spread to scores of countries and billions of viewers; although not the best work ever produced by Hollywood, it was apparently among the most easily translatable.

Another difference in this era is that the volume and diversity of art and cultural products in circulation are staggering compared to previous generations. Beyond the expanded audiences and possibilities for professionals, technological advances have made many artforms accessible to vast populations of amateurs and dilettantes. Digital photography and video, music synthesizers, computer-based editing tools and software, and a range of other products have given people tools to create the kinds of art that once were the product of the very few. These tools, especially software such as Photoshop, have also given people the ability to revise and remake extant art in order to give it a particular message. To distribute the products of their work, today's artists can call on a range of media for their exhibition. Desktop printing allows for innumerable high-quality prints. Photography web sites such as Flickr allow people to share their work globally, instantly. Digital formats and CD burners permit the mass distribution of recorded music. It is true that much of what is being produced and disseminated is shoddy and superficial, but it is also probably true that this flood of creativity is changed and growing faster than critics can process it.

These changes mean that not only are artists and their art increasingly able to appeal to audiences around the world but also that even the fraudulent knockoffs of their work are a multi-million-dollar global industry. For example, a lobbying group for the recording industry estimated the cost of piracy of their products in 2005 by Chinese counterfeiters to be $200 million, and the growing problem of piracy of this and other types of intellectual property is fast becoming a thorn in U.S.-Chinese relations.[2] Furthermore, the production of physical counterfeits is likely not as big a threat as digital file sharing. Although the financial figures are perhaps a problem of business executives and shareholders, where art is concerned they point to the widespread reach of cultural products. A computer user in any part of the world can log on and download music, film, and videos of performances; shop for high fashion; browse online museum collections; or visit virtual manifestations of architectural landmarks.

The spread of art and culture has become so pervasive that it has engendered a backlash. Many people believe that globalization is leading to the erosion and disappearance of cultural and artistic diversity, an idea especially championed by Benjamin Barber.[3] In response, governments are establishing more rules and barriers to protect their domestic culture from invasion and dilution by foreign (often U.S.) influence. The most obvious example of this phenomenon is the Convention on the Protection of the Diversity of Cultural Contents and Artistic Expression recently adopted by the United Nations Educational, Scientific, and Cultural Organization (UNESCO). Part of the text of the treaty reads: "The processes of globalization, which have been facilitated by the rapid development of information and communication technologies, afford unprecedented conditions for enhanced interaction between cultures, [but] they also represent a challenge for cultural diversity, namely in view of risks of imbalances between rich and poor countries."[4]

The problem with efforts like this is that they misattribute the sources of culture change. By representing foreign cultures as invasive or infectious and as posing a "challenge" to cultural diversity, this kind of protectionism ignores both the people who are producing the art and culture and the people consuming it. It takes a certain degree of patronizing to decree that a foreign musician's work poses a threat to domestic artists, if the domestic audience genuinely prefers the foreign music, and otherwise, the foreign musician poses no threat at all. But because artists act as cultural vanguards, their work is fraught with implications for national and social identity, and so in crossing boundaries art frequently becomes politicized whether or not the artists intended it to be.

Art as Politics

That art is often politicized should not overshadow the fact that artists often intend their art to be political—to engage or expound on political issues and to present ideas about those concerns to a broader audience. Novelists of the late nineteenth century, for example, were the first to anticipate the advent of World War I.[5]

In few societies was art as politics more evident than in the Soviet Union. Authors, filmmakers, painters, and poets all felt pressure to produce work to praise and perpetuate the state. Artists who allowed the wrong kind of politics to slip into their work were often severely punished as political criminals.

Art also helps interpret political events and eras; for example, painters and other artists of the New Objectivity movement in interwar Germany helped record and reframe the malaise and discontent of those years.[6] During the U.S. war in Vietnam, books such as Vonnegut's *Slaughterhouse Five* and Heller's *Catch-22* and movies such as Altman's *M*A*S*H* helped shape and mediate public opinion about the conflict. More recently, the terrorist attacks of September 11, 2001, and subsequent militarism by the U.S. government have been reinterpreted in a number of movies, television programs, books, comics, songs, and other works.

Artists as Activists

The celebrity of successful artists can lead readily to invitations and inclinations to speak out on public issues. Some are eager to use their influence on behalf of their values, whereas others prefer to remain silent insofar as the political stage is concerned. The latter tend to view their celebrity as tenuous, as vulnerable to shifting public agendas. On the other hand, the celebrity that accompanies success in the arts can lead to support from one or another individual in the entertainment field. The potential political roles of artists are indicated by the large extent to which political candidates in the United States are lured to Hollywood by their need for funds and endorsements.

Even when their art is not particularly political, artists can embrace roles as activists. Especially for those who are celebrities, their views and opinions carry inordinate weight in public discourse. They often offer or are asked their views on a range of issues and subjects, whether or not they have formal training or even expertise in the matter above that of the average noncelebrity. Because of the increasingly global nature of celebrity, many of these people can draw on worldwide recognition and popularity to become global activists. The comment by

Natalie Maines in the epigraph of this chapter was incidental to her performance in Britain, immediately prior to the U.S. invasion of Iraq. Nonetheless, her remarks were picked up by the media and quickly became controversial in the United States, leading many former fans to shun or protest the Dixie Chicks. This is not to claim that all artists are or should be engaged in world politics; rather it is to note that the changing global landscape creates a potential for activity that many artists have seized. Some are eager to use their influence on behalf of their values, whereas others prefer to remain silent insofar as the political stage is concerned. For those who choose to be heard, their voices can carry very far indeed.

The U.S. experience demonstrates the potential political roles for artists, and not just in the extent to which political candidates in the United States are lured to Hollywood by their need for funds and endorsements. Indeed, much of the interaction between artists and politicians in the United States comes from the television and film industries, the most obvious examples of which are the many actors who have entered politics: Ronald Reagan, Arnold Schwarzenegger, and Fred Thompson, among others. Many more have been active with specific political issues and organizations but have not (yet) run for office, such as Warren Beatty, Al Franken, and Susan Sarandon. Charlton Heston, an actor and one-time advocate of gun control, later served as president of the National Rifle Association. A brief survey of news articles suggests that the step from actor to politician is not exclusive to the United States, but is also quite common in India, and probably anywhere that democracy and a well-established film industry coincide.

Even though many artists—especially actors in the United States and India—have global audiences for their work, there are few institutional offices available with the same breadth and reach. This has not prevented actors and other artists from taking on positions of global responsibility. Perhaps the most famous of these in recent years has been Angelina Jolie, the actor turned UN goodwill ambassador. In that capacity she has toured a number of refugee camps in the developing world, working to bring awareness of those places to a wider audience. The Irish musician, Bono, has also taken a global role, especially as a spokesman for the One campaign to eliminate poverty. Unlike Jolie's films, many of the songs Bono has written and recorded with his band, U-2, have been explicitly political.

Conclusion

The spread of art and cultural artifacts around the world is one of the most important consequences of globalization. Indeed, their distribution has enabled more and more people to assimilate and integrate foreign culture as ordinary parts of their everyday lives. Whether art is inherently political, subsequently politicized, or used as a platform for the artists' political views, it is clear that artists count.

PART IV

People in Unorganized Groupings

CHAPTER TWENTY-ONE

Marginals

In every society some people are marginal to its daily life, either out of choice or because of circumstances. Yet, people on the margins also count! One way they count is through the problems they pose for those in the mainstream. They often require government intervention to help them cope with their age, illness, disabilities, and other limitations. Second, each of the various groups of marginals—as I shall call them—is numerous and potentially susceptible to mobilization as a political force that can have considerable consequences.

Their potential as a political force, however, is limited because the individuals who comprise the various groups on the periphery of society are normally so apathetic with respect to public affairs that they are difficult to mobilize. In most cases their apathy is pervasive and profound precisely because their circumstances are debilitating. Due to poverty, age, or health, they are either unable or unwilling to participate in the affairs of their communities. Nonetheless, not only are public policies designed to alleviate their plight, but marginals are also the focus of organizations that seek to speak and act on their behalf, thereby ensuring that they count.

In relatively few cases the apathy stems from a conscious rejection of the mainstream's values that leads to alienation, to a purposeful retreat from society's affairs and an isolated lifestyle. Such individuals may have wealth, health, and youth, but their choice to live on the periphery is so thoroughgoing that they become people who do not count. With one exception, no attempt is made to include alienated persons in the ensuing analysis. The exception is that small fraction of those whose rejection of the community takes the form of violence against it. They become, in effect, terrorists or criminals.

The Poor

To distinguish between those individuals in a society who do and do not have enough resources to get from one day to the next is to locate them above or below what is known as the "poverty line." Most definitions of the poverty line differentiate between those people who can and cannot afford to purchase all the resources they require to live. The poverty line is not constant across countries and communities. Where it is drawn depends on the circumstances and resources of a country or community. The International Labour Organization estimated in 2004 that some 1.4 billion people lived below a US$2 a day poverty line and roughly a third of these individuals were living below the US$1 a day poverty line.[1] The country with the smallest proportion of its population below the poverty line was Taiwan (1 percent), followed by Austria (3.9 percent), and Belgium and South Korea (4 percent). Of 121 countries ranked, the one with the highest proportion below the line was Zambia (86 percent). The U.S. ranked thirteenth, with 12 percent below the poverty line.[2]

But these figures are somewhat misleading inasmuch as most of those numerous persons only minimally above the poverty line are not likely to have the resources to enable their voices to be heard and their pressures to be felt. The stratum of the society comprised of poor people is larger than can be defined by a line, no matter how systematic and logical it may be.

To be sure, the poor, like other societal groups, are beneficiaries of the skill revolution. Increasingly they are likely to acquire the intellectual tools to move beyond apathy; and eventually more and more of them are likely to use the tools as a means of getting their collective goals appreciated and acted upon. Accordingly, efforts to mobilize them are increasingly likely to intensify and be successful. But this trend will not occur overnight, and the mass apathy induced by poverty is thus likely to persist for the foreseeable future.

A prime and inescapable manifestation of those who live below the poverty line is to be found in the homeless people who populate most cities. Often accompanied by a supermarket cart that holds their few belongings, they sleep in doorways and on the street. In so doing they are conspicuous reminders of the poor being among us, not to mention the limits and failures of a country's economic system and the drain on its charitable impulses.

At the same time there are offsetting sources of support for the poor. The Gates Foundation, recently supplemented by a huge gift from George Soros, has devoted extensive resources to fighting the AIDS epidemic in Africa. Likewise, the singer Bono has used his fame to raise nearly $9 billion for charitable purposes and allocated $5.2 billion to fight disease in 130 countries.[3]

Another technique for enabling the poor to move to higher income levels has been developed by a program called SkillWorks, located in Boston and organized by its Brigham and Women's Hospital. The organization seeks to train poor persons who are working below their potential in menial jobs for more skilled work. Many examples are cited, one being the janitor who "could be trained and guided into work as a painter, an electrician, a groundskeeper or a custodial supervisor." Or, to use another example, "Why shouldn't someone who changes sheets in a hospital, or delivers meals to patients, be offered the education and training necessary to become a surgical technician, or radiologic technologist, or registered nurse?"[4] In short, although the ranks of the poor are not likely to be greatly diminished, neither are they constant. They can be lessened as poor people gain the skills and knowledge necessary to lift them above the poverty line.

The Elderly

As stressed in Chapter 4, the ranks of the elderly are growing rapidly in several societies experiencing a drop in their birthrates. The growth is further stimulated by people living longer, a pattern that is known as the "graying" of a society. In the United States, for example, the median age increased from 22.9 in 1900 to 35.3 in 2000. By 2030 the baby boomers were projected to underlie a rise to 39.0. Stated in terms of life expectancy, the average from birth rose from 47.3 years in 1900 to 76.9 years in 2000.[5]

To a large extent these increases have occurred among the elderly segment of the population (i.e., those aged sixty-five and older). Again the data on Americans are illustrative: the elderly in the United States are projected to increase from 35 to 72 million between 2000 and 2030, a figure amounting to nearly 20 percent of the population in the latter year. Likewise, the oldest old population (those eighty-five and older) was thirty-four times larger in 2000 than in 1900, and its ranks are expected to grow rapidly after 2030 as surviving baby boomers turn 85.[6]

Although not as pronounced, similar patterns mark the world in general. In 2000, individuals sixty-five or older comprised 7 percent of the global population, a figure projected to increase substantially by 2030. Some 59 percent of the world's older population lived in developing countries in 2000, a proportion that was anticipated to rise to 70 percent by 2030.[7] A goodly proportion of this growth can be traced to China and India, where life expectancy was forty years around 1950 and, as a result of the eradication and control of numerous infectious diseases and advances in agricultural technology, had grown to sixty-three years by 2000.[8]

Implicit in the statistics on aging is a huge political reality, namely, that the elderly constitute a substantial stratum of the population that, if aroused and mobilized, can have important consequences for the social, economic, and political processes of society. More so than other strata, the elderly tend to be alert to and knowledgeable about the issues that comprise their society's agenda, and they are thus more ready to be mobilized on behalf of problems that affect their well-being. In democratic systems politicians are therefore especially sensitive to currents of thought at work among the elderly. As a report of the U.S. Census Bureau put it, "Rapidly expanding numbers of very old people represent a social phenomenon without historical precedent, and one that is bound to alter previously held stereotypes of older people."[9]

The likelihood of elderly groups banding together in protests has increased with the lengthening of life expectancies. The increases have led to a drain on pension funds, which were framed when people were not supposed to live long after they retired. The fact that this expectation has been negated, that the retirement years have been of increasingly long duration, has led to a pension crisis. More than a few pension funds in the developed world have had to renege on their commitments, a circumstance that has led to disarray and posed questions as to whether governments should take on the burden of bankrupt pension systems.

The Sick

With the threat or advent of global diseases such as HIV/AIDS, SARS, and bird flu, it is hardly surprising that the World Health Organization (WHO) estimated that 18 million people died from communicable diseases in 2002, 15 million of whom were less than sixty years old. A further 34 million deaths were attributed to noncommunicable diseases, 8 million of them people under sixty. Illness accounted for 51 million deaths, ten times those from injuries, accidents, and violence. The WHO estimates for regions made it clear that in certain parts of the world the challenges to health care are far greater than the capacity of communities and governments to meet them. It is telling, for example, that 40 million people worldwide are infected by HIV and another 45 million new HIV cases are projected to occur by 2010.[10] No less important, the costs and arrangements through which health care is provided are highly controversial in most societies, often serving as issues high on the political agenda. Perhaps the most controversial of these issues involves the potential for conflict between the solvency needs of insurance companies and the health needs of their customers, especially in the United States. Hardly less contentious is the role that drug companies, their research commitments, and their production procedures play in the provision of health care. Indeed, the struggle of the drug companies to increase their funds for research and consumers' opposition to their practices (such as co-opting members of the medical profession) and prices are profound instances of fragmegration.

Another set of differences revolves around the question of what constitutes disease, on the one hand, and good health, on the other. Indeed, controversy can also ensue over what agency is authorized to define what constitutes sickness, with corporate advertisers often offering definitions in the absence of public agencies performing the definitional task. Balding, shyness, and normal aging, for example, are among the conditions that have been defined as ill health, usually by pharmaceutical companies with products designed to treat such conditions.[11]

Many of these issues converge around the procedures and practices employed by U.S. health management organizations (HMOs) in dealing with physicians. Some HMOs employ a system of "capitated" payments to control their costs. It is a system wherein doctors receive a small fixed rate per patient per month, regardless of how sick patients are and how much treatment and care they need. This rate poses a problem for physicians: they lose income if they take on patients with serious diseases that require substantial time devoted to improving their health. As a result, some doctors are reluctant to accept HMO patients and will see only those who can pay out of pocket for their services. Another result is even more distressing: doctors come to see patients with diabetes, heart disease, or cancer as financial losses rather than as sick individuals.[12]

People with Disabilities

The label used to designate persons whose physical, mental, or sensory capacities are impaired is a matter of considerable importance to them. They are sensitive to labels that imply a lack of competence or otherwise reflect prejudice. Terms such as *cripple* or *handicapped* are illustrative in this regard, and they have progressively gone out of use. By a process of elimination, then, the current label of choice is *disabled* or *disability*. Some contend that the correct term is *disabled people* because the words *disabled* and *disability* highlight how society treats them, not their impairment, which is a medical matter.[13]

Depending on the definitions used, of course, estimates of the number of disabled people can vary. Estimates for the world population of disabled people are nonexistent, and the most reliable estimates by country are based on the support that government agencies provide. In the United States, for example, about 6.5 million people receive disability benefits from the Social Security Administration, and another million are registered as looking for work with state agencies.[14] About 50 million disabled people live in Europe, and official surveys in Germany found 6.4 million severely disabled people.[15] The disabled may be a minority, but like the elderly and the sick, they are not small minorities in any country.

Indeed, their numbers are sufficient to serve as the basis for a disability rights movement. Established in the 1970s, the movement has focused on issues of safety and accessibility. Wheelchair ramps, automatic doors, wide doors and corridors, and special parking spaces are among the innovations the movement has successfully championed.

Still another recent resource that has aided the disabled involves a wide array of technological developments. Most of these facilitate use of the computer, including tools such as voice synthesizers that turn text into speech and software that enables blind people to use a keyboard instead of a mouse. Such technologies enable the disabled to work from home and thereby avoid having to travel in order to earn a living. More than that, it enables them to communicate with others without their disabilities being evident.[16]

In sum, the disabled are adaptive and increasingly able to enhance their own well-being even as they contribute to the well-being of society. Rather than being burdens for the society, many disabled persons are contributors to its structure and content.

Gays and Lesbians

In some societies, the United States being one, the stigma of being a homosexual has dissipated considerably. As a result, sexual orientation has become less salient in these societies, and both gays and lesbians are publicly acknowledging their orientation, or "coming out." To be sure, there are still pockets of antigay or anti-lesbian actions, some of them quite brutal. But more often than not such actions are condemned. More than that, in the United States and elsewhere gays and lesbians have formed organizations—such as the Parents, Families and Friends of Lesbians and Gays (PFLAG)—and voting blocs that politicians ignore at their peril.

There is one issue, however, where the much larger "straight" (as those with heterosexual orientations are called) community has been less lenient toward the gay and lesbian community, namely, the issue of legal marriages between gays or between lesbians. Although a couple of states in the United States have adopted legislation allowing for such marriages, many have refused to do so, and the courts have thrown out as unconstitutional such marriages in those states that adopted the legislation. Subsequently an attempt to adopt a constitutional amendment banning same-sex marriages in the House of Representatives was turned back by a vote of 237 to 187, not nearly enough yea votes to meet the two-thirds majority required to amend the Constitution.[17] A succinct statement of the problems faced by gay couples seeking to marry was made in a dissent by the chief judge of the New York Court of Appeals: "Indeed, the true nature and extent of the discrimination suffered by gays and lesbians is perhaps best illustrated by the simple truth that each one of the plaintiffs could lawfully enter into a marriage of convenience with a complete stranger of the opposite sex tomorrow, and thereby immediately obtain all of the myriad benefits and protections incident to marriage. Plaintiffs are, however, denied these rights because they each desire instead to marry the person they love and with whom they have created their family."[18]

Clearly, the gay rights issue is pervasively fragmegrative, with couples trying to come together as a family and society denying them the right to do so, preferring to call such arrangements "civil unions" rather than marriages. Compared to the practices that prevailed in past history, on the other hand, gays and lesbians have advanced in substantial ways, and the likelihood is that these advances will continue in industrial societies. Indeed, this issue is globally divisive. Many developing and tradition-oriented countries still ban homosexuality; in some places it is punishable by death. Muslim fundamentalists often cite the West's permissiveness of homosexuality as evidence of the evil and danger it poses to moral order. Pim Fortuyn in the Netherlands was opposed to Muslim immigration in part because of their cultural lack of tolerance for gays and lesbians, and he was subsequently killed because of his views.

The Unborn

Although neither a role nor a group that can speak or organize for itself, the unborn are at the center of two central issues in U.S. politics. One is abortion and the other concerns stem cell research. Although the abortion issue is perhaps most intensely waged in the United States, the International Society of Abortion Doctors has offices in many cities of some fifteen countries. The opponents of abortion in the United States are mostly conservative, and often they are moved by their religious convictions. Many opponents allow for abortions if the mother's life is threatened, and still others say it is permissible if done in the first trimester of a pregnancy. But a large proportion of the opponents believe that abortion is never permissible. Those who believe in abortion see it as a matter of the right to self-determination, to make their own choice about whether to give birth to and raise a child. In short, the issue of abortion is fundamentally about life and death, a matter about which people feel very strongly indeed.

Yet, this succinct summary of the issue doesn't begin to indicate the intensity with which it is contested. Opponents have picketed clinics where abortions are performed and in a couple of instances have resorted to violence against the doctors involved. Proabortion advocates have gathered around the same clinics to protect the pregnant women wishing to enter, a situation that is always on the verge of collapsing into violence. Perhaps the best indicator of the centrality of the issue is the number of entries under abortion found on Google on April 4, 2007: about 334,000,000.

Although not nearly as heated or widespread as the abortion issue, the question of whether to fund stem cell research has become a major preoccupation in the United States. The research is a public issue because the stem cells derive from live embryos, and although many scientists and supporters of the issue believe the stem cells may some day be used to cure or greatly alleviate major diseases such as diabetes, opponents regard embryos as forms of life and the use of them for research as, in effect, destroying human life. These opposing viewpoints are an issue because of the question of funding the research. Early in his presidency, George W. Bush announced his policy of restricting federal money for stem cell research to the use of then-existing embryos, thus prohibiting the use of federal funds to acquire new embryos on the grounds that doing so amounted to destroying life. Then, in 2006, the Congress passed legislation to expand federally financed embryonic stem cell research, legislation that evoked the first veto of Bush's six years in office. The veto heightened tensions around the issue and became central to several political campaigns, with two governors immediately setting aside state funds for stem cell research and with other governors contemplating similar actions.

To some extent, however, the issue subsequently became moot when research yielded a new technique for recovering embryos without destroying life.

Conclusion

The various marginals may live on the periphery of society, but they are very much a part of its daily life. And there are many other types beside those discussed here. There are the recluses who disdain society even as they live off it, just as there are the apathetic who derive gains from society without contributing to its welfare, as well as the wealthy who live apart in gated communities and also disdain society even as their wealth derives from one or another aspect of its economy. Nonetheless, although their numbers are not trivial, the marginals are not nearly as relevant as those in the mainstream assessed in previous chapters.

Chapter Twenty-Two

Generations

I really want to move to Antarctica. I'd want my cat and Internet access, and I'd be happy.

—*Sixteen-year-old boy in Pittsburgh*[1]

· Occupancy of a generational role involves acceptance of a widespread consensus as to the characteristics and attitudes of people born in a particular time period. Such roles are defined by the values and practices induced by the historical circumstances that are seen as marking people born in that period. In some sense, consequently, a generational role is a grand generalization that does not correspond to the particular life experiences of particular individuals. More accurately, if there is a correspondence between a person's generational role and his or her life experiences, he or she is not likely to be conscious of it. Few people move through time aware of the ways in which others say their conduct mirrors the generation into which they were born. Put differently, unlike the roles assessed in previous chapters, few people consciously occupy the generational role assigned to them and conduct themselves according to its precepts. Expectations attach to generational roles in only vague and ambiguous ways.

Some observers argue that our generational roles matter even if we are unaware of them. As two analysts put it, "through our generational memberships, we all take part in history-bending moments. And through our cross-generational relationships, we communicate across eras of mind-bending length."[2] Such reasoning is precisely why the literature on generations is huge and growing. People think generational differences matter even if they do not consist of role expectations to which they are consciously responsive.

Some indication of the minimal degree to which people purposely occupy a generational role is evident in arguments over the labels attached to generations and the time span that each covers. One formulation lists eighteen generations since 1584,[3] but most formulations focus on four or five more recent generations, namely,

The Traditionalists, born between the turn of the last century and the end of World War II (1900–1945), combine two generations who tend to believe similarly and who number about 75 million people. The Baby Boomers (1946–1964) are the largest population ever born in this country and number about eighty million. The Generation Xers (1965–1980) are a small but very influential population at 46 million. And the Millennials (1981–1999) represent the next great demographic boom at 76 million.[4]

To be sure, some people defy lifestyle changes and resist generational precepts. I, for example, have had difficulty accepting the limits imposed by my aging. I still think of myself as capable of engaging in all the activities that I undertook years ago and doing so with the same zest and skills that I brought to any challenge. It is a defiance that can be dangerous when one gets behind the wheel of a car.

The Contemporary Generation

One distinction that can be drawn with confidence between different generations and different stages of the life cycle concerns the impact of fragmegrative dynamics. Interaction among integrating and fragmenting forces has marked every period of human history, but the time span across which the interactions occur varies considerably in different historical periods. This is most conspicuous in the current era: the computer and the Internet have rendered the distant much more proximate than was the case in earlier times. Where people in the eighteenth century, for instance, had to wait several weeks for news to cross oceans or continents, today it takes only milliseconds for distant proximities to be experienced.[5] On the other hand, even as people today can be considered the Internet generation, life cycle distinctions can be drawn. Widespread are the observations about how much more skilled in using computers and the Internet the present generation of young people is today than are their parents and grandparents. The habits, practices, and capabilities of older individuals are not readily adaptable to new and innovative technological changes, a difference that can conduce to misunderstandings and conflicts across generations.

The Internet, e-mail, and text messaging have become so salient that some have referred to the most recent age cohort as Generation Txt.[6] Whatever may be the appropriate label for the present and future generations, it does seem likely, to repeat, that the availability of new microelectronic technologies will be a source of both greater integration and intensified fragmentation among their members. Like-minded people in age groups are likely to be more conscious of their shared aspirations and fears as they communicate readily with each other across huge geographic distances, just as the differences between them and their elders or juniors are likely to seem more salient.

Even though the concept of generations and differences among them is elusive and questionable, it would appear unlikely to disappear from popular thought and observations. It seems bound to serve as the link people have with history, especially their own historical circumstances. Indeed, it is precisely the historical context of generations that underlies the longevity of the concept and its relevance to individuals and their daily lives.

The Impact of New Technologies

The remainder of the chapter probes whether the generations now in their early thirties or younger are likely to differ from their predecessors by virtue of being the first to be fully comfortable and literate with information technologies—the computer and its Internet, e-mail, and search capacities—when they come to occupy positions of power and prestige in the decades ahead. Will their decision-making skills be more incisive, their grasp of complexity more substantial, their dexterity in framing and implementing policies more proficient, their respect for knowledge and expertise more secure and temperate, their talent for forming consensuses and reaching compromises more extensive, their attitudes more subtle and nuanced, their organizations more effective? In short, in what ways might it matter that children today have been found to be "much heavier users of the Internet and all its services than were their parents"?[7]

It would be premature to offer definitive answers to such questions. Only time will tell whether generational changes will stem from much greater Internet literacy. At this point, with many in the older generation relatively illiterate in comparison to their offspring, we can only speculate about the consequences that might flow from an age group that can fully exploit all the resources offered by computers.

Although one analyst argued that, "in some ways, global satellite TV and Internet access have actually made the world a less understanding, less tolerant place,"[8] here a less precise, more open-ended response is developed: even though it is much too early to assess the full consequences of the Internet for individuals and societies because the Internet-literate generation has yet to fully replace its predecessors, it seems likely that, when the replacement occurs and the present young generation enters the ranks of elites, activists, and thoughtful citizens throughout the world, the nature of politics and economics within and between countries will be, for better or worse, profoundly different than is the case today. To be sure, generational change has always been a primary dynamic in the life of societies, but the changes that lie ahead flowing from the combination of more extensive satellite television and ever-greater Internet literacy may be as profound as (if not more profound than) any that have previously marked the modern era. Anticipating whether the result will be diminished or enlarged understanding and tolerance on a worldwide scale, below I argue that information technologies are morally neutral and that therefore the generational changes that accompany the growth of the Internet are more likely to affect the skills with which the technologies are employed rather than the degree of understanding and tolerance they engender. But this point is best explored after elaborating on how the extensive Internet literacy among those in today's younger generation sets it apart from their elders.

Actually, usage of both the Internet and satellite dishes has undergone rapid growth in recent years, with each medium having contributed substantially to the spread of ideas, pictures, and information to every corner of the earth. But although the spread via television may be approaching a point of saturation, the same cannot be said of the Internet, partly because large numbers of people still do not have access to computers and partly because the skills required to use the Internet vary from rudimentary to sophisticated, whereas the use of television involves little more than turning on the set. Thus, as more and more people acquire access to the Internet and replace their rudimentary skills with a greater capacity to exploit its many facets, so will the relationship between generational change and information technologies come into focus. Among other things, for example, satellite television is a one-to-many medium that can facilitate the spread of ideas, pictures, and information and thereby expand or diminish understanding and tolerance, but the Internet is a many-to-many medium that can serve as a means for mobilizing people and translating their levels of understanding and tolerance into action.[9] The more the Internet skills of individuals are refined, in other words, the greater is their involvement in political processes likely to be.

The Resistance of Older Generations

Based on considerable anecdotal evidence as well systematic findings, it is reasonable to conclude that today's older generations have been largely perplexed and intimidated by the Internet and its potential uses, so much so that many of their members assume that their learning curve does not allow for keeping up with and using the access to the knowledge and communications afforded by the Internet. More than a few of us in the older generations have experienced pride in the computer skills of our children and their children, but our pride is usually accompanied by the assumption that there is no way in which we can match the successor generations in this respect. Indeed, some of us happily acknowledge that we are Neanderthals when it comes to taking advantage of the computer and surfing the Web, contending that after all we have gotten along fine without such skills and thus have no need to acquire them at this late date.

I wrote the previous sentence while looking at my e-mail in the office of a small hotel on the Greek island of Hydra. When I asked the owner if he used the computer, his answer in broken English was unqualified: "No, I have no idea how it works. I got it for my daughters when they visit." And he is not alone. I have encountered a number of persons and intellectuals of my generation in the United States whose Neanderthal attitudes are more elaborate but no less clear-cut, often indicating they have no idea whatever of the potential ways in which the Internet may be of assistance to them.

Others of us sense the potential utility of the Internet and the computer, and we have even mastered some of their rudimentary uses such as e-mail and eas-ily accessible databases, but we remain humble and perplexed when faced with more sophisticated tasks.[10] Partly the perplexity stems from an inability to grasp the underlying processes on which the Internet and its numerous dimensions are founded; partly it derives from a resistance to evolving the habits necessary to employing the various routines and alternative mechanisms through which the Internet may serve diverse and complex needs; partly it is linked to a sense of inundation over the vast amounts of knowledge that have suddenly become available;[11] and partly it may be rooted in a conviction that our capacity for remembering detail has waned and is thus not up to mastering all the wrinkles of which the Internet consists. Stated differently, our perplexity originates with long-standing immersion in empirical and visible phenomena and, consequently, a difficulty in envisioning cyberspace as a place that confounds "the wider array of familiar distinctions—e.g., presence/absence, body/persona, offline/online—through which we have tended to understand what we see and what we do not see, who we are, where we are, and the communities to which we belong."[12] Although younger generations are quite content to have cyberspace liberate them from "the confines of apartment walls, office cubicles, and state borders precisely by presenting users with a seeming boundless frontier space, enabling the freedom of movement to travel, within seconds, to sites across the country or, for that matter, across the world,"[13] older persons tend to be set in their ways and thus not ready for liberation on this scale. It is not that they resist liberation; it is simply that they do not comprehend its availability. Unlike their juniors, they do not have the immediate impulse to turn to the Internet for any problem that may arise—from simple questions like the weather or the automobile route for a trip to the complex issue of Internet usage in diverse foreign countries.

I include myself among this perplexed generation. Even though I am in awe of the fact that I can communicate with my office easily, quickly, and cheaply from an island in the Aegean, and even though I am invariably stunned whenever I find and access obscure articles in obscure journals, age has filled my memory bank and I am endlessly turning to others for help in using the Internet effectively—and even then the help I receive seems more a form of magic than a logical exploitation of available equipment. Admittedly this may be a personal failing, but I suspect it is more an instance of the old adage about the limits of teaching old dogs new tricks. The contrast between my computer skills and those of my students is too sharp to dismiss the discrepancy as simply one older person's quirks.

The Competence of Younger Generations

In Chapter 3 and elsewhere I have argued that people everywhere in the world have undergone a skill revolution, a three-part upheaval consisting of an expansion of analytic, emotional, and imaginative competencies.[14] The Internet, global satellite television, and the computer are not the only sources of this upheaval—more education, more travel, and coping with the challenges of complex urban communities are among the other major sources—but the newer communications technologies are certainly one of the prime factors that underlie the relatively greater competence of younger generations. One national survey, for example, found that children in the United States ages 2 to 5 averaged 27 minutes a day at the computer, and the figures for children 6 to 11 and 12 to 17 averaged 49 and 63 minutes a day, respectively.[15] In short, for many young people, taking full advantage of the diverse uses of the Internet borders has become a second nature, a set of talents and proclivities they do not even know they possess unless they encounter the Internet illiteracy of their seniors.[16]

Perhaps the best, though hardly the only, example of this second nature is to be found among techies and hackers, most of whom entered the computer world before they turned twenty years old and a preponderance of whom are still under thirty years old. Unable to resist the challenge of solving difficult computer problems, and knowing that the problems are capable of solution if worked at hard and long enough, techies and hackers can spend hours in front of their monitors, depriving themselves of sleep and having junk food at their side in order not to waste time in finding the solutions. Where older persons tend to become sufficiently frustrated to abandon quickly a task when the Internet fails to yield the desired solution in a reasonable time, techies and hackers are driven by the knowledge that a solution exists and do not quit until it is found. Thus did their all-consuming fascination with the virtual world opened up by cyberspace contribute substantially to its expansion and growth. Although some hackers have an unforgiving contempt for those they view as novices in their usage of the Internet—as "clueless newbies"—techies tend to be very helpful to those who seek assistance, thereby serving to empower individuals and advance the skill revolution.[17]

Of course, hackers do not always use their competence on behalf of such worthy purposes.[18] Many are loners who, like vandals, simply try to cause damage for its own sake. Yet, the fact that virtually all of the known less-high-minded hackers in recent years have been young poses interesting questions about the ways in which the older and younger generations may differ in their values as well as their skills and whether such differences portend more contentious eras in the future. It is accepted wisdom that people and generations tend to become more conservative as they age, but have the Internet and other information technologies altered the scope and depth of these tendencies? Could it be that the hackers are an expression of a readiness on the part of the younger generation to challenge authority and thus contribute to what elsewhere I have referred to as pervasive crises of authority that plague governments and nongovernmental institutions throughout the world?[19] And if so, will significant changes unfold as the hacker generation becomes middle-aged and then elderly? The answers are as elusive as they are provocative and must be posed as highly tentative.

On the other hand, this is not to imply that hackers are likely to dominate younger generations. Rather, it is to illustrate an extreme version of a culture in which older generations do not readily participate. Most persons in the younger generations will lead more "normal" lives and will be comfortable in cyberspace, knowing that the Internet is a valuable tool they can use efficiently and effectively when situations warrant it. Indeed, as they mature and take on leadership responsibilities they may well be required to contest egregious hackers who invade privacy and pose other threats to the well-being of their organizations.

Nor should the foregoing finding that young Americans are heavier users of the Internet than their parents be interpreted as confined to the United States. The generational differences in Internet literacy are worldwide in scope, with the difference between younger professionals in Asia, Africa, and Latin America and their elders probably even greater than in the United States, where experience with technological innovations has long been a part of daily routines. Indeed, although the proportion of persons in the developing world who have access to the Internet is substantially less than is the case for the United States and Europe, the concentration of users among young people in Asia, Africa, and Latin America is probably greater than elsewhere in the world. A random sample of patterns for 2001 and 2002 in these regions illustrates this probability: in India, "75% of all adults who access the Internet are in the age group of 15–34 years";[20] in Thailand, "most Thai users are in the age group of 20–29 years";[21] in Malaysia, "it can be stated that the number of middle-aged and older persons surfing the Net will be far smaller than the number of youths.... It has been estimated that more than 90 percent of Malaysian users are young people below 30 years, and the majority are school children or college students";[22] in China, "new survey results show that younger people, and people with less education than previously are getting online.... [Their] average age ... is 28";[23] in twelve Arab countries, 79 percent of those with Internet access are under thirty-five years of age;[24] in the Philippines, 81 percent of Internet users are under thirty years old, "because they are not intimidated by technology and it has become a part of their lives";[25] in Lithuania, "61 percent of all computer users are under 30 years old," with "the higher the age group, the lower the incidence of computer use";[26] in South Africa, "the average age of web users is 35, but with the biggest age group being those between 20 and 30";[27] and in Malta, "the main users were registered amongst the 16–24 bracket [and] the use of Internet decreased proportionally with the rise in the age groups, fading away to practically nil for the over 65 years age group."[28]

It bears repeating that these data represent only the small proportion of persons in these countries who have Internet access. Their ranks are growing rapidly, but their number still remains far short of those in the developed world, thus contributing to what is known as the digital divide that separates the relative access of the rich and poor within and between countries. Although interesting programs are designed to narrow the divide among youth in developed countries,[29] many of the younger people in the developing world who do have access acquire it by visiting the numerous Internet cafés that are opening throughout the cities and towns of the developing world.[30] As the newer technologies become increasingly available in the offices, homes, and cafés of the developing world and thus increasingly integral to its daily routines, presumably Internet literacy will spread rapidly through upcoming generations.

Speculations

Assuming, then, that younger generations are more Internet literate than their seniors, let us return to the questions raised at the outset, to speculating about the ways in which politics might change when societies come to consist of elites, activists, and thoughtful citizens who are fully at home with computers and their diverse uses. Needless to say, the task is to trace just noticeable differences (JNDs) rather than wholesale changes.[31] But small as they may be, tracing JNDs is not a trivial exercise. If statisticians are correct in hypothesizing that normally everything, people included, regresses to the mean, then identifying possible ways in which the computer-literate generation might be different from their predecessors by one or more JND is a challenging undertaking. At the very least such an effort may spur further research into what could prove to be important political phenomena.

My inclination is to answer the original questions in the affirmative. It is plausible that the decisionmaking skills of computer-literate generations—those in the private sector as well as public officials—will be more refined than their predecessors. Having become sensitive to, and adept at exploiting, the vast array of knowledge offered by the Internet, they will have a more acute respect for knowledge and its complexity and, accordingly, a greater inclination to offset their temperamental impulses and a lesser readiness to fall back on their intuitive, undocumented feelings about situations. When one is fully familiar with the depth and breadth of information available on the Internet, it becomes difficult simply to dismiss the need to check out, confirm, modify, or reject what seems at first glance to be self-evident. In addition, knowing the huge range of available information and insights available on the World Wide Web is likely to enable people to give more license to their imaginations, to ponder alternatives that earlier generations might consider unexplorable and thus not worth an investiture of time. More than that, familiarity with extraordinary resources of the World Wide Web may heighten inclinations to acknowledge that innumerable grays exist between blacks and whites. To be sure, those with high responsibilities may not have enough time to thoroughly surf the Web for clarity on the problems they face, but they are likely to be less quick to rush to judgment and they can also assign the surfing tasks to subordinates. This greater appreciation of complexity and nuance may, in turn, facilitate greater proficiency in framing and implementing policies as well as helping to develop consensuses and achieving compromises in contentious organizational meetings. To repeat, such changes may involve no more than one JND. People will continue to have their failings, prejudices, and bureaucratic loyalties, and thus they will surely continue to sift information that affirms their prejudices; nevertheless, such weaknesses are more likely to be contested the more people are conversant with what the Internet offers.

At the societal level several changes seem likely. First, the capacity to mobilize like-minded others may lead to one or more JND between Internet-literate generations and their predecessors. The former now form "smart mobs," a label for "groups of people equipped with high-tech communications devices that allow them to act in concert—whether they know each other or not."[32] Although collective actions are marked by a long history, today smart mobs form among the young who are adept at using the new electronic equipment, with one observer arguing that the "convergence of wireless communications technologies and widely distributed networks allow swarming on a scale that has never existed before, a shift along the lines of those that began to occur when people first settled into villages and formed nation-states." Indeed, as a result of this shift, "we are on the verge of a major series of social changes that are closely tied to emerging technologies."[33] Put in more political terms, as whole generations possess the new equipment and acquire the habit of using it unthinkingly, street clashes seem likely to become more frequent and widespread, with larger numbers of protesters on both sides of any issue than has previously been the case.

Second, even if it is less conspicuous, another generation-induced societal change may be no less significant. It concerns the circulation of ideas and opinions relevant to public affairs. Thoughtful citizens in today's younger generations are accustomed to surfing the Internet for news on, say, CNN or MSNBC—even to assuring that they receive the news they want, as such sources allow site visitors to request e-mail on issues of interest to them—whereas their elder counterparts wait until they get home to catch the evening news. The technology of the Internet thus empowers individuals to receive the content that is important to them at times that are convenient, whereas those who rely on television wait until the end of their workday before focusing on the events elsewhere in the world. Accordingly, it can be argued that as the younger generations age, they will be more consequential than the present older generations in the sense that they will initiate the cascades of information that frame public opinion earlier in the day. By the time the evening news comes on the air, much of the public may already have formed its opinions. The Drudge Report's role in the Clinton-Lewinsky affair is illustrative in the regard. Once the Internet publication reported the existence of a stained dress, public opinion cascaded so quickly that the evening newscasts had little role in that political situation. One could probably cite numerous such cases that mark the Israeli-Palestinian conflict, not to mention the increasing frequency of steep intraday climbs and falls in stock markets.

Conversely, some changes seem unlikely to become pervasive. The aforementioned reasoning by George Packer that "in some ways, global satellite TV and Internet access have actually made the world a less understanding and tolerant place" is a misleading statement. If information technology is essentially neutral in the sense that it can be used to promote both good and bad outcomes, depending on a host of other circumstances,[34] there is no reason to presume that the understanding and tolerance of younger generations is likely to be altered as a consequence of being more adept at using the Internet than their elders. Shifting degrees of understanding and tolerance, or misunderstanding and intolerance, stem from circumstances other than the technologies that purvey them. To be sure, frequent scenes of young people protesting in the streets of Palestine and elsewhere in the Middle East suggest that satellite broadcasting and the Internet have lately fostered increasing levels of anger and misunderstanding. As one observer put it,

> At its best, the Internet can educate more people faster than any media tool we've ever had. At its worst, it can make people dumber faster than any media tool we've ever had. The lie that 4,000 Jews were warned not to go into the World Trade Center on Sept. 11 was spread entirely over the Internet and is now thoroughly believed in the Muslim world. Because the Internet has an aura of "technology" surrounding it, the uneducated believe information from it even more. They don't realize that the Internet, at its ugliest, is just an open sewer, an electronic conduit for untreated, unfiltered information. Worse, just when you might have thought you were all alone with your extreme views, the Internet puts you together with a community of people from around the world who hate all the things and people you do.[35]

Be that as it may, to conclude there is less understanding and tolerance in the Muslim world since September 11 and the onset of hostilities between Israelis and Palestinians is neither to describe the direction of change in other regions nor is it to allow for Muslims who are not taken in by untreated and unfiltered information.[36] More than that, such an observation ignores the skill revolution and the ways in which increasing Internet literacy have facilitated more penetrating analysis on the part of more and more people. For every person made dumber by the new technologies, there may well be one or more persons whose horizons have been pushed back and whose levels of understanding and tolerance have been elevated. Certainly there are hundreds of millions of people in various parts of the world other than the Middle East who accept that the victims of the terrorist attacks were people from all walks of life and religions, that none were warned to stay away from their jobs on that day. The outcome of the worldwide competition between understanding and misunderstanding and between tolerance and intolerance is far from certain and will depend on much more than information technologies.

Conclusion

In short, generational change and Internet literacy do appear to be causally linked at this time. But the links can be overstated, especially as Internet Neanderthals will no longer constitute the older generation in another couple of decades. There will doubtless be new information technologies, but it is hard to imagine them making generational differences of the kind that presently prevail.

CHAPTER TWENTY-THREE

Classes

Whatever delineation of the various socioeconomic classes may be used, everyone belongs to one, often by their own definition or otherwise by observers who specify the characteristics of each class. Persons aware of class differences tend to view their membership in a class as a role with expectations to which their conduct should conform. The subject of a voluminous literature, class is especially salient for Marxists and socialists, who refer to this awareness as class consciousness and assign considerable importance to the ways in which this consciousness serves as a guide to conduct and, in some cases, exploitation and conflict. On the other hand, most people are not sensitive to their class roles and rarely think about them, just as they rarely think about the generation into which they were born. Likewise, among those who are class conscious, few are ready to be mobilized on behalf of their class interests.

If one thinks of a country's class structure as a pyramid, a small sliver at the tip is the upper class, and the bottom is the lower class whose size varies from country to country. Between the two is the middle class, a broad swath that encompasses individuals and their families whose income is sufficient to cope with challenges and serve their needs. It is the middle class that shapes the course of society even as the elites in the upper class articulate the values that sustain it. But the values held by diverse segments of the middle class are likely to vary considerably, with the result that the middle class is best thought of in the plural, as the various middle classes shape the course of society in different ways. More accurately, various institutions and practices at work in a society are shaped differently by different segments of the middle class. The upper middle class, for instance, serves as a recruiting ground for the elites and tends to more closely emulate their values and practices than the other segments of the middle class. Likewise, the lower middle class tends to have many orientations in common with the lower class.

Even for those who are class conscious, however, their other roles outlined in previous chapters tend to be the main source of their conduct and attitudes. Their class orientations may underlie their behavior in some respects, but most people are unaware that they are conforming to class practices. To repeat, class consciousness is more an aspect of socialist and Marxist philosophies than it is a routine of daily life.

At least in the United States, with its history of expanding opportunities, people tend not to think of horizontal divisions among them. If anything, they are inclined to think vertically along occupational, educational, and geographic lines, orientations that further blur class distinctions.

Conclusion

Class differences are evident in the way people dress, the way they talk, and the life styles they lead all aspects of individuals that are readily observable and thus readily reinforced through observation. Anyone who is conscious of class can easily affirm their attitudes by watching others and their ways. And chances are that such individuals are keenly aware of the class they regard themselves as belonging to. Many of these are also likely to denigrate those they believe to be below them on the ladder.

While class differences are no less conspicuous in the United States than elsewhere, consciousness of them is not nearly so great as in Europe and Asia. The commitment of American society to the values of individuality and personal accomplishment serves to downplay the relevance of class. Most Americans tend to accept the differences and not to dwell on them. They tend not to look down on those below them or up to those above them. To be sure, the upper classes set the standards in dress and manner that are emulated by others, but concern with such matters is neither intense nor prolonged. The American class structure is fluid and not rigid, a characteristic that minimizes preoccupation with status and class differences. Rightly or wrongly, most people tend to assume they can move up the class ladder if they are inclined to do so.

Chapter Twenty-Four

Recounted People

Despite their titles, neither this book nor this chapter are about people so much as both of them are about the roles people occupy. Conceptually, this perspective allows for variable thought and behavior on the part of those who occupy the same role, but at the same time it permits generalization across the diverse people that occupy the role. No person perfectly conforms to the characteristics conceived to comprise the role he or she occupies. Yet, despite their diversity, all the role's occupants do have important attitudes in common, and faced with the same expectations embedded in their roles, they do engage in similar behavior under the same conditions. It is these similarities that set them apart from those who occupy other roles. And it is these similarities that justify generalizing about the way otherwise unalike people shape and are shaped by the course of events.

Put differently, the role concept is sufficiently powerful to prevent fragmegrative dynamics from obscuring the complex patterns that sustain the human condition. Accordingly, this summarizing chapter is limited to recounting the utility of role analysis and stressing how communities and countries do and do not manage to accommodate to the diversity of their people in an ever-more complex world.

A major similarity that marks any role involves what might be called "role relationships"—those expectations inherent in a role that pertain to what its occupants are required to think and do as they interact with others in particular situations. The similarities that mark the response of members of Congress to executive officials, for example, are different from those that underlie how they respond to members of their family. The number of relationships built into any role is as great as the variety of other persons with whom its occupants interact.

Given the tensions that can mark interactions among roles, it seems remarkable that normally most families, communities, and societies can contain the tensions sufficiently to move through time intact. Their coherence cannot be taken for granted. The complexity of fragmegrative issues throughout the world is such that role expectations are subjected to continuous challenges. Divorce, factional fighting, and rivalries within families, groups, and communities can bring them to an end, as can rapid transformations of most prevailing situations. Indeed, often it seems more surprising that most collectivities persist intact than that they do on occasion break down.

Coping with Diversity and Complexity

The persistence of most coherent collectivities is more understandable when it is appreciated that few roles have a resort to conflict with other roles embedded in them as expectations. With the exception of the police and military, most roles either lack expectations of conflict with other roles in their larger systems, or they involve limited forms of conflict when tensions mount. The absence of conflict expectations is a major source of the capacity of systems to manage diversity and complexity. In most roles the expectation that their occupants will not undermine the systems in which they are located predominates over other expectations, thus facilitating the management of diversity and minimizing a readiness on the part of role occupants to allow conflicts to degenerate into physical violence.

There are, of course, roles that encompass expectations of resort to violent action under given circumstances. The role of criminal is illustrative in this regard. This is not the case, however, of the soldier's role. Soldiers are expected to use violence against persons outside their system, but directing it toward members of their own system is prohibited.

Avoiding conflict and persisting through time, however, is not the same as creatively and successfully managing diversity. Although most people can accommodate to the expectation of avoiding conflict that fosters violent action, they may nonetheless engage in actions that heighten tension and lead to nonviolent conflicts. Indeed, more than a few roles encompass expectations that encourage resort to nonviolent action under specified circumstances. The role of protesters is illustrative in this regard.

It should be stressed that the diversity of social systems is much greater than the preceding chapters suggest. So as to avoid an encyclopedic presentation, a number of roles have not been subjected to analysis. The roles played by scientists, for example, have not been included. Nor have the various subroles encompassed by the examined roles been investigated. Some artists are musicians, others are painters, still others are architects, and their attitudes and behavior in these subroles may vary systematically from each other even as all of them share some of the aspirations, problems, and expectations embedded in their common, more encompassing role of artist.

Coping with the complexity of social systems is no less difficult than grasping their diversity. Not only are individuals and their subgroups extraordinarily complex, but their complexity is magnified many times when efforts are made to account for the complexity that stems from the presumption that both the individuals and the subgroups sustain networked relationships. Understanding individuals is difficult enough, but viewing them as members of various networks adds a significant measure of challenge to the task. Networks of individuals are not immune to careful and successful analysis, but understanding their behavior in networks requires the inclusion of a wide range of variables that are otherwise held constant and that are not easily probed.

Role Choices

Since everyone occupies a number of roles, which set of expectations a person honors in any situation can amount to a crucial decision. What priority among his or her roles should be given to any set of expectations is normally not built into a role. All roles allow their occupants a measure of choice to freely select among the expectations that may be relevant to the situation in which they find themselves. At the same time all roles, by definition, have boundaries that allow for some choices and preclude others. Is it possible, for example, that the shrinking of time and distance is encouraging networked individuals into seeing themselves as global citizens? Those occupants of a role who ignore and transgress its boundaries are likely to be ineffective at best and ousted from the role at worst. To be sure, role expectations can undergo transformation as the issues and circumstances of the systems in which they are located change. For the most part, however, role expectations are stable and serve to minimize the likelihood of abrupt and swift alterations in the behavior of their occupants.

Indeed, the relative constancy of the expectations that comprise society's roles serves as a barrier to rapid and frequent upheaval. The more circumstances induce pervasive shifts in role expectations, the greater the uncertainties at work in a society. In effect, the stability of micro roles can be a prime source of the stability of macro collectivities, just as the instability of the latter can foster uncertainty in the former.

Conclusion

In short, as our messy and shrinking world becomes ever-more complex, so do the roles that people occupy become increasingly crucial to the course of events. The foregoing chapters have probed only a small sample of the roles that comprise the structure of families, communities, and societies, but clearly more than ever people count!

Notes

Notes for Chapter One

1. *Turbulence in World Politics: A Theory of Change and Continuity* (Princeton, NJ: Princeton University Press, 1990).
2. *Along the Domestic-Foreign Frontier: Exploring Governance in a Turbulent* World (Cambridge: Cambridge University Press, 1997).
3. *Distant Proximities: Dynamics beyond Globalization* (Princeton, NJ: Princeton University Press, 2003).
4. A refined version of the skill revolution is presented here in Chapter 3.
5. Most universities have a rule that limits leaves of absence for government service to two years at a time.

Notes for Chapter Two

1. For an extensive elaboration of this concept, see James N. Rosenau, *Distant Proximities: Dynamics beyond Globalization* (Princeton, NJ: Princeton University Press, 2003).
2. Such an assessment is a central preoccupation of Rosenau, *Distant Proximities*.

Notes for Chapter Three

1. William G. Chase and Herbert A. Simon, "Perception in Chess," *Cognitive Psychology* 4 (1973): 55–81.
2. A cogent and wide-ranging discussion of the knowledge explosion can be found in Paul R. Ehrlich et al., "Knowledge and the Environment," *Ecological Economics* 30 (1999): 267–284.
3. For a cogent discussion of emotional skills, see Daniel Goleman, *Emotional Intelligence* (New York: Bantam Books, 1995).
4. The links between the imagination and skills are compellingly developed in Arjun Appadurai, *Modernity at Large: Cultural Dimensions of Globalization* (Minneapolis: University of Minnesota Press, 1996).
5. James N. Rosenau and W. Michael Fagen, "Increasingly Skillful Citizens: A New Dynamism in World Politics?" *International Studies Quarterly* 41 (December 1997): 655–686.
6. It should be noted, however, that sixteen of the twenty countries are in Europe or the English-speaking world, two are predominantly of European culture (Israel and urban Brazil), and two are Asian (Japan and urban China). James R. Flynn, "IQ Gains over Time:

Toward Finding the Causes," in Ulric Neisser, ed., *The Rising Curve: Long-Term Gains in IQ and Related Measures* (Washington, DC: American Psychological Association, 1998), 26.

7. See the various essays in Neisser, *The Rising Curve.*

8. An elaborate set of data depicting educational enrollments across twenty-five years in every country but North Korea can be found in James N. Rosenau, *Turbulence in World Politics: A Theory of Change and Continuity* (Princeton, NJ: Princeton University Press, 1990), 358–360.

9. All the quoted observations can be found in Steven Johnson, "Dome Improvement," *Wired* (May 2005), available at http://www.wired.com/wired/archive/13.05/flynn_pr.html. p4. For an elaboration of the notion that television and video games serve as sources of the skill revolution, see Steven Johnson, "Watching TV Makes You Smarter," *New York Times Magazine,* April 24, 2005, 55–60, and Steven Johnson, *Everything Bad Is Good for You: How Today's Culture Is Actually Making Us Smarter* (New York: Riverhead Books, 2005). See also Seth Schiesel, "Redefining the Power of Games," *New York Times,* June 7, 2005, E1.

10. Matt Slagle, "Poll: 4 in 40 Play Electronic Games," May 7, 2006, available at http://www.ap-ipsoresults.com.

11. For data on computer access and global television, see, respectively, Jonathan Aronson, "Global Networks and Their Impact," in James N. Rosenau and J. P. Singh, eds., *Information Technologies and Global Politics: The Changing Scope of Power and Governance* (Albany: State University of New York Press, 2002), 43, 46; and Rosenau, *Turbulence in World Politics,* 339–342.

12. Gretchen Ruethling, "Almost All Libraries in the U.S. Offer Free Access to Internet," *New York Times,* June 24, 2005, A14.

13. Sharon LeFraniere, "Cellphones Catapult Rural Africa to 21st Century," *New York Times,* August 25, 2005, A1.

14. Editorial, "Measuring the Blogosphere," *New York Times,* August 5, 2005, 14.

15. Matt Richtel, "The Lure of Data: Is It Addictive?" *New York Times,* July 6, 2003, sec. 3, p. 1.

16. Alma Tugend, "Making the Flight, without the Stress," *New York Times,* April 28, 2007, p. C5.

17. James N. Rosenau, *Distant Proximities: Dynamics beyond Globalization* (Princeton, NJ: Princeton University Press, 2004), 63–65.

Notes for Chapter Four

1. A recently married marketing expert, quoted in Michael Specter, "Population Implosion Worries a Graying Europe," *New York Times,* July 10, 1998, A6.

2. A thirty-one-year-old biologist who works in Sweden, quoted in ibid.

3. See, for example, Stephen Kinzer, "$650 a Baby: Germany to Pay to Stem Decline in Births," *New York Times,* November 25, 1994, A4.

4. Ibid.

5. Norimitsu Onishi, "South Korea, in Turnabout, Now Calls for More Babies," *New York Times,* August 21, 2005, 4.

6. Ibid.

7. C. J. Chivers, "Putin Urges Plan to Reverse Slide in the Birthrate," *New York Times,* May 11, 2006, A1.

8. Editorial, "Mr. Putin's State of the Union," *New York Times,* May 12, 2006, A26.

9. A sharp declination of the birthrates in the countries of the former Soviet Union

after the Cold War ended offers a striking illustration of the puzzle posed by demographic trends. See Nicholas Eberstadt, "Marx and Mortality: A Mystery," *New York Times*, April 6, 1994, A21; and Michael Specter, "Climb in Russia's Death Rate Sets Off Population Implosion," *New York Times*, March 6, 1994, 1.

10. Quoted in Specter, "Population Implosion Worries a Graying Europe," A1.

11. Ibid., A6.

12. Reuters, "Japan: It's Just What the Doctor Ordered," *New York Times*, June 23, 2006, A14.

13. William Fry, a demographer, quoted in Richard Bernstein, "An Aging Europe May Find Itself on the Sidelines," *New York Times*, July 6, 2003, 3.

14. Bernstein, "An Aging Europe May Find Itself on the Sidelines," 3.

15. Ibid.

16. Karin Strohecker, "Germans Urged to Be More Fruitful," *Washington Times*, January 21, 2006, A1.

17. William Branigin, "White-Collar Visas: Imported Need Skills or Cheap Labor?" *Washington Post*, October 21, 1995, A1.

18. Pam Belluck, "Short of People, Iowa Seeks to Be Ellis Island of Midwest," *New York Times*, August 28, 2000, A1.

19. Roger Cohen, "Europe's Love-Hate Affair with Foreigners," *New York Times*, October 24, 2000, sec. 4, 1.

20. Nurith C. Aizenman, "At the War's End: A Conflict in Duties," *Washington Post*, April 19, 2003, B1.

Notes for Chapter Five

1. In some twenty countries, citizens pay a fine if they do not vote. This does not include authoritarian countries, which do not hold competitive elections; in those countries voters are, in effect, coerced to vote on a ballot that lists the leader as the only choice. A listing of the countries that require nonvoters to pay a fine is available at http://www.idea.int/vt/compulsory_voting.cfm.

2. Thomas E. Patterson, *The Vanishing Voter: Public Involvement in an Age of Uncertainty* (New York: Knopf, 2002), 84.

3. Normally the wait is not more than a few days in most countries. In the case of presidential elections in the United States, the results are usually known early in the morning of the day after the election. The outcome in the 2000 election, however, was so close that it took thirty-six days before George W. Bush was declared the winner. A close vote in the 2006 Mexican presidential election also resulted in a long delay before the winner was announced. In this case, moreover, the delay was marked by considerable tensions and mobilized street protests.

4. Walter Kirn, "Don't Count Me In," *New York Times Magazine*, April 6, 2003, 15–16.

5. For a study of the flow of postal mail (in the days before e-mail) from the public to newspapers, as well as the White House and Congress, see James N. Rosenau, *Citizenship between Elections: An Inquiry into the Mobilizable American* (New York: Free Press, 1974).

6. Matthew Ericson, "The (Inexact) Science of Crowd Counts," *New York Times*, March 23, 2003, sec. 4, 3.

7. Matthew A. Crenson and Benjamin Ginsberg, *Downsizing Democracy: How America Sidelined Its Citizens and Privatized Its Public* (Baltimore, MD: Johns Hopkins University Press, 2002), 21.

8. Ibid., 46.

9. Ronald Inglehart and Gabriela Catterberg, "Trends in Political Action: The Developmental Trend and the Post-Honeymoon Decline," *International Journal of Comparative Sociology* 44 (March 2003): 300–316.

10. Ibid., 301.

11. Pippa Norris, "Global Governance and Cosmopolitan Citizens," in David Held and Anthony McGrew, eds., *The Global Transformations Reader: An Introduction to the Globalization Debate*, 2nd ed. (Cambridge: Polity Press, 2003), 295.

12. The notion that citizenship is in crisis around the world is a central theme of Stephen Castles and Alastair Davidson, *Citizenship and Migration: Globalization and the Politics of Belonging* (New York: Routledge, 2000), 156.

13. In 2004, twenty-four countries permitted resident aliens to vote in their elections. David C. Earnest, "Voting Rights for Resident Aliens: Nationalism, Postnationalism, and Sovereignty in an Era of Mass Migration," PhD diss., George Washington University (Washington, DC, 2004).

14. James Brooke, "A Campaign as Japanese as Baseball and Apple Pie," *New York Times*, April 24, 2003, A4.

15. Jon Henley, "End Right to Citizenship by Birth, Says French Minister," *Guardian*, September 21, 2005.

16. Warren Vieth, "GOP Faction Wants to Change 'Birthright Citizenship' Policy," *Los Angeles Times*, December 10, 2005.

17. See, for example, Carol Morello, "Granting a Wish to a Slain Marine: Citizenship Conferred on Vietnam Native," *Washington Post*, January 28, 2005, B1.

18. Yvonne Abraham, "Test of Principles, Not Presidents: U.S. Will Redesign Citizenship Exam," *Boston Globe*, January 22, 2006.

19. Lynda Hurst, "Canada among First to Allow Dual Citizenships," *Toronto Star*, August 20, 2005, A1.

20. Ingrid Peritz, "Uproar as Artists Turn Back on Sovereignty," *Globe and Mail*, April 13, 2006, A1.

Notes for Chapter Six

1. A thirty-three-year-old airline flight attendant born in Turkey, who arrived in Denmark at the age of two, quoted in Roger Cohen, "For 'New Danes,' Differences Create a Divide," *New York Times*, December 18, 2000, A1.

2. J. W. Meyer, "The Changing Cultural Context of the Nation-State."

3. Table 6.1 is reproduced from Stephen Castles and Alastair Davidson, *Citizenship and Migration: Globalization and the Politics of Belonging* (New York: Routledge, 2000), 65.

4. U.S. immigration policy became much tighter subsequent to September 11, 2001, though the probabilities are high that it will not become so tight as to undermine the need for certain skills that are in short supply.

5. Carlotta Gall, "China's Migrants Find Europe's Open Back Door: The Balkans," *New York Times*, August 22, 2000, A1.

6. R. Jeffrey Smith, "Nightly, a Furtive Invasion via Italy," *International Herald Tribune*, July 24, 2000, 1.

7. Norimitsu Onishi, "Out of Africa or Bust, with a Desert to Cross," *New York Times*, January 4, 2001, A1.

8. Roger Cohen, "Illegal Migration Increases Sharply in European Union," *New York Times*, December 25, 2000, A1.

9. Steven Erlanger, "Poland Finds Itself the Border Cop of West Europe," *New York Times,* August 28, 2000, A3.

10. Some 1.5 million Mexicans are arrested annually trying to cross the border illegally, with one per day dying in the effort. Tim Weiner, "Mexico Chief Pushes New Border Policy: Free and Easy Does It," *New York Times,* December 14, 2000, A14. For a lengthy and compelling analysis of this flow of illegal immigrants, see Peter Andreas, *Border Games: Policing the U.S.-Mexico Line* (Ithaca, NY: Cornell University Press, 2000).

11. Human Rights Watch, *Human Rights News* (March 2, 2004).

12. A severe Australian policy that put undocumented refugees—"boat people"—in mandatory detention centers was moderated five years and several sea disasters after its adoption. Raymond Bonner, "Pressed, Australian Leader Makes Changes in Handling of Refugees," *New York Times,* June 20, 2005, A7.

13. Steven Erlanger, "The Gypsies of Slovakia: Despised and Despairing," *New York Times,* April 3, 2000, A10.

14. Sarah Lyall, "Irish Now Face the Other Side of Immigration," *New York Times,* July 8, 2000, A6.

15. Ibid.

16. Roger Cohen, "The German 'Volk' Seen Set to Let Outsiders In," *New York Times,* October 16, 1998, A4.

17. Roger Cohen, "German Faults 'Silence' about Attacks on Immigrants," *New York Times,* August 1, 2000, A7.

18. Roger Cohen, "Call for 'Guiding Culture' Rekindles Political Debate in Germany," New York Times, November 5, 2000, 10.

19. Sarah Lyall, "Britain Raises Barriers High against the Asylum Seekers," *New York Times,* April 3, 2000, A1. For a discussion of the problem of asylum seekers throughout the European Union, see Deborah Hargreaves, "Borderline Cases," *Financial Times,* October 17, 1999, 8.

20. Available at www.abroadviewmagazine.com/fall03/dutch_politics.html. See also Roger Cohen, "A Danish Identity Crisis: Are We Europeans?" *New York Times,* September 10, 2000, 1.

21. Donald G. McNeil Jr., "Europeans Move against Austrians on Nativist Party," *New York Times,* February 1, 2000, A1.

22. David C. Unger, "How Immigrants Are Transforming the Politics of Europe," *New York Times,* November 30, 2002, A30.

23. President Franklin D. Roosevelt once addressed the Daughters of the American Revolution, a conservative organization, with the salutation, "Fellow Immigrants."

24. "One U.S. Resident in Ten Is Now Foreign Born," *New York Times,* September 19, 1999, 37.

25. James Dao, "Immigrant Diversity Slows Traditional Political Climb," *New York Times,* December 28, 1999, A1.

26 Anthony DePalma, "'A Tyrannical Situation': Farmers Face Conflict over Illegal Workers," *New York Times,* October 3, 2000, C1.

27. D'Vera Cohn, "Immigrants Account for Half of New Workers," *Washington Post,* December 2, 2002, A1.

28. Jane Gross, "For Latino Laborers, Dual Lives," *New York Times,* January 5, 2000, B1.

29. John Micklethwait, "How the U.S. Is Changing Colour," *Strait Times,* March 19, 2000, 48.

30. Rachel L. Swarns, "House Votes for 698 Miles of Fences on Mexico Border," *New York Times,* December 16, 2005, A31.

31. Associated Press, "Parts of U.S.-Canadian Border Disappear in Brush as Maintenance Money Is Tight," *New York Times,* April 4, 2004, 21.

32. Ceclia W. Dugger, "U.S. Plan to Lure Nurses May Hurt Poor Nations," *New York Times,* May 24, 2006, A1.

33. Ginger Thompson, "A Surge in Money Sent Home by Mexicans," *New York Times,* October 28, 2003, A12.

34. The data on remittances are reproduced from Cerstin Sander, "Migrant Remittances to Developing Countries" (Bannock Consulting/UK Department of International Development, 2003), 6, available at http://www/bannock.co.uk/PDF/remittances.pdf.

35. Using a "make money, help the motherland" theme, India has sought to increase the remittances by offering Indians abroad a government-guaranteed bond at 7.75 percent interest. Somini Sengupta, "India Taps into Its Diaspora," *New York Times,* August 19, 1998, B1.

36. Laurie Goldstein, "To Bind the Faith, Free Trips to Israel for Diaspora Youth," *New York Times,* November 16, 1998, B8.

37. Six of these problems are outlined in Benjamin Pauker and Michele Wucker, "Diminishing Returns: For Developing Nations, Cash Sent Home Is a Net Loss," *Harper's Magazine,* December 2005, 68–69.

38. Jan Aart Scholte, *Globalization: A Critical Introduction* (New York: St. Martin's, 2000), 180.

39. Cohen, "A Danish Identity Crisis," 1.

40. "Ranking the Rich," *Foreign Policy* (May–June 2003): 56–66.

41. Cohen, "A Danish Identity Crisis," 10.

42. Randal C. Archibold, "Strategy Sessions Fueled Immigrant Marches," *New York Times,* April 12, 2006, A16.

43. Robert D. McFadden, "Across the U.S., Growing Rallies for Immigration," *New York Times,* May 10, 2006, A1.

44. Monica Davey, "For Immigrants and Business, Rift on Protests," *New York Times,* April 15, 2006, A1.

45. For a similar four-category formulation in which distinctions are drawn among assimilation, exclusion, integration, and multiculturalism, see Stanley J. Tambiah, "Transnational Movements, Diaspora, and Multiple Modernities," *Daedalus* 29, no. 1 (2000): 167–168.

46. A more extensive discussion of the four categories and the hybrids located among them can be found in James N. Rosenau, *Distant Proximities: Dynamics beyond Globalization* (Princeton, NJ: Princeton University Press, 2003), 193–196. Good examples of hybrids are provided in the next chapter. For another formulation organized around the notion of new transnational spaces, see Thomas Faist, "International Migration and Transnational Social Spaces: Their Evolution, Significance and Future Prospects" (Bremen: Institut für Interkulturelle und Internationale Studien, 1998).

47. Tambiah, "Transnational Movements, Diaspora, and Multiple Modernities," 170.

Notes for Chapter Seven

1. Reproduced from James N. Rosenau, *Distant Proximities: Dynamics beyond Globalization* (Princeton, NJ: Princeton University Press, 2003), 184–185.

2. Virginia Barreiro, graduate student in the Elliott School of George Washington University. The quote is from a paper she wrote for a course on the Dynamics of Globalization (March 1999).

3. James H. Liu, senior lecturer in social psychology at the Victoria University of

Wellington, New Zealand. The quote is a composite of comments from notes for a paper entitled, "The Psychology of Fragmegration."

4. Mark Nerney, undergraduate student at the Elliott School of George Washington University. The quote is from a paper he wrote for a course on the Dynamics of Globalization (December 2000).

5. Tiger Woods, golfer; quote available at http//204.202.128.130/archive/news/Todays_Stories/970423/4_23_97_woods.htm.

6. George Konrad, *Antipolitics* (New York: Harcourt Brace Jovanovich, 1984), 209.

7. For data on the background of cosmopolitans, see J. N. Rosenau et al., *On the Cutting Edge of Globalization: An Inquiry into American Elites* (Lanham, MD: Rowman and Littlefield, 2006), 42–44.

8. Benjamin R. Barber, *Jihad vs. McWorld* (New York: Times Books, 1995), 16–17.

9. Ulf Hannerz, "Cosmopolitans and Locals in World Culture," in Mike Featherstone, ed., *Global Culture: Nationalism, Globalization, and Modernity* (London: Sage Publications, 1990), 239.

10. Christopher Lasch, *The Revolt of the Elites and the Betrayal of Democracy* (New York: W. W. Norton, 1995), 34.

11. Peter L. Berger, "Four Faces of Global Culture," *The National Interest*, no. 49 (Fall 1997), 24.

12. Hannerz, "Cosmopolitans and Locals in World Culture," 240–241.

13. Lasch, *The Revolt of the Elites and the Betrayal of Democracy*, 6.

14. Ibid., 35.

15. Barber, *Jihad vs. McWorld*, 17.

16. Ibid., 29.

17. Lasch, *The Revolt of the Elites and the Betrayal of Democracy*, 47.

18. Robert Reich, *The Work of Nations: Preparing Ourselves for 21st-Century Capitalism* (New York: Alfred A. Knopf, 1991), 304.

19. Ibid., 309.

20. Jonathan Friedman, *Cultural Identity and Global Process* (London: Sage Publications, 1994), 86.

21. Ibid., 204.

Notes for Chapter Eight

1. Available at http://tinet.ita.dc.gov/view/f-2005-05-001/Arrivals%20Departure.

2. Ibid.

3. Howard W. French, "Next Wave of Camera-Wielding Tourists Is from China," *New York Times*, May 17, 2006, A3.

4. Nicola Clark and Matthew L. Wald, "Hurdle for U.S. in Getting Data on Passengers," *New York Times*, May 31, 2006, A9.

5. Available at http://world-tourism.org/aboutwto/eng/aboutwto.htm, 13.

6. French, "Next Wave of Camera-Wielding Tourists Is from China," A3.

7. "Airport Crowds," *New York Times*, May 23, 2006, C9.

8. John Tagliabue, "The Gauls at Home in Erin," *New York Times*, June 2, 2006, C7.

9. Donald E. Lundberg, M. Krishnamoorthy, and Mink H. Stavenga, *Tourism Economics* (New York: Wiley, 1995).

10. Joel Garreau, "Home Is Where the Phone Is: Roaming Legion of High-Tech Nomads Takes Happily to Ancient Path," *Washington Post*, October 17, 2000, A1.

11. Sidney Tarrow, *The New Transnational Activism* (New York: Cambridge University Press, 2005), chap. 3.

12. For empirical data on the local–global balances maintained by rooted cosmopolitans, see James N. Rosenau et al., *On the Cutting Edge of Globalization: An Inquiry into American Elites* (Lanham, MD: Rowman and Littlefield, 2005), 54–56.

13. Alessandra Stanley, "For Ambitious Entrepreneurs, All Europe Is Just One Nation," *New York Times,* December 14, 1998, A1.

Notes for Chapter Nine

1. Jonathan Schell, "The Other Superpower," *Nation,* April 14, 2003, 12. See also Patrick E. Tyler, "A New Power in the Streets," *New York Times,* February 17, 2003.

2. Howard French, "Power to the People: Activists Rise in China," *New York Times,* April 12, 2006.

3. For an extensive listing of guidelines that activists might follow to be successful in their efforts, see http//www.casagordita.com/tools.htm.

Notes for Chapter Ten

1. Scott Shane, "Fighting Locally, Fighting Globally," *New York Times,* July 16, 2006, sec. 4, 1, citing the research of Robert A. Pape in *Dying to Win: The Strategic Logic of Suicide Terrorism* (New York: Random House, 2005).

2. Ibid.

3. Robert A. Pape, "Al Qaeda's Smart Bombs," *New York Times,* July 9, 2006, A13.

4. Jo Thomas, "New Face of Terror Crimes: 'Lone Wolf' Weaned on Hate," *New York Times,* August 16, 1999, A16.

5. Amy Waldman, "Seething Unease Shaped British Bombers' Newfound Zeal," *New York Times,* July 31, 2005, A10.

6. Douglas Jehl, "Experts Fear Suicide Bomb Is Spreading into the West," *New York Times,* July 13, 2005, A10.

7. Dan Eggen and Scott Wilson, "Suicide Bombs Potent Tools of Terrorists," *Washington Post,* July 17, 2005, A1.

8. Josi Glausiusz, "The Surprises of Suicide Terrorism: Interview with Anthropologist Scott Atran," *Discover Magazine* 24 (October 2003): 2, available at http://www.discover.com/oct_03/gthere.thml?article=fetdialogue.html.

9. James Bennet, "How 2 Took the Path of Suicide Bombers," *New York Times,* July 30, 2003, A1.

10. Nicholas D. Kristof, "All-American Osamas," *New York Times,* June 7, 2002, 27.

11. Glausiusz, "The Surprises of Suicide Terrorism," 2.

12. Ibid.

13. Craig Whitlock, "Keeping Al-Qaeda in His Grip: Al-Zawahiri Presses Ideology, Deepens Rifts among Islamic Radicals," *Washington Post,* April 16, 2006, A1.

Notes for Chapter Eleven

1. Since soldiers in armies carry out most of these tasks, they are the focus of the ensuing discussion. Personnel in navies and air forces are, of course, also central to the war-fighting capacities of countries, but here the main focus is on the officers and enlisted men and women assigned to fighting or working on the ground. Also excluded from the analysis are

persons who perform military functions under private contracts rather than as members of a country's armed forces. For a host of reasons, the ranks of those privately affiliated with armed forces are growing, though their numbers are relatively small compared to those in government uniforms.

2. After the terrorist attacks of September 11, 2001, a small proportion of those who volunteered for service in the U.S. Army were moved to do so out of a sense of patriotic duty during a perceived national crisis.

3. Samuel A. Stouffer et al., *The American Soldier: Combat and Its Aftermath*, vol. 2 (Princeton, NJ: Princeton University Press, 1949), chap. 3.

4. Bob Herbert, "Uncle Sam Really Wants You," *New York Times*, June 16, 2005, 27.

5. Bob Herbert, "The Army's Hard Sell," *New York Times*, June 27, 2005, A15.

6. Seth Mydans, "New Violence Puts Indonesia's Military at a Crossroads," *New York Times*, November 16, 1998, A3.

7. Steven Erlanger, "Russia's Military in Need of New Goals," *New York Times*, May 23, 1994, A5.

8. Available at http://www.amnestyusa.org/children/document.do?id= B0275B42F3B4C25380256900006933EF.

9. David J. Francis, "International Conventions and the Limitations for Protecting Child Soldiers in Post-Conflict Societies in Africa," in W. Andy Knight, ed., *Children and War: Impact, Protection, and Rehabilitation* (Calgary: University of Alberta Press, 2006), 8.

10. The table is available at http://www.wrei.org/projects/wiv/wim/t7.pdf.

11. Eric Schmitt, "First Woman in 6 Decades Gets the Army's Silver Star," *New York Times*, June 17, 2005, A16.

12. See, for example, Damien Cave, "Normally Quiet, a Military Town Talks of Casualties," *New York Times*, June 27, 2005, A10.

13. Aaron Belkin, "Don't Ask, Don't Tell, Don't Work: A Ten-Year Evaluation of Military Personnel Policy Concerning Homosexuality," available at http://online.logcabin. org/issues/gay_military_LEF_White_Paper.html (2003).

14. See, for example, James Brooke, "Brazil's Army Joins Battle against Drugs," *New York Times*, November 20, 1994, 4.

15. Rare incidents in South Korea suggest another consequence that can follow from the requirement to follow orders. At least twice soldiers have killed fellow soldiers on the grounds that they had been habitually harassed by their seniors. See Norimitsu Onishi, "South Korean Private Kills 8 Soldiers after Being Hazed," *New York Times*, June 20, 2005, A6.

16. Owing to a technological innovation whereby handheld computers have the potential of becoming standard equipment for all the members of a military unit, the hierarchical structure of such units may undergo change. The technology provides all the members of the unit with the same information about their combat circumstances, thus tending to reduce the unit's degree of hierarchy. Joel Garreau, "Point Men for a Revolution: Can the Marines Survive a Shift from Hierarchies to Networks," *Washington Post*, March 6, 1999, A1.

17. Quoted anonymously in Eric Schmitt and Thomas Shanker, "Posts Considered for Commanders after Abuse Case," *New York Times*, June 20, 2005, A1.

18. Thomas Shanker and Eric Schmitt, "Young Officers Join the Debate over Rumsfeld," *New York Times*, April 23, 2006, 1.

19. Thomas Shanker, "Young Officers Leaving Army at a High Rate," *New York Times*, April 10, 2006, A1.

Notes for Chapter Twelve

1. Monica Davey and David Leonhardt, "Jobless and Hopeless, Many Quit the Labor Force," *New York Times,* April 27, 2003, A1.

2. Codirector of international migration policy at the Carnegie Endowment for International Peace, quoted in Steven Greenhouse, "Foreign Workers at Highest Level in Seven Decades," *New York Times,* September 4, 2000, A1.

3. Development director at United Students against Sweatshops, quoted in David Gonzales, "Latin Sweatshops Pressed by U.S. Campus Power," *New York Times,* April 4, 2003, A3.

4. See Gustavo Capdevila, "Global Unemployment Rises to One Billion, Says ILO Report," Geneva: InterPress Service, November 26, 1996.

5. Davey and Leonhardt, "Jobless and Hopeless, Many Quit the Labor Force."

6. Quoted in Clifford Krauss, "Some Skilled Foreigners Find Jobs Scarce in Canada," *New York Times,* June 5, 2005, 6.

7. Thomas L. Friedman, *The World Is Flat: A Brief History of the Twenty-first Century* (New York: Farrar, Straus, and Giroux, 2005), 217.

8. Peter T. Kilborn, "Job Security Hinges on Skills, Not on an Employer for Life," *New York Times,* March 12, 1994, 1.

9. Robert B. Reich, *The Work of Nations: Preparing Ourselves for 21st-Century Capitalism* (New York: Knopf, 1991).

10. See, for example, Chidanand Rajghatia, "American Firm Reverses Outsourcing to India," *Times of India,* April 22, 2003.

11. Greenhouse, "Foreign Workers at Highest Level in Seven Decades."

12. Claire Fagin and Corinne Rieder, "Nursing Wounds," *New York Times,* June 10, 2003, A27.

13. Steven G. Friedman, "Anyone in the O.R.?" *New York Times,* June 10, 2003, A27.

14. Torben Iversen and David Soskice, "An Asset Theory of Social Policy Preferences," *American Political Science Review* 95 (December 2001): 875–893.

15. Gonzales, "Latin Sweatshops Pressed by U.S. Campus Power."

16. Mark Landler, "West Europe Is Hard Hit by Strikes over Pensions," *New York Times,* June 4, 2003, A6.

17. Mary Williams Walsh, "Pension Bill Cuts Amounts Put Aside for Union Workers," *New York Times,* May 6, 2003, A1.

Notes for Chapter Thirteen

1. Substantial data descriptive of these distinctions can be found in James N. Rosenau et al., *On the Cutting Edge of Globalization: An Inquiry into American Elites* (Lanham, MD: Rowman and Littlefield, 2005).

2. David Woodruff, "Across Europe CEOs Get No Respect," *Wall Street Journal Europe,* June 17, 2002, A9.

3. Jeffrey E. Garten, former dean of the Yale School of Management, quoted in William J. Holstein, "Armchair M.B.A.: Are Business Schools Failing the World?" *New York Times,* June 19, 2005, sec. 3, 13.

4. John J. Fahy, commenting on the Tyco trial, in Kurt Eichenwald, "Big Paycheck Is Exhibit A," *New York Times,* June 19, 2004, 20.

5. Ira Lee Sorkin, in Eichenwald, "Big Paycheck Is Exhibit A."

6. Eichenwald, "Big Paycheck Is Exhibit A," 1.

7. Geraldine Fabrikant, "Executives Take Company Planes as if Their Own," *New York Times,* May 10, 2006, A1. See also Andrew Ross Sorkin and Eric Dash, "Private Firms Lure C.E.O.s with Top Pay," *New York Times,* January 8, 2007, A1.

8. David S. Hilzenrath, "For Many Top Executives, It's Ask and You Shall Receive," *Washington Post,* June 27, 2005, D1.

9. Jad Mouawad, "For Leading Exxon to Its Riches, $144,573 a Day," *New York Times,* April 15, 2006, A1.

10. Gretchen Morgenson, "Outside Advice on Boss's Pay May Not Be So Independent," *New York Times,* April 10, 2006, A1.

11. David Leonhardt, "Who's in the Corner Office?" *New York Times,* November 27, 2005, 1.

12. A qualification is in order here. Some twenty-eight business schools throughout the world have developed courses or programs in social entrepreneurship, a focus that highlights societal problems rather than simply the profitability of businesses. See Emily Eakin, "How to Save the World? Treat It Like a Business," *New York Times,* December 20, 2003, A19.

13. Garten, quoted in Holstein, "Armchair M.B.A."

14. Steve Lohr, "New Economy: 'Scenario Planning' Explores the Many Routes Chaos Could Take for Business in These Very Uncertain Days," *New York Times,* April 7, 2003, C3.

15. Survey conducted by the Center for Global Assignments, in Robert E. Abueva, "Expatriate, Ex-Employee: When Returnees Don't Fit," *International Herald Tribune,* May 18, 2000, 11.

16. Rosenau et al., *On the Cutting Edge of Globalization,* chap. 4.

Notes for Chapter Fourteen

1. Available at http://news.bbc.uk/2/hi/uk_news/politics/3099378.stm.

2. For example, see www.washingtonpost.com/wpdyn/content/article/2006/11/01/AR2006110103269.html.

Notes for Chapter Fifteen

1. For an incisive analysis of the consumer and advertiser roles, see Benjamin Barber, *Consumed: How Markets Corrupt Children, Infantilize Adults, and Swallow Citizens Whole* (New York: W. W. Norton, 2007).

2. J. Mandese, "Internet Wasn't a Blip, the Recession Was: Report Defines a 'New Media Order,'" *Economist,* August 16, 2005.

3. B. Streisand and R. Newman, "The New Media Elites," *U.S. News and World Report,* November 14, 2005.

4. Available at http//www/consumersinternational.org.

5. Available at http//europa.eu.int/pol/cons/index_en.htm.

6. Lars Perner, "The Psychology of Consumers: Consumer Behavior and Marketing," available at http://www.consumerpsychologist.com (italics in the original).

7. Simone Pettigrew, "Consumption and the Ideal Life," *JRConsumers* 9 (2005), available at http//web.biz.uwa.edu.au/research/jrconsumers/consumer/cons_article.asp.

8. Available at http//www.dmaconsumers.org/offmailinglist.html.

9. Leslie Wayner, "Think Globally, Flirt Locally," *New York Times,* June 17, 2005, C6.

Notes for Chapter Sixteen

1. Robert D. Putnam and Kristin A. Goss, "Introduction," in Robert D. Putnam, ed., *Democracies in Flux: The Evolution of Social Capital in Contemporary Society* (New York: Oxford University Press, 2002), 8.

2. As this sentence implies, networks and relationships can embrace essentially the same phenomena. The advent of the Internet, however, has highlighted the extent to which networks may be less intimate than relationships inasmuch as many of them exist in cyberspace and, unlike relationships, are less likely to involve face-to-face interactions. Indeed, the proliferation of networks in cyberspace has led me to refer to people as "networked individuals" rather than simply as "individuals."

3. Pierre Bourdieu, quoted in Putnam and Goss, "Introduction," 5.

4. Ibid., 3.

5. Putnam, *Democracies in Flux*.

6. Jonathon Aronson, "Global Networks and Their Impact," in James N. Rosenau and J. P. Singh, eds., *Information Technologies and Global Politics: The Changing Scope of Power and Governance* (Albany: State University of New York Press, 2002), 46.

7. R. Alan Hedley, *Running Out of Control: Dilemmas of Globalization* (Bloomfield, CT: Kumarian Press, 2002), 44.

8. Internet Usage Statistics, November 20, 2006, available at http://internetworldstats.com/stats.htm.

9. Thomas L. Friedman, "Have I Got Mail," *New York Times,* June 8, 2003, sec. 4, 13.

10. June Kronholz, "After the Science Fair: Dear World, Please Stop Writing Me," *Wall Street Journal,* February 13, 2003, 1.

11. Anitha Reddy, "108 People per Second Tell FTC Hotline: 'Do Not Call,'" *Washington Post,* June 28, 2003, A1.

12. It should be noted, however, that even though most online interactions do not culminate in face-to-face contacts, some do. Evidence of this possibility can be seen in social network sites such as Friendster or MySpace, organizing networks such as MeetUp, and dating sites such as eHarmony or Match.com.

13. For a comparison of cyberspace and face-to-face networks working on the same issue (rebuilding ground zero in New York City), see Amy Harmon, "Vox Populi, Online," *New York Times,* September 26, 2003, E1.

14. "People Power" (editorial), *New York Times,* April 12, 2006, A22.

15. Amy Harmon, "Sad, Lonely World Discovered in Cyberspace," *New York Times,* August 30, 1998, 1.

16. Ibid., 22.

17. Katharine Q. Seelye, "Hands-on-Readers: Why Newspapers Are Betting on Audience Participation," *New York Times,* July 4, 2005, C1.

18. Manuel Castells, *The Rise of the Network Society* (Cambridge, MA: Blackwell, 1996), 469.

Notes for Chapter Seventeen

1. Adam Cohen, "Could a 15-Year-Old with a Laptop Be the Next Campaign Media Guru?" *New York Times,* June 14, 2005, A22.

2. Available at http://www.blogger.com/tour_start.g.

3. For a finding that a majority of bloggers are still in high school, see http://perseus.com/blogsurvey/iceberg.html.

4. For an analysis in which it is asserted that increasingly journalists are circulating their articles through the World Wide Web, see Katharine Seelye, "For Journalists, Politics Not as Usual," *New York Times,* January 8, 2007, C1.

5. For a lengthy account of this sorry episode in the history of the paper, see Dan Barry et al., "Correcting the Record; *Times* Reporter Who Resigned Leaves Long Trail of Deception," *New York Times,* May 11, 2003.

6. Sheryl Gay Stolberg, "Bush Says Report on Bank Data Was Disgraceful," *New York Times,* June 27, 2006, A1.

7. Charles Babington, "The House GOP Chastises Media," *Washington Post,* June 30, 2006, A25.

8. A succinct analysis of these issues was coauthored by the editors of the *Los Angeles Times* and the executive editor of the *New York Times*; see Dean Baquet and Bill Keller, "When Do We Publish a Secret?" *New York Times,* July 1, 2006, A27. Subsequently, the *New York Times'* public editor, Byron Calame, "who serves as the readers' representative," responded to "roughly 1,000 e-mails" he received, "about 85 percent of them critical of the decision to publish the story and a large fraction venomous," by writing a column in which he argued his paper "was right to publish the financial-data story." See "Secrecy, Security, the President and the Press," *New York Times,* July 2, 2006, sec. 4, 10.

9. Quoted in Carl Hulse, "House Assails Media on Disclosing the Tracking of Finances," *New York Times,* June 30, 2006, A4.

10. Tina Rosenberg, "The Long, Hard Road of Investigative Reporting in Latin America," *New York Times,* July 2, 2006, sec. 4, 9.

Notes for Chapter Eighteen

1. Daniel Philpott, "The Challenge of September 11 to Secularism in International Relations," *World Politics* 55 (October 2002): 68.

2. Douglas Miller, the president of Environics International, quoted in Peter Steinfels, "Restoring Trust in Religion," *New York Times,* January 18, 2003, A14.

3. Three of the forty-four countries are not included in Table 18.1 because the question was viewed as too sensitive in Egypt, Jordan, and Lebanon, and the question was not permitted in the Chinese survey.

4. Lizette Alvarez, "Fury, God, and the Pastor's Disbelief," *New York Times,* July 8, 2003, A4.

5. Samuel Loewenberg, "As Spaniards Lose Their Religion, Church Leaders Struggle to Hold On," *New York Times,* June 26, 2005, sec. 4, 4.

6. Craig S. Smith, "A Casualty on Romania's Road Back from Atheism," *New York Times,* July 3, 2005, 3.

7. Frank Bruni, "Faith Fades Where It Once Burned Strong," *New York Times,* October 13, 2003, A1.

8. Ibid.

9. Somini Sengupta and Larry Rohter, "Where Faith Grows, Fired by Pentecostalism," *New York Times,* October 14, 2003, A1.

10. Michael Luo, "Billy Graham Returns to Find Evangelical Force in New York," *New York Times,* June 21, 2005, A1.

11. Neela Banerjee, "Methodist Divisions over Gays Intensify," *New York Times,* October 21, 2005, A16.

12. Laurie Goodstein and Neela Banerjee, "Anglican Plan Threatens Split on Gay Issues,"

New York Times, June 28, 2006, A1; and Laurie Goodstein, "Episcopalians Shaken by Division in Church," *New York Times,* July 2, 2006, 10.

13. Jane Perlez, "Saudis Quietly Promote Strict Islam in Indonesia," *New York Times,* July 5, 2003, A3.

14. John Lancaster, "Reshaping Pakistan along Religious Lines," *Washington Post,* June 20, 2003, A1.

15. Laurie Goodstein, "Seeing Islam as 'Evil' Faith, Evangelicals Seek Converts," *New York Times,* May 27, 2003, A1.

16. Michael Slackman, "Egyptian Police Guard Coptic Church Attacked by Muslims," *New York Times,* October 23, 2005, 8.

17. See, for example, Laurie Goodstein, "Anglicans in Angry Split over Homosexuality Issue," *Washington Post,* October 12, 2003, 14.

18. James Bennet, "How 2 Took the Path of Suicide Bombers," *New York Times,* May 30, 2005, A1.

19. Craig S. Smith, "Muslin Group in France Is Fertile Soil for Militancy," *New York Times,* April 28, 2005, A15.

20. Ibid.

21. Jim Hoagland, "Globalization's Evil Offspring," *Washington Post,* May 14, 2003, A29.

22. Ian Reader, *Religious Violence in Contemporary Japan: The Case of Aum Shinrikyo* (Honolulu: University of Hawaii Press, 2000).

23. One need only tour the monasteries perched on mountainsides in northern Greece to encounter gruesome wall paintings of earlier centuries that make one avert the eyes and wonder that religious conviction can foster such horrid images.

24. Dexter Filkins, "Sunni Clerics Call for End to Attacks on Iraqis," *New York Times,* March 1, 2004, A8.

25. Isabel Hilton, from a book review of Jessica Stern, *Terror in the Name of God: Why Religious Militants Kill,* in *New York Times Book Review,* November 16, 2003, 50.

26. Peter Watson, "The Wages of Fundamentalism," *International Herald Tribune,* June 22, 2005, republished in *YaleGlobal Online,* June 25, 2005.

27. Ibid.

28. Jerry Markon, "In Tribute to Activist, a Call to Forgive," *Washington Post,* April 23, 2006, C3.

29. Alan Cooperman, "Religious Right, Left Meet in Middle: Clergy Aim to Show That Faith Unifies," *Washington Post,* June 15, 2005, A1. See also Nicholas D. Kristof, "Giving God a Break," *New York Times,* June 10, 2003, A27.

Notes for Chapter Nineteen

1. Quoted in Thomas L. Friedman, "'What, Me Worry?'" *New York Times,* April 29, 2005, A25.

2. U.S. Census Bureau, Current Population Survey, October 2003.

3. "Video Gamers Make Good Surgeons," available at http://www.cbsnews.com/stories/2004/04/07/health/main610601.shtml.

4. Sam Dillon, "Literacy Falls for Graduates from College, Testing Finds," *New York Times,* December 16, 2005, A23.

5. Frank Rich, "Harry Crushes the Hulk," *New York Times,* June 29, 2003, sec. 2, 1.

6. Ibid., 27.

7. Larry Rohter, "Chileans Promised a New Deal; Now Striking Youth Demand It," *New York Times,* June 5, 2006, A9.

8. Julia Preston, "University, Mexico's Pride, Is Ravaged by Strike," *New York Times,* January 20, 2000.

9. Seth Mydans, "Indonesia's Students: An Unrelenting Force for Change," *New York Times,* November 13, 1998, A3.

10. Neil MacFarquhar, "Student Protests in Tehran Become Nightly Fights for Freedom," *New York Times,* June 14, 2003, A3.

11. Lloyd Norris, "U.S. Students Fare Badly in International Survey of Math Skills," *New York Times,* December 7, 2004, A17.

12. Sam Dillon, "Test Shows Drop in Science Achievement for 12th Graders," *New York Times,* May 25, 2006, A18. See also Brent Staples, "Why American College Students Hate Science," *New York Times,* May 25, 2006, A26.

13. Editorial, "How to Rescue Education Reform," *New York Times,* October 10, 2004, sec. 4, 10.

14. David M. Herszenhorn and Susan Saulny, "What Lifted Fifth-Grade Scores? School Say Lots of Hard Work," *New York Times,* June 12, 2005, 1.

15. Michael Janofsky, "Education Official Suggests Expansion of Testing," *New York Times,* July 9, 2005, A11.

16. Michael J. Petrilli, "School Reform Moves to the Suburbs," *New York Times,* July 11, 2005, A17.

17. Diana Jean Schemo, "Republicans Propose National School Voucher Program," *New York Times,* July 19, 2006, A17.

18. See, for example, Sara Rimer, "Bright, Eager, and Willing to Cheat," *New York Times,* July 2, 2003, A18.

Notes for Chapter Twenty

1. Speaking to a British audience in 2003 and quoted in Kelefa Sanneh, "It's Dixie Chicks vs. Country Fans, but Who's Dissing Whom?" *New York Times,* May 25, 2006, E1.

2. David Lazarus, "Piracy Eludes Solution," *San Francisco Chronicle,* April 16, 2006, J1.

3. Benjamin Barber, *Jihad vs. McWorld* (New York: Ballantine, 1996). See also Fareed Zakaria's critique of the book in "Paris Is Burning," *New Republic* (January 22, 1996).

4. Available at http://portal.unesco.org/en/ev.phpURL_ID=31038&URL_DO=DO_TOPIC&URL_SECTION=201.html.

5. Noted in Harry Eckstein, *Internal War: Problems and Approaches* (Westport, CT: Greenwood, 1980).

6. Francine Prose, "Berlin Stories: The Caustic Energy of Weimar Art," *Harper's Magazine,* April 2007, 91–99.

Notes for Chapter Twenty-One

1. International Labour Organization, *World Employment Report 2004–2005: Employment, Productivity, and Poverty Reduction* (Geneva: ILO, 2005).

2. Available at http://www.geographyiq.com/ranking_Population_Below_Poverty_Line_aall.htm.

3. Eric Pfanner, "Cellphone Companies Join Bono's Efforts to Help Africa," *New York Times,* May 15, 2006, C12.

4. Bob Herbert, "Untapped Talent," *New York Times,* June 5, 2006, A23.

5. U.S. Census Bureau, *65+ in the United States: 2005,* (Washington, DC: U.S. Department of Commerce, 2005), 1.

6. Ibid.

7. Ibid.

8. Available at http://en.wikipedia.org/wiki/Life_expectancy, 2.

9. Kevin Kinsella and Victoria A. Velhoff, *An Aging World: 2001* (Washington, DC: U.S. Department of Commerce, 2001), 2.

10. WHO, "Revised Global Bureau of Disease Estimates for 2002," available at http://www.who.int/entity//healthinfo/statistic/gbdwhoregion mortality2002.xls.

11. Daniel De Noon, "Are Drug Companies Making Us Sick?" 1, available at http://curezone.com/art/read.asp?ID=133&db=1&CO=1.

12. Suzanne Gordon, "HMOs Fight the Sick Instead of the Sickness," *Los Angeles Times,* June 15, 2000. See also Peter Salgo, "The Doctor Will See You for Exactly Seven Minutes," *New York Times,* March 22, 2006, A27.

13. Daman Rose, "Don't Call Me Handicapped!" BBC (October 4, 2004), 1, available at http//news.bbc.co.uk/1/hi/magazine/3708576.stm.

14. David S. Joachim, "Computer Technology Opens a World of Work to Disabled People," *New York Times,* March 1, 2006.

15. Henrike Gappa and Stefanie Mermet, "Interface Adaptation in a Teleworking Environment for Disabled People," ERCIM News 28 (January 1997): 1, available at http//www.ercim.orgpublication/Ercim_Newsenw28/gappa.html.

16. Estelle Thoreau, "Ouch! An Examination of the Self-Representation of Disabled People on the Internet," *Journal of Computer-Mediated Communication* 11, no. 2, available at http://jcmc.indianaedu/vol11/issue2/thoreau.html.

17. Kate Zernike, "House G.O.P. Lacks Votes for Amendment Banning Gay Marriages," *New York Times,* July 19, 2006, A17.

18. Judith Kaye, quoted in a full-page advertisement, *New York Times,* July 25, 2006, A5.

Notes for Chapter Twenty-Two

1. A substantial portion of this chapter was originally presented at the annual meeting of the American Political Science Association, Boston, Massachusetts, August 29, 2002. Quoted in Tamar Lewin, "Children's Computer Use Grows, but Gaps Persist, Study Says," *New York Times,* January 22, 2001, A11.

2. William Strauss and Neil Howe, *Generations: The History of America's Future, 1585–2069* (New York: William Morrow, 1991), 425.

3. Ibid., 428.

4. Lynne C. Lancaster and David Stillman, *When Generations Collide: Who Are They. Why They Clash—How to Solve the Generational Puzzle at Work* (New York: HarperCollins, 2002), 13.

5. See my *Distant Proximities: Dynamics beyond Globalization* (Princeton, NJ: Princeton University Press, 2003).

6. Howard Rheingold, *Smart Mobs: The Next Social Revolution* (New York: Perseus Books, 2002), 20.

7. Lewin, "Children's Computer Use Grows, but Gaps Persist, Study Says," A11.

8. George Packer, quoted in Thomas L. Friedman, "Global Village Idiocy," *New York Times*, May 12, 2002, sec. 4, 15.

9. "'Many-to-many' communications is the paradigm that best represents the character of communication on the Internet. Personal communication, face-to-face, by phone or by fax, is 'one-to-one' while mass media is characterized by 'one-to-many.' 'Many-to-many' communication includes the characteristics of 'one-to-one' as well as 'one-to-many,' while at the same time allowing 'many-to-many' communications." Michael Dahan, "Internet Usage in the Middle East: Some Political and Social Implications," available at http://www.mevic.org/papers/net-mena.html, 17n6.

10. There are considerable data indicating people in the oldest age groups are increasingly mastering the rudimentary uses of the Internet. Ireland, for example, had a higher proportion (16 percent) of Internet users in the twelve- to seventeen-year-old age group in 2001 than did any other country, but at the same time data for that country showed that "the information society is not being totally confined to younger surfers." The same survey found that "Internet usage [grew] rapidly amongst 'grey' users," available at http:www.acnielsen.com/news/European/ie/2001/20010502.htm. In 1997 similar growth patterns were uncovered for older age groups in the United States, who had a desire "to keep in touch with their grandchildren and to learn the same things their grandchildren were learning about in regard to computers and the Internet." Joyce Philbeck, "Seniors and the Internet," *Cybersociology* 2 (November 20, 1997): 1, available at http://www.cybersociology.com. Likewise in the United Kingdom it was found that "many elderly users are encouraged to use the net by younger relatives, and then discover they have more time available for web browsing." "UK Internet Usage Surges," *BBC News*, August 20, 2001, available at http://news.bbc.co.uk/hi/english/business/newsid_1500000/1500668.stm. Quite the opposite pattern was uncovered in a 1998 Canadian survey, however, with 47 percent of the 35- to 54-year-old age group being most likely to use the Internet and the proportion of those under 35 being nearly as high (45 percent), whereas the figures for the 55–64 and the 65 and over groups were, respectively, 27 percent and 7 percent. Available at http://www.statcan.ca/Daily/English/900715/d990715a.htm. I am grateful to David Earnest, who is less than half my age, for the ten minutes of his time he devoted to helping me locate these Internet sites and those in subsequent footnotes.

11. In preparing to write this chapter, I initially searched the World Wide Web by using the key word *Internet Usage,* a heading that yielded 1,194,032 citations. Stunned, I then used what I assumed would be a more manageable key word, *age group Internet users,* only to come upon 117,411 citations.

12. Diana Saco, *Cybering Democracy: Public Space and the Internet* (Minneapolis: University of Minnesota Press, 2002), 41.

13. Ibid., 189.

14. James N. Rosenau, *Along the Domestic-Foreign Frontier: Exploring Governance in a Turbulent World* (Cambridge: Cambridge University Press, 1997), chap. 14. A considerable extension of the skill revolution hypothesis can be found in my *Distant Proximities,* chap. 10. For an empirical test of the hypothesis, see James N. Rosenau and W. Michael Fagen, "Increasingly Skillful Citizens: A New Dynamism in World Politics?" *International Studies Quarterly* 41 (December 1997): 655–686.

15. Lewin, "Children's Computer Use Grows, but Gaps Persist, Study Says," A11.

16. It is interesting to note research findings indicative of "a significant physical alteration" linked to generational differences: "The thumbs of today's electronic-gadget generation of children have become more muscled, more dexterous, and often more used than fingers.

This is because modern youngsters grow up using hand-held gadgets where the devices are cupped in the hand and held firm by fingers, giving thumbs the pivotal role of pushing buttons." Those who undertook the research, "after studying hundreds of children in Beijing, Tokyo, and other big cities, say today's youngsters have become the 'thumb generation.'" Alfred Lee, "Thumb Generation," *Straits Times* (Singapore), March 25, 2002.

17. Saco, *Cybering Democracy,* 123.

18. For cogent arguments that "hackers" is an imprecise concept, that for hackers it is a term of respect, that hackers are often helpful to those who turn to them for assistance, and that they "possess qualities that serve the public," see Verna V. Gehring, "Do Hackers Provide a Public Service?" *Philosophy and Public Policy Quarterly* 22 (Summer 2002): 25. See also Douglas Thomas, *Hacking Culture* (Minneapolis: University of Minnesota Press, 2002).

19. Rosenau, *Distant Proximities,* chap. 12.

20. Available at http://www.bangalorenet.com/internetindia.

21. Available at madans@planetasia.com.

22. Available at http://www.interasia.org/malasia/ramanathan.html.

23. Available at http://virtualchina.org/archive/archive/news/jun00/'/cgi-bin/adrotate/ad/cgi.

24. Available at http://www.mevic.org/papers/net-mena.html.

25. Available at http://www2.seasite.niu.edu/tagalogdiscuss/_0000070c.htm.

26. Available at http://www.dtmedia.lv/raksti/EN/EIT/200101/01010832.stm.

27. Available at http://www.thos.co.za/news/240498_sao.html.

28. Available at http://www.nso.gov.mt/cosnews/news02/news02102.htm.

29. Michel Marriott, "Not Just Closing a Divide, but Leaping It," *New York Times,* July 18, 2002, E1.

30. One database lists 4,208 Internet cafés in 141 countries (available at http://www.cybercafe.com). In China, for example, more than 200,000 cyber cafés are spread around the country. Erik Eckholm, "Taboo Surfing ... and Click Here for China," *New York Times,* August 4, 2002, sec. 4, 5.

31. Although there are problems operationalizing JNDs as instruments of measurement, they are metaphorically useful as a means of tracing phenomena marked by change. See James N. Rosenau, *Turbulence in World Politics: A Theory of Change and Continuity* (Princeton, NJ: Princeton University Press, 1990), 32–33.

32. John Schwartz, "In the Tech Meccas, Masses of People, or 'Smart Mobs,' Are Keeping in Touch through Wireless Devices," *New York Times,* July 22, 2002, C4, an article anticipating publication of a book by Howard Rheingold, *Smart Mobs: The Next Social Revolution* (New York: Perseus Books, 2002).

33. Ibid.

34. James N. Rosenau, "The Information Revolution: Both Powerful and Neutral," in Thomas E. Copeland, ed., *The Information Revolution and National Security* (Carlisle, PA: Strategic Studies Institute, 2000), 9–27.

35. Friedman, "Global Village Idiocy." The Internet also has enabled student groups in the Middle East to launch and broaden boycotts of U.S. goods. See Neil MacFarquhar, "An Anti-American Boycott Is Growing in the Arab World," *New York Times,* May 10, 2002, A1.

36. For data affirming that more than a trivial number of Muslims are independent in thought and action, see Dahan, "Internet Usage in the Middle East."

Index

Abortion, 119, 142. *See also* the Unborn
Abu Ghraib scandal, 78
Activists, 63–66; amateur and professional, distinction between, 63; artists as, 130, 133–134; elderly people as, 139; gays as, 141; and globalization, 64; goals of, 65; lesbians as, 141; and mobilization, 63, 64; people with disabilities as, 140; responses to, 64, 65; single-issue and multi-issue, distinction between, 64, 65; skills of, 65–66; sources of, 64–65; students as, 125–126; temperaments of, 65. *See also* Mobilization; Political activists; Protests
Adelphia Communications, 89
Advertising, and consumers, 97–98, 99
Afghanistan, 75
Africa, 137; and immigrants, 29, 44, 48; information technology in, 21–22; Internet literate in, 150; religion in, 115, 116–117, 118
Age of the networked individual, 8
Aggregated structures, 7–8
AIDS. *See* HIV/AIDS
Albania, 44
Alienation, 136
Al-Jazeera, 113
Al Qaeda, 68, 69, 119
Altman, Robert, 133
Amnesty International, 75
Analytical skills, 20. *See also* Skills
Anarchist movement, 67
Anglican church, 118
Angola, 115 (table)
Apathetic, the, 143
Arab countries, Internet literate in, 150

Argentina, 115 (table)
Art: and cultural diversity, 132–133; globalization of, 131–133, 135; and piracy, of intellectual property, 132; as politics, 133; and technology, 131–132. *See also* Artists
Artistic vision, 130–131
Artists, 130–134; as activists, 130, 133–134; and artistic vision, 130–131; and computers, 132; and culture, 130; and globalization, 131–133, 134; and politicians, 134
Asia: and immigration, 44; Internet literate in, 150
Australia, 44
Austria, 87; and immigration, 45 (table); poverty in, 137
Automatic weapons, 75

Baby boomers, 138, 145
Balkans, 44
Baltics, 74
Bangladesh, 115 (table)
Barber, Benjamin, 132
Barreiro, Virginia, 53
Beatty, Warren, 134
Belarus, 44
Belgium: and immigration, 45 (table); poverty in, 137
Bernstein, Carl, 110
Bird flu, 139
Birth control, 28–29
Birth rate, 25–29; and immigration, 29–30
Blair, Jayson, 110
Bloggers, 108–109. *See also* Journalists

About the Author

James N. Rosenau holds the distinguished rank of University Professor of International Affairs at The George Washington University. This honor is reserved for the few scholar-teachers whose recognition in the academic community transcends the usual disciplinary boundaries. Rosenau has held a Guggenheim Foundation Fellowship and is former president of the International Studies Association. He is a renowned international political theorist with a record of publication and professional service acknowledged worldwide. He is the author of more than 140 articles and author or editor of more than 40 books, including *Turbulence in World Politics: A Theory of Change and Continuity* (1990), *Governance without Government: Order and Change in World Politics* (1992), *Information Technologies and Global Politics: The Changing Scope of Power and Governance* (2002), *Along the Domestic-Foreign Frontier: Exploring Governance in a Turbulent World* (1997), *Distant Proximities: Dynamics beyond Globalization* (2003), and *The Study of World Politics* (2006).